MW01248052

SWING TRADING, FOREX TRADING.

THE COMPLETE CRASH COURSE ON OPTIONS & DAY TRADING.
LEARN ALL THE BEST STRATEGIES TO INVEST IN THE STOCK
MARKET AND MASTER THE TRADER'S PSYCHOLOGY

JACOB ELDER

THIS BOOK INCLUDES

BOOK 1: 6

SWING TRADING

BOOK 2: 200

FOREX TRADING

SWING TRADING

Table of Contents

Introduction

swing trader doesn't need to sit at his computer watching the stock markets all day long, although you certainly can if that is an option for you and you like doing it. Swing traders can also start small and grow their business over time. Day trading involves lots of upfront costs instead. Rather than building a long-term retirement account, swing trading is all about earning profits in the short term. While substantial profits are possible, it's not a get-rich-quick scheme and although it can be done on a part-time basis, we want you to start thinking of swing trading as a business from this point forward. The goal is to earn profits, and you can use those profits as ordinary income if you like or reinvest them to build your retirement account or some combination of the two. That is entirely up to you. But keep in mind one thing: very few people are going to make a million bucks in their first year and go right into retirement.

That said, swing trading can be a very lucrative way to make a living, and if you are interested in business and finance, it can be a lot of fun! In order to get there, you are going to have to study and become an expert in the field. The journey can start with this book.

Inside this guidebook, you will learn what swing trading is all about, the benefits of swing trading, and even how to get started in the market. You will then learn the three best strategies that you can try out if you want to see real profits with swing trading. Whether you are a beginner to investing or you have been in the market for some time and want to try out something new, this guidebook will help you to see success.

So, in this book, you will learn several trading strategies that will help you as a beginner to hopefully make an increasing income through swing trading. You shouldn't be confused by the simplicity of some of the strategies, rather, you should read these strategies and paper trade with each of the strategies to find out the one that suits you better and profits more. Let's get started!

Chapter 1:

What is swing trading

swing trade can be defined as a technical approach to recognizing potential trading opportunities especially the trades that are moving in the direction of the most recent market trend. It doesn't completely rely on a company's fundamentals, rather a trend may be caused by a fundamental catalyst, however, the trade will be a full technical decision. Every market has certain price actions which professional traders call "momentum," they have natural ebbs and flows over time which is often followed by moments of rests and the stocks are no exception. Although some of these types of momentum can really be short-lived, they often move significantly, and this is the ideal swing trading opportunity that traders can capture in the market on a short-term basis like 3-10 days.

Swing Trading and the DOW Theory

Basically, according to the Dow theory, three trends exist at the same time in the market:

- The short-term or day-to-day fluctuations

- The long-term trend and

- The intermediate trend

Ideally, swing traders should always focus on the intermediate trend. The long-term trend provides direction for traders while a confirmation of the trend is provided by the intermediate trend. The short-term price action helps swing traders to target their entry and exit points. This basically constitutes a well-formed swing trading plan and having a strict money management plan will help you position properly to capture extraordinary moves in the market.

Investing can be a smart way to watch your money grow. You can put your money to work and earn some more in the process without having to go back to working another job. Depending on the type of investment you go with, you could end up making a lot of money in the process without doing a ton of work. Learning how to pick out a good investment opportunity that will make you as much money as possible while also limiting your risks can be a challenge. Luckily, there are a lot of options that you can work with and the risk can be limited if you learn the proper methods to be successful in them.

Those who are working with swing trading will often work with the fundamental or intrinsic value of the stock. They will also need to take some time to look at the price trends and other patterns that come with a stock because this helps them to make some good decisions for which stocks will make a profit with swing trading.

So, you may be curious how a swing trader is going to work compared to investors in other opportunities. To begin with, all swing traders are going to act quickly because they need to be able to find situations where a stock is about to move upwards over a short amount of time. It doesn't matter how that stock will do over time. If there is a big piece of news that is about to happen with a stock that will drive the price up for at least a few days, then these are the ones that you want to work within swing trading.

To see the biggest profits, these upward trends need to be extraordinary. Otherwise, lots of other investors are going to jump into the market as well and your profits will be limited. You'll need to look at the history of the stock, some of the news that is surrounding the stock, and other factors to determine that this particular stock is going to have a big upward trend for you to capitalize on. If you are right, you'll purchase the stock at a low price and then sell it within the next few weeks in order to make a nice profit.

There are some similarities between a swing trader and a day trading, especially considering that the individuals who do both will work this kind of market on their own from home. You aren't going to have a big financial institution that is working with this option because the movement is too quick and the profits from each trade may not be huge. The point here is that when you do quite a few of these trades over a few weeks, your profit will add up. But the individual trades may be small on their own.

As a day trader, you're going to hold onto either a position that is long or one that is short. You won't hold this position for a long time. Most traders will get rid of the stock within a few days, but you can hold onto the stock for up to a few weeks and still be considered a swing trader. You are assuming that there is going to be a large price move in the stock, so you need to be careful about picking out the position you want to work with, or your risk will not be limited. In addition, if you are working with some time frame charts, you need to rely on some that take on longer ranges, like daily and weekly charts, to help you determine how the market is going to behave.

Advantages of Swing Trading

Generating consistent income

Long term investors are more bothered with wealth creation or wealth preservation. They aren't bothered about generating consistent monthly income. On the other hand, successful swing traders can easily generate consistent income for themselves on a monthly basis.

Holding different securities to diversify your risk

Swing trading is active investing in the true sense of the term. Swing traders actively trade a basket of securities and try profiteering from moves on both sides. Buy and Hold investors are passive investors and invest into a security or a basket of securities using mutual funds which might not yield very high returns.

Profit from shorting stocks, which long term investors simply can't replicate

Shorting a stock is something a long-term investor cannot replicate. A swing trader takes maximum advantage of price declines. This is done because a swing trader actively manages his own portfolio and with the use of technical indicators can enter or exit stocks and maximize overall returns on one's portfolio. Many believe the advantage of shorting is that it leads to good price swings as a result of panic selling which helps the swing trader maximize his returns.

Lower risk compared to day trading

When you compare the amount of risk that you're taking with swing trading compared to day trading, it's much lower with the former. This is because you are going to have some more time to work on the market. Sometimes it's hard to estimate how the market is going to do in one day because there's a lot of up and down movement based on how other traders are behaving that day. But it's easier for a lot of traders to predict whether their stock is going to do better over a couple of days, especially if there is some big news coming out about the company. This lower risk is going to make swing trading a more profitable option for many traders.

Do swing trading and other trades

Many traders like swing trading because they can do these trades along with day trading. During market hours for the day, the trader may focus a lot of their energy on the position they took for day trading and focus on the swing trade later. They can do this by placing their swing trade position the night before, or at least before the market opens that day. This helps prevent confusion while trading.

Having the advantage of trading overnight

Some traders find that trading overnight is a risky endeavor and that it's going to harm their profits. They worry that there's going to be a big trend that occurs overnight and that they will be able to do nothing about it because they are asleep. Sometimes there are a few gaps that will occur overnight and whether they will go with your trade or not will vary. In many cases, this overnight position is going to help you out, giving you more time to wait for the trend and make big profits the next day.

Time to look at the market

With day trading, you're only able to look at the market over one single day. If something goes wrong with your trade, you don't have a lot of time to wait for it to turn around. Even if the market is going to go the way you predict, that may not happen until the next day and you would miss out on day trading. With swing trading, you can stay in the market a little bit longer and wait for that uptrend to happen, even if it happens to take a few extra days to get there. This helps to reduce the risk and can make many investors more comfortable with using this option.

Potential to reach the trades better

When you compare this to day trading, you are more likely to reach the trade that you want when using swing trading. You get more time to watch how the market will behave, to predict the trades and how they will behave over a longer period, and you can end up making more money in the process. In fact, you can even make a lot of money overnight if you choose the right stocks at the right time with this trading method. Or if your position needs to be held over a few days rather than a few hours, swing trading can make this happen.

Freedom throughout the day

You literally need to spend your whole day watching the trade. And when little changes happen, whether they are up or down changes, they can make big differences in how well you'll do in day trading. This can be stressful and can turn a lot of people away from even trying. Often those who go with swing trading are ones who tried out day trading and didn't like all the work and stress that came with it. They wanted to make some good money over the short-term, without needing to spend all their day in front of a computer screen watching how the market was doing.

What Is Important to a Swing Trader?

Typically, positions will be held for less than a week when swing trading, with buy and sell decisions being taken purely on price movement and not company fundamentals. In fact, most swing traders use analytical tools to 'trawl' the market for potential tradable stocks.

Because of this trading profile, and the short time frame of position holding, it is right to assume that swing traders have no concern for what a company makes or sells, nor its balance sheet, profitability, market sector, state of the economy, etc. A long-term investor, of course, would analyze all these factors before making an investment decision.

There are only two factors which concern swing traders:

- Flows of funds in and out of a target stock

- Risk to capital and ease of trading the target stock

How Swing Traders Make Trading Decisions

With no reference to company fundamentals, it's clear that swing traders use other indicators as a basis for trading in and out of stocks: predominantly price and the way the price is moving initiates a buy or sell indication.

The Idea of Predictability in an Unpredictable Market

Markets are unpredictable. No one can say with certainty in which direction a market will move, nor how far or how fast on any given day, week, month, or year. Outside factors create fear and greed which moves markets up and down, seemingly at will. However, what can be predicted to a far greater degree is the nature of humans, so investors.

When a stock is moving up, investors tend to buy and when it's moving down, investors tend to sell. This is the foundation of swing trading, and what makes it a close cousin to momentum trading.

Swing Trading and the Psychology of the Crowd

This predictability of the crowd is what causes stocks to move up and down.

As a stock's price moves up, with buyers stepping in, this creates a situation where the increasing price encourages further buyers as traders and investors pile in, not wishing to miss out on the market move. This is the psychology of greed, fear, and hope, literally forcing investors to buy in reaction to what others do.

However, each move will eventually run out of steam when those that bought stock early seek to realize profits and sell out. When this happens, the stock forms a peak and reverses direction, causing greater numbers of investors to sell, providing momentum to the downside until the stock is deemed to have fallen far enough.

16

Basic Swing Trading Concepts

One of the easiest ways to identify swing-trading opportunities is to find financial instruments such as equities or currency pairs that are trading within a channel.

Channels

A channel is a trading range defined by an upper resistance level – the price at which sellers' step into the market and the price starts to fall – and a lower support level, where buyers enter the market and the price starts to rise. When the market is consolidating, channels will typically run horizontally, but ascending and descending channels can also occur in rising and falling markets.

Price Baselines

One of the most important ways that traders identify these potential opportunities – although there are others – is by establishing a price baseline.

This baseline is the price that the stock or other financial instrument tends to oscillate around in a liquid market. Typically, this baseline is calculated by using the exponential moving average (EMA) of the price. The EMA is basically a weighted average of the price over a period, with more recent prices being more heavily weighted. This is different from a simple moving average (SMA), where all the prices are weighted equally. The advantage of using an EMA is that it tends to react more quickly to changes in price momentum, giving traders an earlier indication of upcoming changes.

How a swing trader thinks

When you are working with swing trading, you have to remember that all of the steps of the investment will occur within a few weeks. You may decide to stick with swing trading for many years and turn this into an income, but the individual trades never last more than a few weeks at most. If you're doing swing trading and the trades take longer than the few weeks, you have exited out of swing trading and the strategy is not going to work as well for you. There are some big differences between long-term and short-term investing, and it will take a specific type of trader to see success when they are working with a swing trader.

So, what does a swing trader need to have, what kind of personality, in order to be successful? First, they need to think things through without emotions. Things can change quickly when you're a day trader and your money can often be at risk. Since you're not working with the investment for the long-term, it's possible to lose that money quickly without a chance to gain it back. This can be hard on a lot of new investors and can often negatively influence the trades that they make.

There are some people who have a lot of trouble keeping their emotions out of their trades. These people are going to get too caught up in the moment and will make some bad trading decisions.

18

This leads them to lose out on a lot of money, money that they could have held onto if they had gone through and thought out their trades the right way. If you are not able to control your emotions during these trades, then it is best to find another investment option other than swing trading.

Another thing that you will need to be aware of is that you need to love looking through charts and doing research. You will never make any money with swing trading if you don't perform some good research ahead of time. You will miss out on important trends, get into a stock at the wrong time, and worst of all, lose money. Often these things would be easy to see if you had just done your research ahead of time. It's important to look at the charts for any stock that you are interested in, as well as look at the charts for the overall market as well. This helps you to see what is going to happen in the future and will make it easier to form predictions before starting your investment.

As a swing trader, you need to have a good sense for making predictions. It doesn't do you any good to enter a trade when the upswing is already occurring. This is often too late to enter the trade and you will pay too much for the stock and may not be able to sell it for a profit. To make the most money, you have to find a stock that is currently undervalued, one that isn't being bought that much right now, so that you can purchase it for a lower price than what it is worth.

You don't want to go for a stock just because it is low, though. You need to pick out a stock that is undervalued. This means that it may be selling for less than it is worth right now, but there is something that will happen in the near future that will raise the price of the stock back to its market value or higher. When this uptrend occurs again, you'll be able to sell the stock and make a profit. With the right prediction, you'll be able to do this within a few weeks and earn a good amount of profit in a short amount of time. If you enter into swing trading and you have trouble reading charts and recognizing when a new trend is about to happen, you are going to miss out on a lot of potential profits because you won't trade the right stocks.

Building a Foundational Investment Strategy

Let's go a little deeper into the world of swing trading. All investing begins with careful analysis (or should at any rate). There are basic trend principles we can look at to develop a baseline, and from there, take in more factors to further develop our probabilities in making a profitable trade.

To start, we have the Pareto Analysis or Pareto Principle, widely known as the 80/20 rule. This rule is based on the observation that eighty percent of activity is generated by twenty percent of people. Originally put forward by an Italian economist, Wilfredo Pareto, who learned that 20% of people owned 80% of land in Italy. After further research and analysis, he discovered the country's wealth distribution as a whole followed the same pattern.

As more research was done on the Pareto Principle, over the decades, economists came to realize how applicable the 80/20 rule was to capital markets and trading. Without delving too deeply into this basic law of investing, we will boil it down to its basics. Which is: twenty percent of your entire efforts will result in eighty percent of your results. With this in mind, you know that most of your efforts will result in negligible losses or gains. Take it as part of your foundation, and let it reinforce in your mind the need for patience and discipline when investing.

Generally, you can count on emotional responses to create market movement. Greed, fear, and uncertainty are the three dominant emotions that influence even experienced traders. When it comes to short-term price aberrations, almost all can be attributed to those emotions affecting buying and selling decisions. To be successful as a swing trader, you must ignore the tendency to react emotionally to price movement and use logic to take advantage of market overreaction. When prices rise quickly, the overall investing market tends to act out of greed, buying to get in on the anticipated profits. But you do not need to have that instant reaction. Yes, let their greed drive the market, and then try to take advantage of that.

That's a basic, and it does depend on the time frame. There are various ways to define what a trend is such as Simple Moving

Averages (SMA), higher highs or lower lows against absolute momentum, which is the emotional traders either buying into the market late or selling off late as they try to stem losses.

Take the uptrend. Within several days of an uptrend, there will be pullbacks. So, how to capture a profitable trade? Trends have the principle of persisting in its trend. Keep in mind though that works both ways and does include range bound patterns. If the trend has peaks and valleys, then it tends to follow that trend and stay range bound.

A good way to track your performance is to give yourself a set number of trades throughout a month. The reason for this is a good run in trading can quickly turn south even for the most experienced trader, and easily turn into a two-month binge of self-destruction, and erase any gains you may have made, as you start to make trades to try to turn your 'luck' again.

Never rely on luck for trading. Yes, sometimes, luck will play a factor, accept it and move on. Set the number of trades you'll make in say, a month; five being a good number for that time frame. This will help instill market discipline and give you a reliable metric to base your performance on.

What are key performance metrics you should track? Certainly, profit and loss are the most important, although it is advisable to have at least one other metric. The ratio of profitable trades to losing trades is a simple measure to calculate your month to month performance. Say, for example, over a ten-trade cycle, you profit $1,500 over $500 in losses, giving you a profit ratio of 3R, or three times more profitable than you lose. You can track your performance over time and quickly identify when you are below your historical average and know you need to take a look at your trading strategy.

You also want to set your maximum drawdown. Set a percentage, say 20 percent, of your account at the start of a trading cycle and determine it as your maximum drawdown. Ideally, as you progress in trading proficiency and take more consistent profits, you will want to limit your maximum draw down even more.

How to Start Trading

Now, it's time to move on and get to some of the basics about doing an actual swing trade. We are going to take a look at some of the steps that you need to take in order to enter the market, the types of positions that you can choose to take, and even how to take each of the positions that you choose. This will help you to get set up when it is time to do that first trade with this kind of trading strategy!

Choosing to Buy Long or Sell Short

The price of a stock is going to do one of three things at a given time. It will either go down, go up, or it will move sideways. When you enter the market as a swing trader, you're expecting that the stock is going to either go up or it will go down. If you think that the stock will see an increase in its price, then they will purchase the stock. This move is going to be considered "going long" or having a "long position" in that stock. For example, if you're long 100 shares of Facebook Inc., it means that you purchased 100 shares of this company and you're making the prediction that you'll be able to sell them at a higher price later on and earn a nice profit.

How to Enter a Trade

If you are brand new to trading, you are probably curious about how you would sell or purchase a security. Any time that the market is open, there are going to be two prices for any security that can be traded. There will be the bid price and the ask price. The bid price is what buying or purchasing traders are offering to pay for that stock right then. The ask price, on the other hand, is the price that traders want in order to sell that security.

You will quickly notice that the bid price is always going to be a bit lower simply because the buyers want to pay less, and the asking price higher because sellers want more for their holdings. The difference between these two prices is known as the spread.

Investment and Margin Accounts

There are two types of accounts that you can choose to open in order to trade stocks. The two main options include the margin account and the investment account. With a margin account, you can borrow against the capital that you have placed in your account.

The investment account, on the other hand, will allow you to buy up to the dollar value you hold in that account. You aren't able to spend more than what you have put in that account at a time.

When you decide to open up a margin account, you might be able to borrow money from the investment or brokerage firm to help pay for some of your investment. This is a process known as buying on margin. This can provide you with some advantages of purchasing more shares that you would be able to afford if you just used the capital in your account, and it can help you leverage to get more profits with your money.

Picking out a Broker

During this process, we also need to take some time to discuss picking out a broker. If you've already gotten into other forms of trading in the past, then you can simply work with the same broker that you already have. But, if you're getting into trading and this is the first one you have done before, then you'll need to search to find the right broker for you.

There are many different brokers out there, and many of them can assist you with swing trading. The biggest thing that you'll want to look at is the commissions and fees that each broker assesses against you. Since swing trading times are relatively short and you'll enter in and out of trades within a few weeks at most with each trade, you want to make sure that the profits you make aren't eaten up by the commissions to your broker.

Picking out How Much You Want to Invest

Finally, before we move into talking about some of the different swing trading platforms that you can work with, we need to discuss some of the basics of about how much you are going to invest in your account. Since we already discussed the importance of working with an investment account rather than trying to do the trading on margin, you will need to decide how much money you would like to put into your account.

First, talk with your brokerage firm and decide how much you need to put in to meet their requirements. Some brokerage firms will ask you to spend a certain amount or keep some amount in your accounts at all times in order to trade. If your chosen firm has that kind of requirement, then make sure that you put in at least that much. Putting in more is up to your discretion.

Learning the Art or Science of Swing Trading

Now that you've decided to try out swing trading you will be glad to know that you can find your feet and learn the basic skills by using simulation trades based on live, real-world stock but using virtual money. Many brokerages offer this service where you can safely learn in a virtual environment. The importance of using these simulations to learn, develop and practice your trading strategies cannot be overemphasized. You will however also need to undoubtedly develop your own trading strategy that suits your pocket and risk profile. After all, you don't want to start out trading using real money without a tested strategy. Therefore, you'll need to first learn how to swing trade and practice using the simulators to hone your skills and develop a strategy. A good way to develop those strategies and skills is to follow the methodologies of experienced swing traders and copy their typical approach to swing trading.

A day in the life of a Swing Trader

What you need to do before the Market opens is essential if you want to be successful. Professional swing trader will often rise and begin working long before the start of trading. Indeed, it is often as early as 6.00 am if they can sleep through their trade notifications chiming on their phones. This is so that the trader can get an early impression of the prevailing conditions that have overnight affected slant of the day's market. Diligent traders also check their existing positions' profitability and the effects on them from overnight trading which can be considerable. They need to be on the look-out for new potential trades, and they may do this by making up a daily watch list.

Get an early impression of the Market

After you shake the sleep from your eyes and get some coffee the next task of the day is to fire up the computer and get an early impression of the market conditions. The most effective way to do this for beginners is via CNBC. There are also other media channels and websites as well as subscription services. However, most professionals are not interested in the actual details and just want to know what is better or worse about something such as is the SP500 up or down, or is the dollar trading higher than the Japanese yen? They don't get too embroiled in the details and only want to figure out what's better or worse today. The beginner should take that as a good tip. You should also keep to the traditional media sources before committing to a long-term subscription service.

Find Potential Trade Opportunities

Traders will always be on the look-out in the morning for new potential high-value trades. Typically, swing traders will first identify and buy stock with what is known as a fundamental catalyst. The experts will then manage or sell the stock based on technical analysis. Now to understand what a fundamental catalyst is and how to find good fundamental catalysts we can use one of three methods:

- Specialist opportunities: These opportunities arise from unpredictable changes in a company's standing include going public, loss of a CEO, takeovers, mergers, and other similar major events that will be reported in the financial and business orientated media. Such opportunities will indicate high risk and are not for the beginner, well at least not without considerable simulated and paper trading experience.

- Focusing on a Specific Sector: Discovering this type of high performing stock is done by studying the business news and focusing on the updates that are relative to that sectors financial news. The objective this fundamental analysis is that it gives you knowledge of which sectors are performing well.

Draw up a Watch List

For you as a beginner swing trader to keep on top of your research and opportunities, you are best to take another leaf out of the professional's book and create a watch list. This is a list of potentially high-performing stocks that are trading which has caught your interest. Typically, these will be a list of stocks that you have been advised on or have yourself detected by some basic fundamental analysis. These stocks will look like having the potential of being a good trade. A more detailed watch list which a professional might make up each day will typically contain a list of stocks with their entry prices and stop-loss prices that they want to keep an eye on.

Calculating the Existing Positions

Most importantly you must check up on the existing positions of your stock but do it on a regular basis not sporadically. The problem with random checks is that you can see losses or gains and then trade reactively trying to chase the losses. To do this, you should first check your current position and if everything is stable look to the overnight financial news to ensure that nothing untoward has happened, that may affect your stocks positions. This can easily be done by entering the assigned stock symbol into Google. If there is a significant change to your position, then you'll have to see how it may affect your current trading strategy. Even if it doesn't, you may want to reconsider where to adjust your stop-loss or where to set your take-profit points.

After-Hours Market

Aftermarket hours is a dangerous time as it is the time when the rest of the world is trading. But it is the time where you can watch what is going on in real time, and if you can't sleep, you may want to do some of your own trading's. But even if you don't want to trade you may want to make adjustments to your position based on global market movements that offer opportunities for future trading.

Where can you use swing trading?

Swing trading can be used in virtually any market. It's a technique, rather than something specialized for a specific market like crypto currency. Nevertheless, swing traders primarily trade on stock markets. But you can use swing trading as a technique when trading commodities, currencies, and anything else that will see price swings up-and-down over periods of interest, and that means you could apply it to anything that gets traded. You could even think of trading options as a form of swing trading since you're hoping to profit on the same moves of the stock, although options are quite a different ball game overall.

Our focus in this book is going to be on stock trading. But keep in mind that you could use the exact same techniques, including the methods of analysis for the most part on currency markets as well.

How Does Swing Trading Differ from Buy and Hold Investing?

Most people come to the stock market thinking about traditional buy-and-hold investing. Buy-and-hold investing is a technique that is focused on the long-term gains of the stock market and highly valued companies.

If you invest in specific companies at all, and many people don't, a buy-and-hold investor is looking for high-quality buys. It's true investing, meaning that you're focused on the fundamentals of the company and its long-term prospects, and you're putting your money into the market to invest in the company over the long-term, which can mean up to 30 years or more.

The buy-and-hold investor is going to dig into a company very deeply when it comes to the fundamentals. That means going over the financial statements and cash flow in detail, seeing how things are changing year to year, and reading all the earnings reports and following the calls. It also means studying the management team to see who they are and what their backgrounds look like. You're going to familiarize yourself with the company's products and what markets they are in.

A good buy-and-hold investor that invests in specific companies will approach it as if a friend or relative said: "hey do you want to invest in my business?" Buy-and-hold investors have low turnover rates in their portfolios. Some buy-and-hold investors are actually income or dividend investors, hoping to make a living off dividend payments either now or in the future, while safely preserving their capital. They may be inclined to invest in a slowly changing stock like Chevron or IBM, as opposed to some stock that sees significant price swings over days, weeks, or months.

Many buy-and-hold investors these days don't even invest in individual companies. With the advent of exchange-traded funds, it's possible to buy and sell shares on the stock market while investing in index funds rather than investing in individual companies or being constrained by stodgy and expensive mutual funds. Given that an index like the S&P 500 is going to go up over the long term barring some unforeseen disaster, a simple buy-and-hold strategy is to load up on index funds like SPY. Of course, the most extreme form of it would be someone who invests in mutual funds, and let the fund manager keep track of all the investments and rarely check on it themselves. Such investors just hope to have a "nest egg" in retirement.

Regardless of whether a buy-and-hold or long-term investor invests in specific companies, index funds, mutual funds, or some combination out of all of these, they will use the same basic techniques. Those techniques involve diversification of your portfolio and using methods like 'dollar cost averaging'. They will also be looking for so-called value stocks, which are undervalued at the present time based on the fundamentals of the company, and so the investor hopes to make cheap buys of quality stocks that will appreciate over the long term.

We see, right off the bat, buy-and-hold investing is quite different from swing trading. Swing trading pays some attention to the fundamentals of the company, but the focus remains on short-term profits. Even when looking at fundamentals, the swing trader is interested in how they are going to impact share prices in the coming weeks, not over the course of decades. Techniques like diversification are of limited interest to the swing trader. You will have a little bit of diversity in that, you're going to be buying and selling multiple securities over time as you get involved with more trades simultaneously. Beginning swing traders may not have any diversity at all and may only be buying and selling one security at a time. Dollar cost averaging is obviously not something a swing trader would consider at all. If you don't know what that means, dollar cost averaging is a strategy that uses investing at regular intervals. The idea is to average out the price paid for shares of stock as it fluctuates up and down. People who use dollar cost averaging have a philosophy that over the long term, those price fluctuations are going to average out, and many believe you can't predict price fluctuations anyway (they might take a dim view of technical analysis).

Chapter 2:

Fundamental Analysis

Fundamental analysis is a process by which you study the fundamentals behind a financial asset. On the FOREX markets, you will be looking at the state of the economy, GDP growth, and political factors that impact the overall picture and stability of the country. If these items are looking good, that means the currency for that country will gain strength. But since currencies are traded in pairs on FOREX, that means you also have to compare fundamentals between countries. If Europe looks strong but Japan is looking even better, then the Japanese yen would strengthen as compared to the euro.

When it comes to stocks and options, the fundamentals include profit margins, price-to-earnings ratios, cash flow and other indicators that give a picture of the overall health and prospects of the company. You'll want to look at quarterly earnings, and reviewing earnings calls for companies that you are invested in. Fundamental analysis also means looking for stocks that are currently undervalued. The price of undervalued stocks is likely to increase at some point in the future, so spotting an undervalued stock could be useful for the swing trader.

Since swing traders have different time horizons as compared to buy and hold investors, short-term results like earnings calls are going to take on a larger role, as compared to looking at trends in revenue and profits over the course of years. A good earnings call can send prices soaring, while failing to meet expectations can send stocks into a rapid decline. When there are events like this as a swing trader you must be ready to seize upon them as quickly as possible.

It's also important to keep your eye on company news of a more general nature. If a product fails or ends up creating legal trouble for a company, it can be an opportunity to short the stock or invest in put options. Alternatively, the release of a new product that exceeds expectations can be an opportunity to go long on the stock.

Financial Reports to Read and Where to Get the Information

The SEC requires that all publicly traded companies make audited financial statements available. This includes a prospectus and an important report filed annually which is called the '10K'. In these documents you'll find audited records that include items such as cash flow, balance sheets, and other financial data. They also include important information about the management team and competition the company is facing in its sector. The company must also give shareholders an overview of its future plans and information about attempts to enter new markets. You can visit company websites to get these reports, or do an online search using the company name with "10K" or "prospectus". Summaries of financial information are also available on many stock websites free of charge. For example, you can get income statements, balance sheets and cash flow on Yahoo Finance for any company that is listed on the stock exchanges.

There is also another important report that may be released from time to time, called an 8K. These contain information similar to that found in a 10K, but they are only filed when important short-term information has to be disclosed to investors. At times, the information contained in an 8K can have a major impact on share price.

Financial Statements in More Detail

There are three general types of financial statements in case you aren't fully aware. These include the following:

- **Income statement:** An income statement will include information such as revenue, gross profit, and operating expenses. These reports can help you determine the overall health of the company, and you can look for trends in revenues and profits over the past few years. Be sure to look for net income as a percentage of revenue. As a swing trader, while you need to have an understanding of the overall health of the company, you'll be more interested in looking at quarterly statements and keeping up with earnings calls and other announcements.

- **Balance sheet:** A balance sheet shows current assets and liabilities for the company. Current liabilities are of particular note on a balance sheet. You want to look at a balance sheet thinking about the financial health of the company. Is it carrying a large amount of debt? Is the amount of debt increasing, and could that prevent the company from being profitable or paying dividends at current levels? These factors may make a company less appealing to investors. When a company is younger and in an aggressive growth phase, investors may be more tolerant.

- **Cash Flow:** Cash flow is a summary of items such as net income, changes to inventory, depreciation, changes to liabilities and financing opportunities, among others. Cash flow can give you a good overview of recent company performance and is another way to gauge the health of the company. Pay special attention to changes in inventory. Ask yourself if it looks like the company is able to move its product.

When examining quarterly data, you'll want to compare quarterly results to the same quarter a year earlier. In many cases, company performance will depend on time of year, so the best way to see trends in the company's performance is to make an apples to apples comparison, rather than just looking at how revenue and net income changed from last quarter to the most recent quarter.

Earnings Calls

On a quarterly basis, one of the most important events for a swing trader is the earnings call of the companies that the trader is interested in. Earnings calls can lead to dramatic swings in stock price, depending on whether it's a good earnings call or a bad earnings call. In the crazy world of Wall Street, earnings call largely depends on what people are expecting out of it, rather than any absolute measure of performance. For example, if investors expect earnings to increase 25%, and the company reports that it only grew earnings by 10%, even though any rational person would view that as a positive, Wall Street is probably going to react negatively. Of course, if the report shows a decline it's going to be that much worse. Now, we swing traders don't know how strongly the market will react. If share price is $200, it might drop to $180, or it might drop to $170. Nobody knows ahead of time, but you should be ready to enter into your trades accordingly.

Things work just as well the other way around. If analysts were expecting a company to see a 10% increase, but they report an 18% or 25% increase in year over year profits instead, this will send the stock soaring. Again, nobody is sure how high it will go. You'll have to have a preset value of profit you are willing to accept on a trade and place a limit order ahead of time. Then you have to live with the results. If your limit order is at $220 a share, you can be happy with your $20 a share gain, even if the stock keeps rising. A disciplined trader that doesn't get greedy is far more likely to succeed over the long-term.

While it's impossible to know ahead of time how an earnings call is going to go, you can gain some familiarity with a company and how the market reacts to it by going over previous earnings calls. Do so by not only reviewing the content of the calls, but by looking to see how strongly the market reacted to them.

Keep in mind that a bad earnings report isn't just an opportunity to short stock or invest in put options. When the stock drops, it's also an opportunity to get in at relatively low price point. Don't set perfection as a goal for your trades. The only thing you should worry about is getting in on the stock when prices are relatively low as compared to the previous price level. If it continues going lower, beating yourself up over missing the opportunity is a waste of energy. Instead, focus on waiting – for the stock to go back up so you can profit at a future date.

If the report turns out to be a good one, you might want to be ready to enter into your position immediately. Then you can ride the wave of rising share prices. It isn't necessary to invest before an earnings call and it could even be a bad decision to do so, because you won't know for sure which way things are going to go. In any case, earnings reports are an important part of your fundamental analysis to see how the company is performing.

Price-to-earnings ratio

An important metric that matches share price and earnings per share is the price-to-earnings ratio. Investors and traders are on the lookout for price-to-earnings ratios that are excessively high, and those that are low in comparison to similar companies in the same sector. If the ratio is excessive when compared to other companies in the same sector, that could mean the stock is overvalued, and might head into a downturn at some point. Conversely, an undervalued stock as indicated by a relatively low price-to-earnings ratio is a stock that is available at a "discount", because it's undervalued. At some point – the thinking goes – the stock is going to rise in price up to its true value.

You shouldn't just take the price-to-earnings ratio at face value. If you notice one that is out of line with the rest of the industry, you should do some research to find out if there is some external reason behind the difference. That may require a detailed check of news about the company on financial websites, as well as reading press releases and 8K reports issued by the company.

An interesting and recent example is Ford Motor Company. At nearly 14, the price-to-earnings ratio of Ford is nearly twice that of other auto companies. Compared to GM, it's actually more than twice as big. At the time of writing, it alone stands out in the automobile sector, where all the other companies are in a similar range. It's extremely unlikely that Ford represents the standard of the sector and all the rest of the companies are undervalued.

That could mean one of two things – Ford is in for a correction at some point in the future, or it has recently made some moves or announcements that make it deserve the high ratio. The first step you should take is to look over financial reports and compare profit margins between the different auto companies. You'll also want to look for any news you can find about Ford in recent months.

It could be something as simple as a stock split. When a company splits its shares, the amount of money invested in the company stays the same but the number of shares changes. Splits can work in both directions. Companies can use them to inflate or deflate price-to-earnings or earnings per share ratios.

In general, if the price-to-earnings ratio appears excessively high or low, this can indicate that the stock is in for a correction in the coming months. If it's excessively high this is an overvalued stock, and the price of the stock might be set to drop in the coming weeks. We would expect it to drop until it reaches a more appropriate level for its sector. On the other hand, if its low and the company fundamentals look good, that can be a sign that the company is poised for gains. So, the price-to-earnings ratio can indicate that an individual stock is set to undergo a "correction".

But keep in mind that there is no "right" or "wrong" price-to-earnings ratio. As we explained above, you'll have to look at companies in the same sector to get an idea of how a given company compares to its competitors. Obviously, you don't want to compare a bank to an auto company or to a social media company. Also make sure you're really comparing the same measurement. A good one to look at is TTM. This means **trailing twelve months**. You will also see past-looking and forward-looking price-to-earnings ratios. I prefer to avoid forward looking and stick to the TTM value. To get a feel of how different they are from sector to sector, since we've already looked at automobile companies, let's compare that to some other industries.

Let's look at a younger and growing sector, social media companies. Looking at Twitter, we find that the P/E (TTM) ratio is 20.61. This is considered a pretty average price-to-earnings ratio. Looking at Facebook, the price-to-earnings ratio is a bit higher, checking in at 28.58. That's almost 42% higher than Twitter, but given the more successful financials that Facebook has, it's probably justified.

Now let's look at a newer company, such as SNAP. In this case, there isn't any price-to-earnings ratio given. That means SNAP is not profitable. Since it's a young and growing company, that isn't relevant, at least not yet. Investors will want to see results at some point – but for now they are relatively patient. Tesla is another example of a relatively young company that is poised for rapid growth – it has yet to have positive earnings.

Searching for some more social media companies, we find one that is way out of whack. YELP is sometimes considered a social media company, and its P/E ratio is 49.89. This is much higher than what we've seen so far. YELP is a popular website to be sure, but it doesn't seem to have any fundamentals to justify a price-to-earnings ratio that high. That could mean it's in for a price correction in the coming months.

We can also find examples on the other extreme. Weibo Corporation has a P/E ratio of 15, which is comparably low.

You can also look at closely related companies that are similar, but not necessarily in the same exact sector. Microsoft is a technology company and they own Linked-In, so that seems like a good candidate. Their P/E ratio is 30 – about the same as Facebook.

With these values in mind, Weibo might be a hidden opportunity. Before deciding, however, you'd want to look at the company financials and read what analysts are saying about it. Something a swing trader should always keep in mind is that looking at a single metric should not drive your decision making. You need to find confirmation elsewhere.

The point of looking at price-to-earnings ratio is that it's a starting point for further research.

Social media is a new and growing sector. It's interesting to look at another more slowly moving sector such as banking. Here is what we find:

Wells Fargo: 10.24

Bank of America: 10.4

Citigroup: 9.81

JP Morgan Chase: 11.72

Notice how they are all clustered around the same value. If you are looking at stocks in the banking sector, any stock that had a price-to-earnings ratio that fell outside of the range 9-11 would be very suspect, possibly representing an opportunity to look at for a future price swing.

Open Interest, Volume, Short interest and Put-to-call Ratios

Looking at options, open interest, volume and short interest are some of the factors to consider. These can also help you determine where traders expect prices to go. There aren't absolute numbers that can be used as a guideline, everything is relative.

Open interest tells you the number of options contracts for a given strike price and expiration date. Options traders seek out a minimum of 100, because this indicates enough liquidity that you can quickly get out of a trade. When you find strike prices with higher levels of open interest, these are probably price levels where expert traders are expecting the stock to go soon. You will want to compare open interest numbers for calls and puts on the stock. Calls are bets that the stock is going to rise in price, while puts are bets that the stock is going to decline in price.

Volume tells you the number of trades that happened on the most recent trading day. This also gives you an indication of the level of interest in the strike price – where people think the stock price may be heading.

You can also look into short interest, and the put-to-call ratio for options related to a stock. Short interest tells you how many investors are shorting the stock. If this number is high, that indicates that the investing community is expecting a stock price to decline in the near future.

This information is also communicated by the put-to-call ratio for options related to the stock. Investors who think that a stock price is going to decline are going to invest in put options. If the ratio is excessive, then it can reflect an expectation of coming price declines in the stock. You can compare the value you find for a given company to similar companies in the same sector. It's also good to check the put-to-call ratios for SPY, which tracks the S & P 500, for a rough comparison. That will give you an indication of what investors are expecting for the market as a whole. Note that options all have different strike prices, so you will want to check the put-to-call ratios for different strike prices.

Futures and after-hours trading

You can look at futures and afterhours trading to see how a stock is moving as a leading indicator, that might help you decide when to enter or exit a position. For futures, S & P 500 and other index futures can indicate the overall direction of the market. For individual stocks you might look at afterhours trading especially after a late earnings report. This will help you determine when to enter your next trade.

Fundamental Variables

There are going to be several questions that come to your mind immediately as you start to perform research on a company. For example, you might ask yourself how long the company has been successful. You'll wonder if this is company will give you a good profit or if it has a history of getting traders high returns. Whatever questions you ask yourself, you need to realize that you have to do more than just ask the basic questions. In fact, you must make sure you take time to look at the fundamental variables.

Positive Earnings Adjustment

In the trading world, there are those who are known as market analysts. These people will often analyze how well companies are doing and then give the companies a review or a forecast, which allows other people to notice where the company is sitting. Market reviewers are typically known as cautious people and don't tend to believe that companies will pass their forecast. However, this does happen and when it does, it brings us into positive earnings adjustment.

Basically, this states that we need to look for stocks which have surprised the market analysts. This is because if companies pass their forecast, they will continue to succeed. Therefore, they become known as one of the best companies to gain a profit from, which is always a great thing for a trader to know. However, you'll still want to make sure that you do your deep analysis before making any moves on a stock.

Positive Earning Revision

Market analysts conduct this process when they're evaluating how well a company is doing so, this gives them a forecast. As stated above, analysts are cautious and very careful to note where they think the company is going. Therefore, when the company goes further than what they initially thought, they need to re-evaluate the company. Of course, admitting they're wrong is not an easy thing for analysts to do as it isn't easy for anyone. However, when they do need to admit this, people can quickly learn what companies they should start paying attention to.

Earnings Momentum

While there are many important fundamental variables to look at when you are making an analysis, earnings momentum holds a special place. This variable is very important, especially when it comes to bull markets. Earnings momentum is the variable which looks at the year to year growth of earnings. Therefore, this is what will often set the price for stocks.

Strong Cash Flow

This is another fundamental variable that will tell you how much free cash a company has. This is a very important variable because it will let you know where a company financially sits after it has paid all of its bills and expenses. When you're getting into trading, you want to pay attention to the companies that are financially stable. You want to make sure that a company can grow because the more they grow, the more profit that you make. Think about it – if you put your money into a stock where the company could barely pay the electric bill, do you think that your money would be secure, if even for a period of time? You want to make place your money in companies which are financially secure.

Earnings Growth

Another variable you want to pay attention to is how much more money the company is making as the years go on. When you look at this variable, you will be looking at the earnings growth variable. This is another company that you would think of investing in because you know that they have seen considerable growth for a certain number of years. Therefore, you analyze that the company will only continue to grow.

Chapter 3:
Risk management and
market planning step by step

R isk management is a grossly neglected area of every unsuccessful trader's strategy. Indeed, most do not even understand the concept and fail to explore it beyond the cursory nod given to stop losses and per trade risk.

Here's the thing: Perfect risk management can save a poor strategy but even the best strategy cannot save poor risk management. Many of you must have heard of this piece of wisdom but probably very few of you truly understand its implications.

You see, most people enter the world of trading with dreams of dollar signs and massive money in a short period of time. They aren't concerned with the possibility of loss and only consider the massive gains on offer. Such traders (gamblers is a more appropriate term) soon find themselves in the red and either quit in disgust or even worse, attack the markets with new capital and a shiny, new, "infallible" strategy.

Risk in trading is quite simple. It is the probability of you losing your capital on a series of trades, including the current one. Not just your capital at stake on that particular trade (your per trade risk amount) but your entire capital. Most traders only see risk as the probability that that trade will be a loss.

Truth is, it doesn't matter what happens on that trade. That's right! It doesn't matter whether your current trade is a win or a loss. All that matters is: despite this trade and the next one and an entire series of them being wins or losses or some combination of both, will you still make money? If the answer is yes, you're managing risk correctly and you are guaranteed to make money even with a rubbish strategy.

How to Limit Your Risk

Discipline is one of the hardest things to ace. In the meantime, it is the most significant component of effective exchanging. It's dependent upon each merchant to set up a pre-showcase routine and construct solid exchanging propensities.

You ought to endeavor to accomplish discipline on the off chance that you ever would like to accomplish any degree of exchanging achievement. Exchanging control is polished most of the time, in each exchange, every single day.

Along these lines, to give you a hand, this blog entry goes for uncovering the 10 brilliant guidelines of exchanging discipline. You should consistently condition yourself to be restrained. On the off chance that you need to be a genuine broker, then read through the standards consistently before the exchanging session starts. It shouldn't take over three minutes to peruse them. Think about the activity as reminding you how to behave all through the exchanging session.

Adhere to a Proven Trading Method

Furthermore, do not transform it. If you have a demonstrated technique but it doesn;t appear to work in a given exchanging session, do not return home that night and attempt to devise another. In case your strategy works for more than one-portion of the exchanging sessions, at that point stay with it. Keep in mind, the Holy Grail of exchanging is cashing the executives.

Effectively Trade the First Three Hours of Each Major Session

It is basic information that the FOREX market exchanges 24 hours every day. In any case, not those hours are practical for day exchanging. If you're an informal investor, you need to focus on the accompanying exchanging perspectives: unpredictability, force, bearing, pattern and difference.

Also, you have to settle on positional exchanging and scalping. Take positions that appear to be the most self-evident, on the grounds that these are the most ideal approach to amplify your benefits. You can figure out how to recognize easy decision arrangements utilizing our investigation and online courses.

Additionally, focus on your exchanging plan. The initial three hours of each significant session are typically the best as far as force, pattern, and retracement. It is then that we brokers will locate the best exchanging potential outcomes.

The Market Rewards You for Your Discipline

Exchanging with control should (all being great) compensate you with a positive cash stream. The purpose of exchanging with control is to have more pips in your record and less pips out. The one consistent truth concerning the business sectors is that exchanging with control ought to furnish you with greater benefit potential.

Consistency is Confidence

How great does it feel to have the option to turn on your exchanging stage the morning realizing that, if you play by the guidelines, the likelihood of fruitful exchanging day is generally high? The appropriate response? Great! Keep in mind: If you make somewhat consistently, at that point you have earned the privilege to exchange greater.

Try not to Let a Winner Become a Loser

We have all abused this standard every once in a while. Be that as it may, it ought to be our objective to invest more energy not to abuse it later on. What I am discussing here is the voracity factor. The market has compensated you by moving toward your position. But, you aren't happy with a little victor. Along these lines, you clutch the exchange the desire for a bigger increase, just to watch the market turn and move against you.

Try not to Chase the Markets

Actually. You ought to abstain from bouncing on a cargo train. This may suck you into a winding of fate as you understand the business sectors may betray you. Quietly sit tight for the arrangement. The business sectors resemble a shadow. So, if you pursue it, you'll never get it. If you stop, it will grasp you.

Proficient merchants that pick Admiral Markets will be satisfied to realize that they can exchange totally chance free with a FREE demo exchanging account. Rather than going to the live markets and putting your capital in danger, you can dodge the hazard and essentially practice until you are prepared to change to live exchanging.

Remember EOD – End of Day Trading

At the point when the London session is going to end, regardless you have roughly a few extra hours to adventure advertised developments. But if you neglect to utilize this time, your exchanging may stop in its tracks until the Tokyo session opens. EOD exchanging is extraordinary, as you often have to exchange against the pattern. Why?

Since when most day exchanging market movers take benefits, the cost follows. Each end of a purchase position is a programmed sell

54

again into the market. The enormous bit of leeway of EOD exchanging is that it doesn't require consistent observing which, thusly, makes it perfect for dealers with a normal everyday employment.

You Are a Long-Distance Runner

Have you at any point wanted to exchange while not having the option to do as such in light of the fact that the value in your record is excessively low and your specialist probably will not enable you to exchange except if you submit more assets? That occurs on the off chance that you go out on a limb. Huge misfortunes hurt, and they hurt excessively. Use influence keenly. Try not to hazard over 4% per exchange. Remeber, you need to have the option to exchange one more day.

Pursue Your Trading Routine

Your exchanging routine should comprise of a significant market hours trading, pre-advertise investigation and end of day (EOD) hours.

Never attempt to break your exchanging schedule. Pursue real markets and exchange just during the significant markets. These include New York, London and Tokyo markets.

The value moves even more detectably during significant market sessions, so you can disregard minor markets. Significant markets furnish you with an incredible number of arrangements as well.

Truth be told, you can now check the day's monetary schedule for any solid financial reports that may impact your arrangements; at that point move to value activity investigation, to check whether the costs have gotten through significant help or opposition levels. My recommendation is to exchange drifting markets.

It is a Step-by-Step Process

Attempt to utilize exacerbating. Aggravating is an incredible method to add benefits to your benefits. It is entirely appropriate for littler estimated accounts. At last, you may even have the option to assemble a six-make sense of whole of two-figure account.

Maintaining a Trading Journal

The final thing that you should consider doing is maintaining a trading journal that will talk about the different trades that you have done. You can do this online or keep a paper copy nearby. When you're done with one trade, make sure to write down what happened during that trade, what strategy you used, what was going on in the market, how much you spent, and more.

More than anything else, your trade journal is what will keep your risk management on track. Your journal should, at a minimum, record your trade date, instrument, direction (long or short), stop-loss size, reasons for entering, exit date, P/L and any comments.

You're free to add other data to your journal as well. There are many platforms online which, for free, can record all this for you.

Excel is probably the easiest to use though some traders also favor handwritten notes. As long as you're recording the relevant information in a manner that can be easily reviewed, choose whatever it is you're comfortable with.

Along with your journal, you should also keep screenshots of your trade at relevant points. This includes, at a minimum, the entry and exit. If there's some special event which happens during the trade you feel compelled to record, feel free to do so. It's helpful to make notes on the screenshot as to what your analysis was in the moment, especially on entry. Tracking this along with your psychological state on entry will give you great insights into how you perform under pressure and where improvement is needed.

The biggest area of improvement for most new traders is on the mental side of things. Technical skill increases by leaps and bounds when you're at an advanced level, already making good money. Newer traders often assume the opposite and thus neglect to track their mindset and thus never become self-aware enough to improve. Always track your mental state and focus on that much more than your technical skill and your ability to develop new strategies. In the beginning, stick to a basic, simple strategy and focus on executing it perfectly. You'll find this makes you money and that you're also learning to think like a trader, not a gambler.

This is a step that a lot of people like to skip, but it can really help you out later on. The more details that you can add to it, the better it is. If you ever get stuck with one of your trades or you aren't sure how to handle one situation or another, you can refer to this journal and see what advice it has. You may be surprised that, after a particularly hard situation in a different trade, you can look back in this journal and find the answers that you need.

Keep Your Emotions in Check

While I have briefly touched on this before, I want to talk about making sure you can keep your emotions in check while trading in more detail. It is a very important factor to remember and once that can decrease your risk greatly.

One of the best examples to give you to control your feelings is the stock market crash of 1929. One of the reasons this crash occurred was because investors and traders started to let their emotions take over as they saw the stock market numbers decrease.

Keeping your emotions in check is especially important when you find a stock going against you. Not only does this make you realize that you made a mistake during your calculations, which carries its own sentiments, but this can also make you go through a series of mental stages. There are many traders and investors who state that this series of five stages is like the five stages of grief. While some people feel that this is a bit over-dramatic, several experienced traders have discussed how they often feel these stages when they see a big loss from one of their stocks.

Follow the 1% Rule

One of the biggest ways to reduce your risk is to make sure that you focus on keeping your proportion low. One of the best ways to do this is by only risking about 1% of the money in your account with each trade. For example, if you have $10,000 in your account, this means that you won't trade more than $100 on a trade. However, many expert swing traders believe that when you are first starting out, you should lower this even more. Therefore, a beginner should look at trading no more than around 0.3% to 0.5%. While this doesn't seem like a lot of money, most stocks generally aren't a large amount of money to buy. Some of the most expensive stocks to buy will be blue-chip stocks.

Of course, there are always traders who often thrive on risk, and following the 1% rule won't feel right to them. While this isn't advised for beginners, if you find yourself more comfortable taking higher risks, then you should think about increasing the percentage. For instance, instead of 1%, you could go up to 2% or 3%. However, it is not recommended that you go much higher than that. It really all depends on your personal preference with risk, your experience, and how much capital you have in your account.

Make sure you have stop-loss orders in place

Previously, we talked about stop-loss orders when discussing swing trading strategies. So, let's revisit the concept.

A stop-loss order is a special type of order that you place with your broker at the time of placing your trade, ordering him or her to automatically close off your trade at a small loss, should the market fail to move in the direction that you predicted.

It is the most basic type of risk management tool you will ever find in the financial markets.

Generally, you should get into the habit of placing a stop-loss order every time you place a trade in the market. This helps protect your capital against unforeseen events that could result in a catastrophic financial loss to your account.

As a trader or investor, you should always assume that every trade that you place in the market carries risk of capital loss. Therefore, you owe it to yourself to keep that loss at a manageable level so that you can afford to trade in the future.

Watch out for high volatility in the markets

If you want to be able to trade profitably and with much ease, then you must stay away from hostile market environments that a very difficult to understand and predict. You should stick to trading during periods when the market is trading uniformly, smoothly and predictably.

If you think about it, trading is like swimming in a river. Imagine for a moment that you are someone who loves to swim. You have a specific spot at the river where you and your friends love to swim and have for years now. This place is always calm, and the water flows evenly and quietly.

Then one day, you arrive at that spot and you find that rain that fell upstream caused that place to flood and the river is flowing violently with huge rapids and some trees have even been carried away. Would you consider swimming at that spot? Of course not, you wouldn't dream of doing that in your worst dreams. If you do so, chances of you drowning and losing your life are very high. And that is the same thing that happens in trading.

When you choose to trade during a time when prices are thrashing around violently and there is a lot of unpredictability in the market, then you are sure to drown, drown financially.

It's better to be patient until the market mood improves, and then you can be sure to start placing your bets. If you do so, you will be like a wise swimmer who only swims at the river when there are no floods or rapids, mainly because his or her life is at risk.

An angry market mood is risky for your wallet and will surely cannibalize your capital faster than you could imagine. Volatility or market mood can always be determined visually. You don't need special tools for this. If you see the prices moving uniformly, then you know it's time to play. If it's the opposite of that, then you should stay away.

Watch out for high spreads

Another risk factor in the financial markets is the spread.

In case you have forgotten, the spread is the difference between the asking price and the actual trading price of an asset or security.

It is how your broker makes his or her living – by taking a commission on every trade you place, whether you make money or not.

For the most part, a reputable broker will charge you fair spreads. But still, you should keep a keen eye on it because there are instances where your broker may raise the spread , sometimes to some unbelievably high levels.

Proper Position Size

The most basic risk management strategy available to us all is simply to control the amount you lose on each trade. This is of course down to personal risk appetite, but the consensus among brokers and traders is that you should cap your risk at about 1% of your capital per trade. For beginners, even after extensive time spent paper trading or on simulations you still might want to go even lower, to begin with, a level at 0.3%. The reason some recommend this is that they'll tell you that paper trading or using virtual money just isn't the same as the real thing. Trading with real money affects you differently psychologically and sometimes makes you trade irrationally. Hence, they recommend lowering your position for at least the first six months to around 0.3% before moving up gradually to 0.5% then 0.7% before moving up to the 1% level. At the lower level of 0.3% means that if you have an $8,000 broker account you can lose $24, but at the recommended level for experienced traders of 1%, that means if you have an $8,000 broker account, you can lose up to $80 per trade.

A critical element of trading success is taking the appropriate position size on every trade. Position size is how much shares you take on a stock trade. However, choosing the right position size should not be just some arbitrary figure, nor should it be related to your confidence in the stock you are trading nor even how convinced you are a trade will be profitable. Rather, the correct position size is determined by a simple mathematical formula. Using this dispassionate scientific approach helps control risk and maximizes returns on the risk that's taken.

Determining the proper position size requires three steps:

Determine Account Risk

Regardless if your account is large or small—$1000 or $500,000–a single trade shouldn't put more than 1% of your trading capital at risk. On an $8000 account, you should not risk more than $80 on a trade, if your account is $2,000 you can risk up to $20 per trade.

Determine Trade Risk

To determine your position's size, you must set a stop-loss level. A stop-loss is an order that closes out the trade to negate the trade thesis if the price moves against us. What it means is you will set a stop order level that is low enough that when triggered after it reaches a specific price will prevent your losses escalating. This order is placed at a logical spot which is out of range of normal market movements caused by volatility for example, but if it hits erroneously it will at least let you know that you have misjudged the current direction of the market.

Therefore, you will need the trade risk to move onto the next step in determining proper position size. Assume you buy a stock at $9.50 and place a stop-loss at $9.40. The trading risk is $0.10.

Always maintain an acceptable risk-reward ratio

The risk-reward ratio is another part of every trade that should always be under your radar.

Risk reward-ratio can be defined as the measurement of the downside risk to the upside profit potential that a trade holds.

This is one of the key areas where many novice traders who fail to make money in the markets mainly go wrong. A study done by **DailyFX** researchers on traits of successful traders, highlighted wrong risk-reward ratios as the number one mistake made by most traders.

The study pointed out that on average; top traders were right 50 to 60 percent of the time. The study also showed that most traders were able to meet this number.

In short, most traders were just about as right as the top traders. So, what made most of these traders lose? This was when an amazing discovery was made.

The top traders were able to make money because they kept a high-risk reward ratio in all their trades. The losing traders allowed for exceptions and therefore most of their winning trades were outdone by the huge losses on their losing trades.

Trade with money you can afford to lose

Lastly, make sure that you trade with money that you can afford to lose.

Trading is one of the riskiest businesses that you could ever go into in this world. In this business, if you aren't making money, then you are losing it. Therefore, it helps to keep this reality in perspective when you decide to risk your money in this business.

Unlike most businesses, where the risk of loss is somewhat manageable, in trading, the risk of losing all your life savings is real. Sadly, there have been stories of people who risked their life savings in the financial markets and lost all of it, only to end their lives. It is for this reason that I have chosen to term this point as a risk management tip.

Only put aside money from either regular savings, from your entertainment budget or some variation of that before investing it in the market. If the money you are holding right now, planning to invest in this business is very important to you, then don't trade.

Only invest a small portion of the money you can risk losing, in the beginning as you trade. Then after you taste some success and start having more confidence in your methods, you can start slowly building up your stake.

But don't be in a rush to borrow money from friends and relatives or from your bank to invest in the markets.

Follow Your Guidelines and Rules

We have already discussed various way to help you eliminate risk when we discussed some of the common mistakes and various tips for beginners. These are important to follow as they will help you eliminate risk. For example, making sure you stay in the right mindset will help you remain positive about trading. This can help eliminate your risk because you will continue to put your best effort into making sure that you make the best decisions when it comes to your trades.

As you get started in your trading career, you will start to develop your own rules and guidelines, such as in your trading plan. It is important that you don't change any of these rules and guidelines without fully looking at your trade as a whole. On top of this, it's important to follow because it will help keep you focused, you'll begin to learn the details of swing trading easier as you won't be so concerned about your next step, and you will feel more comfortable in your abilities.

Don't Trade Alone

Earlier I discussed the importance of finding a broker as they will not only help you with your trades, but they will also advise you through your swing trading career. This is especially important for beginners as it is a great way to lower your risk. There's a lot you will still learn as you start to trade. Even when you begin trading with simulations, which means you don't use real money, to get a feel of what trading in the stock market is really like; you'll still feel different once you start using real money. Therefore, it is important to make sure that you have someone you trust that you can bring your questions, concerns, and can help teach you how to manage your account and all the other facts that go into trading.

Of course, this doesn't mean that you always need a broker. In fact, there are a lot of swing traders who don't have brokers. However, at first, you should always make sure that you have someone to help guide you until you learn the world of swing trading a little better and become more comfortable making decisions on your own. For example, you might have a broker for the first couple of years you are a swing trader and then decide that you are content with making your own decisions.

Money Management

The Concept of Leverage in Trading

Earlier in this book, we talked about leverage, although briefly. We described it as a way of borrowing money from your broker so that you can control larger financial transactions than the amount you have available for trading. So, let's dive deeper.

Leverage can be defined as a special type of loan that is extended to you as an investor, so that you can increase the returns form a certain type of investment. In other words, it is simply borrowing to invest more.

As an example, let us look at how leverage works in the world of real estate. Particularly, let us look at how mortgage financing works. When you want to buy a home valued at say $100,000, it is common practice to invest part of your money first and then borrow the rest.

So, you may put up say $30,000 first and then borrow the remaining $70,000 from your bank to finance the rest of the purchase.

Now let's say that you bought the house purely for investment purposes. So, maybe in a year's time, the house grows in value to say $150,000. If you sell it and pay back the bank's money plus interest (let's say interest was 8% per annum), you will have made a profit of around $44,400. This is a whopping 148% return on investment.

That is the power of using leverage in your investments.

In trading, it works the same way. You open an account with your broker and deposit an amount in it. This amount which you invest upfront is always known as your margin. Then your broker will provide leverage so that you can magnify your investment.

Chapter 4:
Monitoring the markets

Stop Loss Levels

A s the name suggests, the stop-loss level is that point on a chart beyond which you do not wish to be involved in the trade and would rather exit at a loss. Practically speaking, when you designate a stop-loss level, your broker places an order at that level for you which close your position for a predetermined loss.

So, in a long trade, your stop-loss would be below your entry point. The stop-loss order would be a sell order which closes your long position at a loss. In a short trade, your SL is above your entry point and the SL order is a buy order which closes your trade for a loss.

Most trading platforms provide easy options for you to place this order and it is essential that you do so. Beginners often fall into the trap of placing "mental" SLs because they feel their stops will be hunted by more experienced players. There is this incorrect belief that the bigger traders in the market push prices to a level where obvious stop losses ought to be, trigger those stop losses and then push the price back in the direction of a profit.

Correct SL Levels

Placing stop-losses is a skill that you will get better at as time goes on. You will probably have the majority of your SLs tripped before price goes in the original direction quite a lot in the beginning. Determining SL levels is a combination of understanding S/R, the volatility of the instrument and a gut feeling which comes with experience and errors.

The true definition of an SL is "the point beyond which if the price were to move your entry doesn't make sense anymore." This is a rather vague statement that doesn't help us when we're starting out, no matter how correct it is. Start off by placing your SL order under or over the closest key S/R levels to your entry point. Why key S/R level?

Well if you recall what constitutes a key level, you'll recall why this level would act as a barrier for price. Key S/R levels are the best options for your SL levels in a balanced environment. In a highly imbalanced environment, you can use a more dynamic level like the 20 EMA to inform your stop less level. In other words, place it beyond the 20 EMA. If you're using a crossover strategy, you can place it below the crossover point as well (in appropriate environments).

The volatility of the instrument determines how far below or above you place the stop-loss order. More volatile instrument requires greater breathing room than less volatile ones. When starting out, I recommended you choose a slightly less volatile instrument. To get an idea of an instrument's volatility, observe how cleanly it respects key S/R levels when it retests them in different environments. Can you draw a relatively thin zone to mark the key level? Or is the zone wide? The wider it is, the more volatile the instrument. Consider a large number of bars when determining this to avoid any recency bias (that is overvaluing the present).

Position Sizing

This is another area where beginners get tripped up. There's all sort of entry strategies out there involving pyramiding and scaling. It always pays to keep things as uncomplicated as possible. As such, leave the pyramiding, etc. to more experienced traders. Simply enter your full position size upfront.

How do you determine position size though? Well this is a relatively straightforward task and we'll use the example below:

Account size: 10,000 $

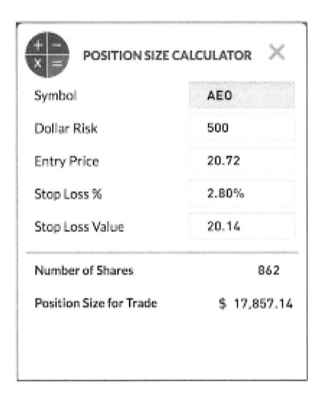

R: 0.25% or 25$

SL distance: 10 points

Position size= (R/SL) = 25/10= 2.5 units

The idea is the maximum loss you can sustain on this trade is the R amount. This is the simplest way to approach position sizing.

Take Profit Levels

Take profits can be approached in two different ways, unlike SLs where your only concern is determining the close key S/R level.

For beginners, a "set and forget" strategy is highly recommended. A set-and-forget strategy means you pick an SL, you pick your T P and then do nothing except observe the market as it moves towards either of those levels. You don't close out the trade at any time, and instead wait for one of those levels to be hit to exit the market.

TP Levels

Your TP level will simply be the place where, once price reaches it, you will make a predetermined R multiple on the trade. When you have lots of data (at least 100 trades), you will know exactly which multiple makes you the most money and can calculate the level accordingly.

For the first 100, picking a 2R level is appropriate. Once you have enough data, you may realize that a 1.5R TP level increases your hit rate and your overall profit or maybe a 3R level decreases your hit rate but increases profits. Either way, you must understand, your first 100 trades are for the purposes of gathering data only. Therefore, it is crucial you keep your risk as low as possible.

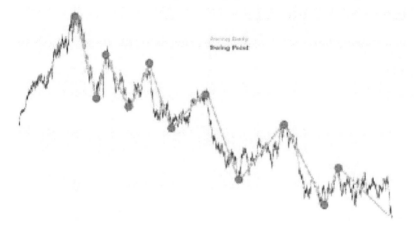

For now, though, let us look at how you calculate the TP price level. The calculation is the exact same formula as the SL one.

Account size: 10,000$

R: 0.25% or 25$

TP: 2R or 50$

Position Size: 2.5 units

TP distance from entry point= (TP/Position Size) = (50/2.5) = 20 points.

So, in the above scenario, if you entered a long position at $100 and have placed your SL at 10 points, your positions size is 2.5 units, your SL sell order is placed at $90 and your TP sell order is placed at $120.

An Alternative

The set-and-forget is what you ought to start with in the beginning. Once you've placed over 200 or so trades, you can begin experimenting with your TP levels. You see, to make the most money possible, it is essential to let your winners run. To let them run, you'll need to evaluate the upcoming S/R and determine whether price is likely to break through it or not.

This obviously requires a degree of emotional detachment from the result of your trade. If you've already made 2R on the trade, will you be strong enough to hold on for a further potential 5R? How would you react if it went up to 5R and then swerved back below 2R? Only you can answer this honestly and this is why it is recommended to stick to the set-and-forget method for at least 200 trades.

This concludes our look at the basics of SL and TP levels. Remember, once you've gathered data over 100 trades, you will need to analyze them to see what hit rate and R multiple makes you the most money. You might need to extend your TP level and reduce your hit rate or reduce your TP level and extend your hit rate. Ultimately, all that matters is which scenario maximizes your profit (not how many trades you were correct on or some such).

The Idea of Predictability in an Unpredictable Market

Markets are unpredictable. No one can say with certainty in which direction a market will move, nor how far or how fast on any given day, week, month, or year. Outside factors create fear and greed which moves markets up and down, seemingly at will. However, what can be predicted to a far greater degree is the predictable nature of humans, and this includes investors.

When a stock is moving up, investors tend to want to buy. When it is moving down, investors tend to sell. This is the foundation of swing trading, and what makes swing trading a close cousin to momentum trading.

Market Rhythms

The markets are never still. They are dynamic, ever changing, ever evolving and always challenging a trader to the utmost. While on a superficial level it may seem almost impossible to discern order beneath the chaos of the market, breaking down the mechanics of the market helps us understand its rhythms and its flow. That's simply a fancy way of saying, let's break a complex structure down to its basics.

77

Order Flow

Those of you who have read other books on this subject might not have encountered what you're about to read previously. Most trading advice usually skips straight to the trading strategies without paying any heed to when to implement said strategies. The market environment, more than anything else, determines your strategy. Always remember.

The market environment is determined completely by the underlying order flow. How many sellers versus buyers are there?

How strong is the dominant side (that is, how much stronger are the buyers compared to the sellers)? What is the probability that the tide is changing, and the dominant side is weakening? The answer to these questions lies on the price chart. We can also use indicators to help us figure out the answer to these questions.

The underlying order flow produces two states of price action in the markets. These are

Trends

Ranges

We'll look at these in more detail now.

Trends

A trend is a state of price action where the price is moving in a direction quite clearly. This movement could be up or down, it doesn't matter, as long as it is moving in a clear direction.

Determining this is quite simple really. Looking left to right on your chart, is the right-hand side at a higher or lower level than the left-hand side? Is there a general direction in which the market has been moving? If the answer to either of those questions is "yes" then you have a trending environment.

Take care to avoid the trap of getting too technical with this. You don't need to get too granular with regards to the price bars or candlesticks (we'll cover these in later chapters). The irony is, when you're first starting out, you're in the best position to evaluate whether a market is trending or not because you don't have enough knowledge to go on. Hence, you'll end up using your gut feeling and this is usually right.

Once you know a bit more, you know just enough to make mistakes, and this is when you'll see most traders over complicate the process. Let's look at the chart below to understand this better.

Figure 1: A Trending Environment, From: (Global Prime-MetaTrader 4, 2018)

The chart above is of the EUR/USD currency pair on the daily time frame. Never mind what you see now, just focus on the price chart. Now this is a candlestick chart, which we'll look at in details later. For now, all you need to know is that each individual bar or candle, represent one day's worth of price movements.

Our task with this chart is really simple: Is this trending or not? Go ahead and try to determine this before proceeding. All the information you need has been given to you in the previous paragraphs.

Your task is perhaps made easier by the huge arrow pointing downwards, but if you answered "yes" to the question above, you're correct! At first glance, it's easy to see how this instrument peaks near the left side of the chart and then starts sliding downwards and then begins a free fall at the right-hand side. This is what all newbie traders and experienced traders alike will recognize.

However, the group in between them, the traders who know just enough to trip themselves up, will probably say this is moving sideways. The position of the first price bar on the left is roughly the same (on a vertical scale) as the final price bar on the right. Hence, it must not be trending right? Wrong! This is an example of how one can overcomplicate things.

Just keep it simple and if all else fails, go with your gut. But if your gut fails too or if you don't trust it enough, stepping aside and saying "I don't know" is a perfectly valid answer. There's no rule in the markets that says you need to participate all the time.

Ranges

The second form of price action activity cause by order flow is called a range. As you've probably guessed by now, a range is a non-trending or sideways market. Determining this is just as simple as determining a trend. You look left to right and if there doesn't seem to be a major commitment to any particular direction from the market, we're in a range.

The chart below illustrates this point.

Figure 2: A Ranging Environment, From: (**Global Prime-**MetaTrader 4, 2018)

Now even in this chart, if we get really technical with it, the first price bar is at a lower point than the final one on the right. However, this is not a trending environment by any means. Yes, the price fluctuates. Moving left to right, we see it go up a bit, go back down, then go up quite a bit and then promptly fall back down before going back up again.

The overall product of this up/down/up action is a sideways movement. Notice how you can draw a straight line across the points when the price reaches towards the bottom of the chart. This is referred to as the bottom of the range. In this particular range, the top isn't clearly marked but you could roughly draw a straight-line right about where the arrow has been placed on the chart.

So now that we've seen what the definitions are of a trend and a range, let's look at the underlying cause of such the price movement.

How Order Flow Produces a Landscape

When reading a price chart like the ones above, it's easy to focus only on the bars or candles in them and forget that these bars are the result of something, not the cause of anything. Put simply, these bars are the result of buyer and seller interactions which make up the underlying order flow.

Many traders approach the markets the other way around and fail to take note of this fact. Looking solely at the price bars without acknowledging the underlying order flow is much like a doctor treating a symptom instead of the underlying disease. That's an unfortunate analogy but let's stick with it for now.

Let's now look at the nature of order flow that results in a trend or a range.

Trending Landscapes

In any instrument, at any time when the markets are open, there are buyers interacting with sellers. These parties mutually agree to exchange the instrument with one another for a given price and it is this price we see on stock tickers and price charts.

If there happens to be a larger number of buyers than sellers, the demand exceeding supply, the price goes up. The degree by which the price goes up is determined by the measure of buyers exceeding the sellers. Put simply, the steeper the price rise, the greater the number of buyers compared to the sellers.

Similarly, when the number of sellers exceeds the number of buyers, supply exceeding demand, the price falls. The degree by which price falls is determined by the measure of how much the sellers exceed the buyers. Please note: We as traders are not concerned with why the numbers exceed one another. All we know is that they do and we're here to take advantage of it. Remember the point previously made about speculation versus investment.

At the start of trends, we often see huge with trend (be it up or down, also called bullish or bearish respectively) participation. One can understand this behavior psychologically. The price usually breaks into a trend after a sideways movement. Traders as a bunch aren't huge fans of prolonged ranges and as soon as the price shows an inclination to break out, everyone rushes in with relief that, finally, the market is headed somewhere. This often results in a steep movement in the with trend direction (again, this could be bullish or bearish).

Nothing is ever unchallenged though. The counter-trend players will soon show up and test the strength of the with trend players. If the with trend push is strong, the counter-trend players are easily overcome, and this usually shows up as a very small countertrend or sideways movement on the chart. In the overall scheme of things, this usually looks like a blip.

As the trend progresses over time though, the number of counter-trend players start increasing and the trend progress becomes slower. The testing periods or sideways movements become longer in duration and sometimes even go sharply against the trend. If a sharp counter-trend movement is observed on the chart, it's a clear indication of the growing strength of the counter-trend players and that we might be seeing the end of the trend.

Eventually, the strength of the counter-trend players equals that of the with trend players and we enter a ranging landscape.

Ranging Landscapes

A range is produced when the underlying order flow in the instrument is roughly equal. In other words, no side is particularly able to sustain its domination. We might see the price hurry in a particular direction but is swiftly pushed the other way by the opposing side.

We often encounter ranges at the end of trends and before the start of new trends. This effectively means, a range functions as a redistribution. Please note, however, that it is not necessary for the trend to reverse. In other words, if we've been in a bull trend (uptrend) for a while and we're in a prolonged range now, it doesn't automatically mean that we'll see a bear trend (downtrend) once the price breaks out of the range.

It could just be taking a breather before continuing upwards. From an order flow perspective, in such a scenario, the buyers are absorbing all the seller's orders and are preparing to push higher. In a trend reversal scenario, the sellers are absorbing the buyer's orders and are preparing to push down.

The price often prints clean boundaries in a range, but we should not expect straight lines. A better approach would be to draw a line through the greatest number of points where price reaches. Even better is to treat these areas as zones. This is something we'll discuss in the next chapter.

Following from all this, we can then conclude the following: Trends are the result of imbalanced order flow and ranges are the result of balanced order flow. The degree of imbalance determines the strength of the trend. Take care to avoid the trap of thinking of "balanced" order flow as being completely evenly distributed between both sides of the market. This is scaling in too much and overcomplicates things.

Take a look at the chart below and walk through it left to right while determining what the underlying order flow characteristics are. In particular, take note of the areas marked in the boxes labeled 1, A, B and C.

Figure 3: Order Flow Differences, From: (Global Prime-MetaTrader 4, 2018)

Follow the same reasoning as described in the previous sections, about how buyers test the strength of the with trend players, observe how counter-trend strength grows and how the order flow balances out. Notice how the size of the boxes keeps increasing as we move left to right. What does this tell you? Does a small box signify greater with trend or counter-trend strength? Will the box be bigger if there's more counter-trend strength or less?

In the chart above, blue represents buyers and red represents sellers. Again, we'll cover this in the chapters on candlesticks, but this is enough to help you understand this price chart. For now, it's time to look at the next key ingredient of the chart landscape, support and resistance.

Chapter 5:
Swing-Trading Example

N ow, let's turn to the stock market for a simple example – although this is far from the most complicated swing-trading strategy. This is based on the use of Bollinger Bands, which consist of an upper, middle and lower band, with the upper band representing the market being overbought and the lower band indicating that the market may be oversold. Most traders who use Bollinger Bands combine these with other indicators, but there are those who advocate just using Bollinger Bands to trigger opening a market position.

Specifically, when the price of a stock closes below the lower Bollinger Band, this is a signal to buy the next day. This is well illustrated with the Intel chart below, with the stock closing below the lower Bollinger Band on December 22, indicating that the stock was oversold. The next trading day – December 26 – the stock started to rise, closing above the Bollinger band and then continuing to rise through January 10. A trader who followed this swing-trading strategy for Intel would have seen the price rise by nearly $1.50 over 10 trading days – a 7.5% gain.

Of course, this is only one of many potential swing-trading strategies, and no strategy offers a guarantee of success. However, it does illustrate how swing-trading can generate significant profits in a relatively short period of time.

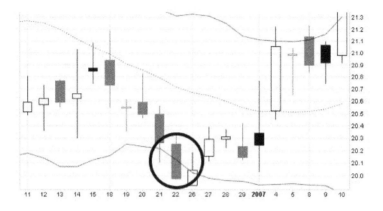

Swing Trading vs. Day Trading

Although both may have great similarities in practice, the main difference between day trading and swing trading is "time." For day traders, they could be in and out of their trades in few minutes or hours, however, swing trading can last for several days and even weeks. Since day traders trade with shorter timeframes, they don't usually hold positions overnight. Consequently, they usually escape the risk of having an open trade during news announcements which could lead to serious moves against them.

Swing traders need to always remember that the opening of a stock might be remarkably different from how it closed the previous day. Swing traders often encounter issues with the widespread between the ask and bid and the commissions which could take a great portion of their profits; however, this problem is much serious for day traders.

Also, unlike day traders that experience serious time commitment when trading since they need to pay attention to all open positions, swing traders may have few transactions in some days while they may not trade at all on other days. When you're a swing trader, you can check your positions periodically or be alerted especially when the price hits critical points. This is much better than monitoring the market constantly which could lead to apprehension and emotional trading.

Simply put, the strategy you have is your edge and it's the reason why you place a new swing trade. While the strategy is the reason why you want to enter a trade, your tactics have to do with how you enter and exit from the trade. Most trading strategies for swing traders are obtained from momentum catalysts or technical analysis.

Swing trading is the art and science of profiteering from the price movements of a security over the short term may be from a couple of days to a maximum of one month. Swing traders can be individuals or institutions like hedge funds. These traders look at low risk opportunities available to themselves before taking any bets in the markets. They try to find out undervalued companies and go long on them and try getting the lions' share of the trade once there is an upswing. They're also known to short companies that they believe are overbought for the time being and ride the wave to the downside.

Swing trading is good for a methodical thinker who likes to have time to plan their trade out in advance - to determine their entry point, analyze the upside and downside, and then settle on their exit strategy - and all before pushing their buy or sell button.

In summary, you are the one who is best able to determine if this trading style is a better approach for you and your personality. It is possible that you may be comfortable doing both types of trading, like myself. People who are comfortable day trading are often comfortable doing swing trading as well, but traders using swing trading strategies may not feel the same way about day trading.

For a day trader, that initial hour of market action often provides the best trading opportunities from a risk-to-reward perspective. So many traders continue to trade throughout the day and get chopped out of trades – eventually giving back all their profits from the open. Others do make additional profitable trades but there is considerable sitting, watching and waiting involved in-between tradable opportunities.

Day trading is a huge time commitment. Day traders can change their positions in a minute, and certainly, trading positions of fifteen minutes or less are very common. This means that you must constantly be monitoring your position.

With swing trading, you have a chance to breathe, you need to monitor your trades, and make sure you're in a favorable position, but obviously not with the intensity and stress of day trading. Also, commissions are lower on swing trading, since you won't be making multiple trades per day, which increases your spread on any given trade.

Best of all, in the end, you should realize greater profits through swing trading, as letting your trades run longer and having greater flexibility should maximize your profits on a successful trade. Both can be profitable, but swing trading allows for more profitability per trade, all other things being equal. Day traders need to exercise far more trades to realize the same profits. Do you want to make one or two trades a week or ten trades a day? For some, it's the latter, simply because that has become the technique they've developed, but for the vast majority of investors, this is simply not the case.

Although there certainly is a place for day trading, and if you have the time and the dedication to put towards it, it can be a profitable venture. Swing trading though is the best option for those who want to trade profitably without devoting their entire lives to it.

Chapter 6:

How much the world's financial market news effects the financial markets.

NASDAQ, NYSE, FTSE, DAX, CAC, Nikkei, FOREX, COMEX and on and on it goes. Anytime you switch the channel to CNBC or one of the many financial news channels, you see all these symbols floating at the bottom of the screen. The news is full of green arrows and red numbers or vice versa. If you're new to the markets, all of this will cause a severe information overload and you might be wondering if all this isn't better left to the professionals after all.

Well, let's take a step back from all this noise and focus on the important stuff. Indeed, more than any other strategy or secret sauce, this is the biggest key to making money in the markets. Any market, as a stroll through your neighborhood farmer's market, will tell you, consists of two parties: a buyer and a seller. The items they're trading might be different but, needless to say, this is a fundamental aspect of every single market out there.

So, in a stock market, we have people trading shares (also called equity) of companies with one another. The options market has people trading options, the bond market bonds and so on. While the mechanics and subtleties of each market are different, the intrinsic motivation of all the players in it are the same: to make a profit. There is only one way of making a profit in a financial market and that is to buy low and sell high.

Buy then Sell or Sell then Buy?

Please note that while you need to buy low and sell high, you don't need to do so in that order. You can sell high and buy back your instrument at a lower price later. This process is known as "shorting" (the opposite of "going long," that is, buying low and selling high) and it is here that a lot of newbies stumble. Most people are accustomed to buying low and selling high and find that, naturally, much more comforting to do as opposed to the other way around. You'll often see people invent excuses like "shorting is unethical/amoral/anti-capitalist etc." and my absolute favorite, "Shorting is Un-American/<insert your nationality>"

Shorting is something that goes against our basic nature since you're making a profit on something losing its value. If you're an investor who likes to hold stock for years on end and doesn't plan on selling soon, it doesn't make much sense to short. However, if you're a trader, irrespective of whether you're holding your stock/instrument for a few minutes, sessions, days, etc., opting to skip shorting is nothing short of suicidal for your financial success in the markets. You need to do whatever it takes to become comfortable with this if you want to have any hope of succeeding.

Opting to short is literally like wading into a pool full of sharks with one arm tied behind your back. This brings us to the next point about the nature of the markets: your trading screen and ticker at the bottom of your television simply display numbers which flash red and green or blue, and it's easy to think of it as a video game of sorts.

You must remember there are real people behind those numbers (and in stock markets these days, robots) whose sole aim is to make money. They aren't there to donate their hard-earned cash or to make things easy for you. It's important that you become mentally comfortable with the fact that if you're making money, the person or program on the other side of your trade has probably lost money. There's no definite way of knowing this but as your skill in the art of trading successfully progresses, you will realize that a lot of strategies aim to take advantage of traders who make mistakes.

Trading successfully is an art, but above all else, a business. It is imperative you treat it as one instead of viewing it as a casino or a get rich quick hustle. More than anything else, this will ensure your strategies are successful instead of losing money like most traders out there. Having got that out of the way, let's look at the two major ways of making money in the markets.

Speculation vs Investment

The debate as to what constitutes speculation and what investment is one which has always raged in the financial community. Benjamin

Graham in his book, 'The Intelligent Investor', was one of the first to put pen to paper and offer a definition. Subsequently, his many disciples such as Warren Buffett, Charlie Munger, etc. have built on that and have offered their own takes on it.

It is essential for you to understand the difference because the philosophy you most identify with will determine not only your approach to the markets but also whether you'll be successful or not. No one would expect a hardcore capitalist to support socialism and similarly, one can hardly be a successful speculator if investing is what appeals to you the most. Without going into too many technicalities, if you purchase anything with a view of treating it as an asset, you're investing. If you purchase something with the sole intention of selling it at a higher price without any care as to the underlying asset or what it represents, you're speculating.

As an example: Let's say someone offers you a book on personal financial advice for $100. You skim through this book and know that the information contained in it is priceless and that you'll probably save thousands and make a few more thousands by following its advice. Suddenly, $100 doesn't seem too steep a price for a book does it? You're investing your money in the book, and yourself, with the hope of using the book's advice to make even more money. You may or may not be able to implement this advice successfully but that's a risk you're willing to take.

Now let's say, when you're offered this book for $100, instead of skimming through this book to see what's in it, you first ask around to see what someone else is willing to pay for it. Let's assume someone you know says they'll pay $150 for it. You promptly buy the book for $100 and resell it for $150 for a quick profit. In this case, you're speculating that someone else is willing to pay a higher price for the book and you aren't particularly concerned with what the book is about. As long as there's someone willing to pay a higher price, you'll always buy that book.

It should come as no surprise to you that all forms of trading, day, swing, position, etc. firmly fall under the category of speculation. The example above simplifies the process a lot, but you should understand the philosophy and approach behind speculation and check to see whether your beliefs are compatible or not. Most beginners look at the money and forget this fundamental step in their education.

This is not to say that one approach is better than the other. You will find a lot of opinion columns on this subject, but you'll discover, as you progress in your learning, that investment vs speculation is a nonsensical debate. All that matters is you identify which one makes more sense and align yourself and your strategies accordingly.

Now that that's out of the way, let's delve more into the types of trading.

Selecting a Financial Instrument to trade

Selecting a market in which to trade will be the first big decision you will have to make as there are several different financial markets and what they call financial instruments to choose to trade in. For instance, you can trade in shares, currency, futures, options or even cryptocurrencies to name just a few. Which one you choose will depend on your interest in that field and largely by the capital you have to trade.

The good news is that there are lots of financial instruments you can swing trade with. And each one of them has its own pros and cons. Here are some financial instruments that are considered suitable for swing trading:

- Exchange-Traded Funds (ETFs): You can trade ETFs just as you would trade a regular company's stock such as Facebook (FB) or Apple Inc. (AAPL). There are ETFs for just about everything; they will track indexes and bonds, futures, commodities, stock sectors, and currencies.

- Individual stocks: Possibly the most popular instrument for swing trading is trading individual company shares. There are some advantages and disadvantages to trading individual stocks compared to trading ETFs. For example, taking a position with an individual stock exposes you to the possibility of 'single event risk.' What it means is that if you're holding a long position on a trending stock, you can be vulnerable to sudden bad news. For example, if bad news about a security breach breaks, say regarding Facebook or Google, the stock can suddenly fall. However, if you were swing trading on a sector like technology that bad news might take time to affect the market. The point is that when trading individual stocks, you are always going to be vulnerable to this type of single event risk. On the other hand, typically individual stocks can outperform other companies' stocks that are in the same sector such as Technology. This means that taking a position on an individual company's stock may mean that you can outperform an ETF covering the related sector.

- Currencies: FOREX trading is another hugely popular swing trading instrument. When trading FOREX, you're comparing the relative performances of two currencies, and so you're looking for one currency to move up or down relative to the other currency. But this requires a huge amount of research into international financial markets, and it's very volatile. For example, the US dollar may go sky high or plummet compared to the Euro because of a late-night tweet by a President or a CEO. FOREX trading is high risk and volatile, but that also makes it attractive and if you are on the right side of the trade extremely profitable.

- Cryptocurrencies: Swing trading these new cryptocurrencies has opened up a whole new market which has attracted very professional, sophisticated but also some very dubious traders and investors. The huge attraction of vast and quick profit has many amateurs entering the market which hugely inflated the realistic price. Nonetheless, the volatility of cryptocurrencies is a dream for swing traders so long as you don't get greedy.

- Options: Options and Futures are a more sophisticated instrument that can be used in hedge funds and hedging positions, but they are also good for swing trading. Trading options and using them in a variety of strategies requires additional education and experience that are not quite covered here, but a swing trader should be aware of their existence and consider using them as they increase their knowledge.

Tools and platforms, you will need

If you are seriously entering the market, then you should do it professionally. You should consider it the way you would any other business startup venture. Therefore, you must have the capital, knowledge and the tools to do the job. The first thing you'll need is an account with a licensed broker as they will do the trades on your behalf. They will also provide you with a way to make the trades typically through an online system. You should, however, shop about and try their online simulators to make sure you are comfortable with the system and the information that they give you.

Fortunately, online brokers and stock trading platforms are in abundance, but your choice may be restricted by the country in which you are currently residing.

However, if you're just starting out and you don't have a trading account, then do a Google search to find a broker in your country that has good reviews.

When considering a broker look for the following things:

Account type – There are several types of accounts that are available to you as a swing trader. There will be an investment account. This style of account allows you to trade within the limits of cash deposited in the account. However, there's also an account called a Margin Account which allows you to use the money or stocks in your account as collateral so that you can borrow money from the broker. This facility of getting a loan from the broker will give you more trading power; however, you must be aware that you are now trading on borrowed money. This means you are taking on far more risk.

Transaction fees – The cost of executing a trade must be taken into account as the commission can vary greatly in price between brokers. However, for a swing trader that is just starting out the transaction fees are not quite so important. This is simply because as a beginner you should only be doing a very limited amount of small transactions a month. If not and you start out over trading, then the brokers' transactions fees are likely to eat up the majority of your profit. The good news is that there are online brokers that charge as little as $3.75 per trade, but the bad news is that if you are working off a $1,000 account and sticking to the safe 1% rule, even that small commission will take most if not all your profit.

Platforms and Tools – You want a trading system that you are comfortable with, but they vary a lot. Some online trading systems give you a lot of added features such as charts and research. Others, however, will give you the bare minimum. Also, the quality of advice and tools can vary across different brokerages. Indeed, it isn't just across brokerages as some firms will offer different classes of service depending on how much you're willing to pay. Nonetheless, to start off you'll want a reliable online system that provides real-time quotes as well as a straightforward ordering procedure. It's also important to have a reliable system that will execute your orders immediately and also confirm your trades. That is the minimum you should be looking for, but it would be nice to have real-time charts, technical analysis tools (moving averages, support/resistance, etc.). If you're going to pay a lot for the broker's services, then you should expect research reports and opinions as well as their analysts' ratings. Fortunately finding a broker and online services is not difficult as there are many free resources and online tools available. Listed below are several excellent resources.

- FINVIZ (finviz.com)

- ChartMill (chartmill.com)

- StockCharts.com (stockcharts.com)

- Estimize (estimize.com)

- StockTwits (stocktwits.com)

- CNBC (CNBC.com)

- Yahoo Finance (finance.yahoo.com)

Before you use your account, you need to use the broker's online simulator or start out paper trading to learn and find your risk tolerance and develop your early skills.

Traditionally the way beginners entered the market was via an apprenticeship and spent paper trading, but today demo accounts are preferred. Nonetheless, paper trading is still an excellent way to find out if swing trading is suitable for you as it does provide valuable feedback on your trading judgment before you put your real money at risk. However, paper trading goes against the grain with many beginners to swing trading as it lacks the excitement of the real thing. Nonetheless, if you're serious about making swing trading a profitable venture then delay opening a trading account until you have practiced and believe you're ready to start live trading.

Starting out Paper Trading

Practicing and learning the art or science behind swing trading is incredibly important. After all, what makes you think as a novice that you can just enter the market and beat the odds. The harsh reality is that you'll need to practice and then learn from your mistakes. It is those defeats and your subsequent analysis that will give you the skills which will enable you to survive let alone be successful. Even if you are a skilled trader in other instruments or a hugely successful day or position trader changing codes means learning new strategies and specialized tactics. Nonetheless, as competitive as the markets are, paper trading does give you a method to develop your skills. This is why and how you should do it:

Before you, as a beginner place a live trade, you should make sure to take the time to test the waters by first trying to trade out on paper. The first step is to decide the amount you want to trade. This amount will be determined ultimately by your capital and your risk appetite. But in this example let us keep the figures easy to work with so let's say it is $10,000

Then you select your stock after some level of fundamental analysis you have concluded that certain stocks look to be on a promising trend wave and worth trading.

Now what you must do is to write on paper or notepad the current stock prices and the number of shares you want to buy with their current selling price.

Then you have to subtract the commission and transaction fees from that figure.

Divide that trading figure by the actual share price but remember to round down as you can't own a 1/3 or 1/2 of a share.

Then sit back and ride the wave as you track your trades. You can easily do this by checking the closing stock price.

An example of paper trading to show you how well it can, work here is an example of paper trading a virtual portfolio.

In this scenario, you start with say $20,000 and five preferred stocks. You have $4,000 per investment, but we must take commission and transaction fees into the equation, so we are less a $20 fee for buying and selling that's $9,980 apiece. Hence, we're likely to buy along with this type of pattern:

Stock A: Bought 100 shares at $20 for $2000

Stock B: Bought 150 shares at $30 for $4500

Stock C: Bought 100 shares at $50 for $5000

Stock D: Bought 100 shares at $60 for $6000

Stock E: Bought 200 shares at $12 for $2400

Now what you want to keep in mind here is that the original share price isn't as significant as the percentage of price movement, i.e., the gain or loss. For example, if Stock B goes up from $4 to $34 per share. You now have $5100 in this position a profit of 11%. But the notable thing is if Stock E also goes up from $4 to $16 per share? Well, then you'd be at $3,200 in this position at a profit of 13%.

This is the thing you must remember it isn't always just about the price it's about your current position – this is determined by both the price and how much stock you hold. Paper trading is educational and can be helpful in surfacing some strange trading anomalies as well as effectively designing your own swing-trading strategy. After all, it is far better to make your mistakes on paper exercises than lose your money trading real stocks. Of course, there is a downside. It's boring, and you don't get the positive feedback that a real trade gives you – a tangible loss or gain – but you must practice and learn the skills and develop those tactics and then see whether your skills and research return a profit. An alternative approach and one many younger people favor is to use a simulator or demo account to test their skills.

Practice trading with a Demo Account

Should you find that paper trading is a bit boring, then an alternative is to use a demo account. Most brokers will give you this facility as it is a simulator that you can practice on. By all accounts, demo accounts are more enticing than paper trading as the simulators give you immediate feedback as to how your trades are performing. But of course, there's always a conflict of interest – remember they are trying to sell you a service - and you may well find that you can do no wrong. Instead, you should try out as many as you can, and practice swing trading with a wide range of tactics. At the end of the day, demo accounts are a great way to gain trading experience without losing your money. They are important to swing traders as they allow you to try out and experiment with new strategies and tactics. They also help you build confidence – but be aware some are vanity orientated - while you learn the basics of market trading.

The problem with simulators and demo market games is that they are often too one dimensional. They do not sufficiently give the experience of losing or winning and one of the problems is they often have little context as the data is historical. But in real life, the market is based on three emotions: Greed, Fear and Hope. With the latter being the deadliest. There's no way to simulate these emotions at the depth required to represent real trading whereby you could be fabulously wealthy or wiped out in a few seconds. Instead, the best that demo accounts can do is to simulate the real trading environment without the emotions. It isn't the same psychologically. Indeed, physically trading with pretend money in many ways can make you learn bad habits. Nonetheless, it is an introduction to the sometimes-overwhelming experience of the financial market's mayhem. Therefore, realistic or not it's still a very good way to practice. There is, of course, a dilemma as most brokers provide you

108

with these free to use demos or simulators. The problem is that they want you to play and to boost your confidence and get you to trade. After all, that's how they make their money. Hence be very wary of demos where you seem to do no wrong and especially those that reward a winning trade with a pop-up acclaiming you to be a top trader.

- **Discovery** – There is a school of thought that every trader should find their niche market by testing their skills and knowledge against different financial instruments. The belief is that it will allow you to get a feel for the market that is best suited to your temperament as markets do behave differently. An example would be that trading stocks will be different to futures or commodities.

- **Gain experience** – Practice your techniques and strategies before you risk your own money. Whatever you do practice at least entering and exiting positions, plus applying stops and limits. Also, you may want to start experimenting with short selling, and you'll gain an understanding of risk and capital margin requirements, as well as in tracking your profit and loss.

- **Charting** – The most important aspect that a beginner to trading needs to learn is how to read a chart. Even if it's just simple pattern recognition, it's invaluable in making informed decisions. Therefore, you should spend time learning how to interpret price charts. What is more, you should also test your tactics and techniques against these charts to validate their effectiveness by testing the technical indicators to surface illusive patterns.

- **Evaluate past performance** – Just about all worthy analysis is based on historical data. Machine Learning and A.I. feed almost exclusively on historical data. These clever algorithms analyze past performance data to find ways to find better solutions. They're a good way to determine and hone your strategy before you put your savings on the line.

- **Trading tools** – There are a myriad of resources available to you such as the financial news, forums, and social media but how you interpret the information is the decisive factor. We all have free access to the same general information, but some make it work for them while others let it drift by. Understanding how world events can affect stocks particularly within a sector is hugely important, so pay attention to news feeds and breaking market data.

- **Watch-lists** – As part of your overall strategy have a list of potential stock that you would like to keep an eye on. These may be stocks that you aren't sure about, but you still should keep them in mind. Many experienced traders regret missed opportunities rather than bad trades so keep track of those borderline stocks.

- **Manage Risk**– A demo account is hugely beneficial as you are betting with virtual money. Therefore, gains and losses are meaningless in real terms, but they should be tactically analyzed to prevent you from repeating the mistake with your own money. Also, demos allow you to practice swing trading so that you make your early learning mistakes in a safe environment and not in the big bad world.

- **Price action** – Demos give you plenty of practice in reading price lines and identifying trends. One of the best ways to interpret a price line is to spot the visual patterns; however, that only comes with experience. Practicing on real price lines on a demo will enable you to interpret those volatile movements that will allow you to profit on future real price fluctuations.

- **Broker and platform** – Trying out a broker's online platform is a good way to evaluate their service. You can, for example, see what research and charts they provide and see what they charge extra for. Also, you can get a taste of how good they are by dipping into their forum and taking account of the sentiments of the regular poster.

Chapter 7:

Tips and tricks used by Top investors

B elow are a variety of tips that you can carry with you into your new swing trading career. These tips are taken from experienced traders who want to give you the best advice that they can, so you can begin your new job with a positive mindset and feel ready to take on the swing trading world.

Learn from Your Mistakes and Move On

Successful traders learn several lessons early on in their career. One of these is that mistakes are going to happen and when they do, you have to learn from it and move on. You can't hang on to the mistake you made as this won't help you psychologically. It's important as a trader to note that you should always be in the right frame of mind. When you start to dwell on your mistakes, then you're more likely to become emotional. This can allow your emotions to make decisions instead of thinking logically.

Even if you make a mistake that you read about on this list. This happens. You don't want to put too much stress on this mistake. Instead, you want to realize that you made the mistake, figure out what you can do so you are less likely to make the mistake in the future, and then move on.

Stay in the Right Mindset

Every successful swing trader knows that one of the most important pieces of the career is having the right mindset. The basis of this mindset is to believe that when you're confident in your abilities and you believe that you can become a successful swing trader, you'll become a successful trader. There are a lot of parts to developing this mindset and it can take time, especially if you lack patience, confidence, and don't believe that you'll be successful.

Be Flexible

Many people get into the swing trading business with the belief that they must follow the rules and guidelines exactly as they are written. On top of this, they believe that they have to stick to their own rules exactly as they were created. But really, when you become inflexible to the world of swing trading, including the rules, then you will start to feel stressed. This stress can put you in the wrong mindset for trading. For example, it can make you feel that you are not capable of becoming a successful trader.

Remember the Research

Learning is a common theme as a trader. It doesn't matter what type of trading you find yourself taking on, you will always want to make sure that you learn as much as you can before you start your career and continue to learn. There are a variety of ways that you can focus on research and learning with swing trading. For example, reading this book is one way that you are researching and learning.

Join an Online Community

Another great way to learn about swing trading and meet other traders is to join an online community. There are several websites that are comprised of forums run by some of the most experienced swing traders today. These forums are extremely beneficial to any trader for a variety of reasons. First, beginners can go join the community and receive more tips, trading lessons, and other information that will help them become successful. Second, this is often a location where beginners meet their trading mentor. Third, this is a place where traders can go to not only get the most up-to-date information on the profession but also get to know people who are like them. It is always important to feel that you aren't alone, especially when find yourself struggling with a part of trading. There will be hundreds, if not thousands, of people who will be interested in helping you.

Below are a few swing trading online communities that you can check out:

The Trading Heroes Blog

This is a swing trading & currency trading education online community. This blog started in 2016 and focuses on FOREX education and trading. Over the last few years, this blog has grown to become one of the top swing trading blogs online. The owner publishes about one post per month; however, he is often found on the blog and is willing to help other swing traders with advice.

Elite Swing Trading

This is one of the most in-depth swing trading websites available. The site is run by Jason Bond Picks and gives not only a place where other traders can converse but also a newsletter with helpful information and tips for everyone involved in the swing trading community.

Morpheus Trading Group

This is an online community that focuses on how to trade stocks. This community started around 2002 and has steadily grown to become one of the most helpful communities online. You will receive about one post per month which will give you all types of helpful information to help you through your swing trading journey.

Ratgebergeld

If you want to find a community that gives you a little more than just one post every month, you can check out Ratgebergeld. This is a site that focuses on both swing trading and day trading. You will receive about two posts a week which focus on the most up-to-date information and a live chat. There are generally several experienced traders who are a part of this chat and are ready to help you with any problems you might be having in the moment.

Align the trade with the market

When you're trying to figure out what trades to do, you always need to look at what the market is doing. The market is not going to behave in the manner that you like, so you need to learn how the market is about to behave and then pick your trades to go with that.

The overall direction the market will take will be measured through the S&P 500. These trends will provide you with some context for making your short-term trades. Remember that such trades will be a bit different than you will find with long-term trends and look at how the market will behave in the next few weeks is more important than worrying about how the market will do over the next few years.

However, you do need to pay some attention to the trends that happen over the long-term with swing trading. These trends will often show up again and again for a stock and look at them can help to increase your profit potential. Yes, it is important to observe the short-term and see what is going on with the market to see if anything is about to change and then trade along with that trend. The more you can look at the charts, both long-term and short-term the more you will be able to make good decisions on your trades.

Go short weakness and long strength

You shouldn't avoid the tape once you figure out what the overall trend is. You need to look at the charts to find long trades that will work during periods of bullishness. And then when you are dealing with periods of bearishness, you need to find the right short trades. These trends will help you to get the results that you would like when it comes to successful swing trading.

Forget to use stop points

The stop points will be so important when you start out as a swing trader. These points will tell you when to get out of the market, whether the market is going up or down and can reduce your risk. You need to have a stop-loss point, which is the point you will get out of the market if you lose so much money, and you need a stop-profit point, which is where you will get out of the market once you earn a certain profit.

Figuring out your risk-to-reward ratio and your profitability

The profitability of the trades that you work with will be the percentage of trades that you complete that end with a profit. So, if you earn a profit on sixty of your trades and you trade 100 times, your ratio will be sixty percent.

On the other hand, the risk-to-reward ratio will be the amount that you end up risking compared to the amount that you are working to gain. As a beginner, it is best to pick a risk-to-reward ratio that is no worse than 1 to 1. This means that if you risk about five percent on the trade, you will try to make five percent on that trade as well.

117

This ratio is not going to make you a ton of money, but it does help you form a base and will build up confidence as you go. Depending on the chart pattern that you work with, you may change the ratio around a bit, but this will vary based on the strategy that you want to use. As you become more of a professional trader, you can increase your risk-to-reward ratio so that you can earn more on each trade.

Enter at the beginning rather than the end

One mistake that some beginners will make is that they will try and enter the trend near the end of it, rather than catching the trend at the beginning. This will limit some of the money that you can make if you wait too long to enter a trend. Of course, it is much better to get into the market at some time for the trend, before it goes down because you will be able to make some money, but the earlier you can get into the trend, the more money you can make.

When looking at the charts, it is important to look for early signs of the change. The earlier you can see these new trends, the less risk you will take with swing trading and the bigger the profits you will make. This means that you must be active. Trends can go quickly and if you aren't careful about what is going on in the market, and you're not looking at the market averages, you will end up missing out on some trends and will miss out on some money, or even lose money.

Looking at the overall market averages on your charts will help with this. When you look at the market averages, you will sometimes see that the stocks have been oversold or overbought. When this has happened, it means that it is likely they will turn around again soon. If the trend looks like it is about to reverse, you can jump in, get the stock for a good price, and sell it over the next few weeks when things start to go back up.

You need to get some of your own indicators in place to figure out when these trends are about to happen. The Volatility Index, the Put/Call Ratio, and the Arms Index are good tools. You'll be able to see, through these methods, when the market is testing a major zone of resistance and support, and it can help you to predict what will happen in the future.

On the other hand, looking at moving average crossovers and trendlines will make you fall behind. These are just going to confirm that a trend is happening and by the time you see them and join in on a trade, it may be too late to make any money. These tools can help you determine if you have made a good decision along the way, but if you're relying solely on them, you'll miss out.

Never trade on one technical concept

With swing trading, things will change on a frequent basis. You need to work with trading quickly, picking up one trade and then selling it within a few weeks. You don't get the benefit of staying with the market for a very long time, or you're missing out on the profits you can make. Relying on just one technical concept will lead you to a lot of trouble along the way.

119

In most cases, the highly profitable trades will occur when you can find at least two (but more is much better) technical tools send you the same message. There are times when several of your tools will show the same indicators, and this means that the stock will rise or fall sharply in the future. This is great news for you. The more indicators that show the same information, the more likely that the trend is about to occur and that you will make a large profit in the process.

However, there are times when one indicator will show that a trend is about to occur. If you only look at that one indicator, you may find out after entering the trade that it is wrong. You want to have at least a few indicators in place to help you make your decisions. The best opportunities for swing trading will show up in at least a few indicators, and when you can get three or more of these to show up with the same message over a two- or three-day period, this will increase your profitability.

Enter the trade with a good plan

There are a lot of different strategies and plans that you can go with. Many of them can be successful when it comes to swing trading, but you do need to pick out a good one and stick with it. One of the worst things that a beginner can do is get started with a strategy, see that maybe ir isn't doing as well as they had hoped, and then jumping over to a new strategy right in the middle of their trade.

This is setting yourself up for failure, and you're more likely to lose money with this method than any other.

It's fine to switch out the types of strategies that you want to use if you find one is not the best for you. But you must make sure that you pick out a strategy and use it for the whole time of your trade. Even if the trade is not going the way that you would like, stick with the strategy. This will limit your risks, and you will learn more from the experience in the long run. If a strategy is not the right one for you, simply switch to a different one the next time.

Try to work the odds

You can't make the market work the way that you would like. The market will behave however it would like. There are a lot of different people who are in the market, and the swing trading will only take place over a few days. You need to learn how to work with the market, rather than trying to influence it.

It is never a good idea to risk a dollar just so you can make a dime. You have to pick out smart trades, trades that will lower your risk as much as possible while making your high profits. There will be some trades that may promise a lot of money if you try them, but the risk is so high that you are likely to lose all your investment plus more without making anything.

The best trades that you can do are ones that will provide you with a strong profit if you make the right types of decisions, but where you can limit your losses as much as possible if you're wrong. The profits may not be as big as some of the trades that you can make, but it ensures that you will not lose out on all your investment either.

Do your trading with a consistent group of stocks

When you first get started with day trading, it's pretty easy to jump around between stocks. You may find on that looks good and then want to jump to another once the trade is all done. There is nothing wrong with following the action, but it is always best to have your core stocks that you track on a regular basis and learn how they work.

Having a few regular stocks is a great way to see regular success with swing trading. These regular stocks will allow you to learn about the market better and can save a lot of time researching. You will have time to learn how the stocks work and understand how they have performed in the past and are likely to perform in the future. It takes some of the work out of it all when you can stick with a few core stocks over the long term.

Of course, there is nothing wrong going with a new stock on occasion if you see some big trends that are coming up. This can be a great way to increase your profit, especially if you've been in the market for some time. But chasing after those new stocks can take a lot of work. Learn as much about your core stocks as possible, and you'll save a lot of effort, reduce your risk, and increase your profits.

Everyone will spend time working with different methods and strategies when it comes to swing trading. And even with different methods, it is possible to see many people make a profit. If you follow some of these rules and learn how to pick the right strategy, you will see some great results when it comes to swing trading.

Putting in more money than you can afford to lose

With any investment that you work with, you need to be careful about the losses that you are dealing with. If you take on too much risk, you'll end up losing all your money and never getting a chance to give it another try. Coming up with a good risk-to-reward ratio will help to limit your losses, but you also must make sure that you never put in more than you are willing to lose.

Understand your strategy

If you don't understand the strategy that you are using, it can be impossible for you to get results when you get started with swing trading. Your strategy will outline exactly how you'll behave in each trade situation. It will tell you how to look at the charts, how to pick out the stocks, when to enter the market, and when to exit the market. Each strategy has the potential to be successful, but you need to understand the strategy and use it properly.

When you get started in swing trading, it is always best to start with a simple strategy. Yes, there are some more complex ones that may sound fun, but since you are already learning about the market and how it works, why add in more complications with a hard strategy. There are a lot of great strategies that are simple, and some even designed for the beginner, that will make you just as much money as the more complex strategies, without all the work.

Have the right tools

As a trader, you need to have some of your own tools in place if you would like to get started with swing trading. This can be a very difficult method when it comes to investing, and without the right tools, you'll miss out on some important information that can help you see trends and make smart decisions along the way.

The first place to go for some tools is to talk to your broker. Often the broker will have a variety of unique tools that they can give to you as part of their fees. If you don't know how to use some of these tools, make sure to ask questions to learn how to make it all work or you will miss out.

You can also bring in some of your own tools to the game as well. Find charts about the market, look online, and ask questions. Remember, the best way to notice a trend is when the same information starts to show up on more than one chart or tool so always strive to have as many of these tools available as possible.

Don't follow the crowd

When you first get started, it can be tempting to find a mentor or a group and then just follow along exactly with what they do each time. This is really tempting if you see that they're making a lot of money and you want to join and make that money as well. But in the long run, no one knows the trading style that you like, and there are times when even an advanced mentor will get things wrong.

Instead of following along blindly with what someone else tells you, it's better to learn your own way. There is nothing wrong with talking to a mentor and others who have been in the market for some time, but you need to learn your own methods, strategies, and behavior. This will help you to stay on track with your trades and will ensure that you don't get misled by others who may not have your best interests at heart.

Cut your losses

Even the best swing traders will make mistakes at times. They will misread the market, they will try out a new strategy that doesn't work for them, or the market just doesn't behave in the manner that they had hoped. And when this happens, the trader will lose their money. As a beginner, it is more likely that you will earn a loss at some point. The important thing is to learn how to cut your losses, rather than staying too long in the market.

Some beginners will see that they are losing money on one of their trades and so they will try to regain that money. Even with the market going down, and no signs of reversal, they will stay in the market and hope that things will reverse. This is dangerous because it results in you staying in the market way too long and you'll lose way too much money in the process.

Instead of sticking with a market that is not working in your favor, it's much better to learn how to cut your losses. Pick out an amount that you are comfortable with losing if the market does not go the way that you would like, put a stop point there, and then withdraw from the market as soon as you reach that point. This will help you to limit your losses and can give you more opportunities to try another trade in the future.

Utilize Technology Wisely

Trading is a focused business. Graphing stages allow dealers a boundless collection of strategies for review and breaking down the business division. When you utilize technology in a clever way, you get well ahead and can access important information you will need.

Learn to control the emotions a little bit

We already talked about this, but I can't emphasize how important this is. The mistake that almost all beginners make is that they let their emotions get in the way of their decision making. They see that they are about to lose out on a trade, or they see that the profits will keep reaching a higher value, and they want to stay in the market longer, despite what all their research and their strategy told them before. This will end up disastrous and is one of the leading reasons that beginners lose so much money and end up having to stop at day trading.

The most important thing that you can do when you get into swing trading is learning how to keep your emotions out of the game. This is important no matter which investment you choose, but it is especially important when you are working with some of these short-term investments. Once your emotions get into the mix, it is a lot harder to make smart decisions and trades that lead to profits.

If you let your emotions get into the mix, you are likely to make poor trading decisions. You will make decisions that will lead you to lose money. You'll stay in the market too long, hoping to earn more money, or hoping that you can recover some of your losses. Basically, when you start letting the emotions get into the mix, you're risking your money, and you'll end up losing out on all your hard work.

For those who aren't able to think through their decisions critically, who can't keep their emotions out of the trades that they will do, it is much better to just stay out of the market completely. Swing trading needs some fast decision making and the help of a lot of research. If you can't do this without all the emotions, you will fail in the long run.

Chapter 8:

Tools for swing trading

To see success with swing trading, you need to make sure that you are working on the right strategy. There are a lot of different strategies that you can work with when you are ready to join the market, and each of them has potential to earn you a profit if you properly use them. But you must know how each of them will work and you need to stick with that strategy throughout your whole-time trading.

Looking at good patterns

One thing that you can look at is the charts for a stock you would like to look through. There are a lot of different patterns that can come up all the time and the way that they look will determine whether they are a good one to use for your trade or if you should go with another option. When you notice these patterns, you will be better able to predict how the stocks that you want to work with will behave in the future and use this to make a profit. Let's look into some of the successful swing trading patterns that you should look for when you get started.

TRIANGLES

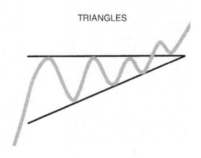

Triangle: The triangle shape is a very successful pattern to look for, and if you see it in one of your stocks, you will be likely to see successful. With the triangle pattern, you will notice that the trend is going either upwards or downwards, but the variations are getting smaller between the highs and the lows. When these starts to get together on the right side of the triangle, you can see that a breakthrough trend is about to happen. This can go the opposite way as well. If you see a triangle that goes in the opposite way of the picture above, it means that the trend is about to go down and you should not join in.

DOUBLE TOPS

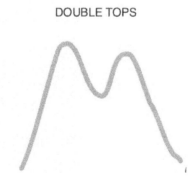

Double Top: this is another pattern that many swing traders will observe, and it can be really successful. It is one that you want to look for when it comes to working with swing trading. The same pattern works even if it is turned around. For example, if you notice that this trend is upside down, you can use this information to help with going long in your stock.

CHANNEL PATTERN

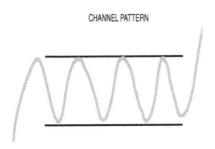

Channel Pattern: This is a great pattern even though it is not always as successful as some of the others. You'll find this one repeating through various instruments that you may be moving. There are two ways that you can trade for this pattern. One is on the channel, and the other is to trade when there is a breakout. It often depends on which way you would like to trade with your swing trade and how the market is doing.

The Moving Average

Another option to use is the moving average. Since swing trading can do quite well with technical analysis and the moving average is considered one of these, it is a good option to go with. The two options that you can use include the exponential moving average and the simple moving average. With the simple moving average, we will look at the average of security over a specified number of time periods, such as over fifteen minutes or another time frame. The exponential moving average will spend more time looking at recent prices. The point of both is to identify the direction of the trend and figure out where the resistance and support levels are to make the most money possible.

One thing to notice is that these moving averages will lag from the current prices because they base themselves on the prices that happened in the past. The longer the time period you use for a moving average, the bigger lag you will deal with. This means that a 200-day MA will have a bigger lag compared to a 20-day MA because of how long of a time period it covers.

The best bet is to use shorter moving averages since you are working with a short-term trading strategy. If you decide to do a longer-term investment, you can go with a longer moving average if you would like. Often going with something near the 50-day MA is a good option because it gives you a good amount of average to work with and when breaks happen, either below or above this moving average, it can be an important signal for your trading.

You'll find that moving averages are also important trading signals all on their own, but they can be important when there are two averages that will cross over. When there is a moving average that rises, it shows that the stock is going through an uptrend, but when the moving average is starting to decline, it means that the stock is starting to go on a downtrend.

In a similar manner, an upward momentum can be confirmed when you see a bullish crossover, which is something that happens when the short-term moving average starts to cross higher than the moving average for the long-term.

The opposite will be true if you are looking at downward momentum with a bearish crossover.

Candlestick charts

These are great technical tools that can hold a lot of data about the stock into one price bar. This can make them easier to look at and more useful than the traditional simple lines that will often connect the closing prices.

These candlesticks will build up patterns that can predict the direction of the price once you are done with it, and the brighter colors make them easier to read through.

There are a few different types of candlestick patterns that you can work with, and each one will help you in different types of markets. You also need to find your own candlestick patterns.

If you follow the ones that are given out by hedge funds and other big companies, you're being led in the wrong direction, and you won't see the results that you want. But, there are always candlestick patterns that you can follow to help you get the best results.

TWO BLACK GAPPING

You can also work with the two black gapping candlesticks. This is a bearish pattern that will occur after the stock has gone through a big top in an uptrend and there will be a gap down that will yield out two black bars that post lower lows. With this kind of pattern, it will predict that the stock will continue to decline even more and that there may be a more regular downtrend in the market. If you see this kind of trend, there is a higher chance that the stock will experience lower prices soon.

Another strategy to work with is the three black crows. This one will start at or near the high of your uptrend, and there will be three black bars that will post lower lows. This is another predictor that a decline will continue in the stock and that this trend may continue for the foreseeable future. The version that is the most bearish will start at a new high point because it will end up trapping some buyers who are entering in on momentum plays. This pattern though is often going to predict that the stock will continue with the lower prices rather than going back up.

You can also work with the abandoned baby candlestick strategy. This is another bullish option that you can use, and it will appear at the low of a downtrend, right after there is a series of black candles that print out some new lows. The market will gap even lower on the next bar, but when there aren't any new sellers to help, it will yield a narrow range Doji candlestick at the opening and closing prints at the same price. Then there will be a bullish gap on the third bar that will help to complete the pattern, and it will predict that the recovery will continue to new highs. This is a good one to work with when you're trying to see if the price is about to go up with the stock you want to work with.

Working with candlesticks can be of great use to figure out which way the market will go. They are not completely accurate all of the time, but they can give you a good idea of how the trend will continue in the near future and will give you a way to determine if it is time to get into the market or if you need to wait until a later time. Many people like to work with the candlestick strategies because this allows them to look at the market accurately and make the best predictions on what will happen in the future.

Use technical analysis and the price action

These are techniques that most swing traders will use. This kind of analysis will make it easier to figure out which stock or option you should trade and for how long you should hold it.

Don't spend all the time with a company

While most long-term investors will focus on the fundamentals of a stock compared to how well it is doing at a moment, this is not something that swing trading will worry about. You may want to pick a few stocks to stick with for your trades because this helps you to learn the history and make better predictions, but you don't need to worry yourself about the particulars of the company. The intrinsic value, who runs the company, who owns the company, and what the company does is not all that important unless it will lead to a big increase in stock value over the next few weeks.

Stick with the trends

Many swing traders will choose to look at the trends in the market and then use those to help them develop their own strategy. For example, they will use a bull trend bar when they are working with a bull market, and then they will do a bear trend bar any time they are in a downward market.

Work against the trend

It is more common for a swing trader to work with the current trend of their stock or the market they pick. But there are some who decide to work against the trend, something that is known as fading. For example, when the stock is swinging high, they will choose to work with a bearish position, but when there is a downtrend, they will take a bullish position.

Japanese candlesticks

Some new traders like to work with candlestick charts because they are a bit easier to understand compared to a bar chart. You can use these charts to identify where there is pressure for buying and when there is pressure for selling. You can also use these charts to figure out how intense the pressure is at a time. If you can read these charts the proper way, it's easier to know which way the market is going, and you can make some smart investing choices.

T-Line strategy

With this strategy, you will go look at your charts and identify where the T-line is located to help you make good trading decisions. If you see that a stock is closing above this line, there is a good probability that the price will keep rising. On the other hand, if the stock ends up closing below this line, it's likely that the stock price will keep falling. In many investment trades, this strategy will prove successful.

Trend Following

No matter what strategy you decide to use, you'll need to make sure that you understand how to read charts and trend lines. You'll use these tools in order to help guide you towards the best time to make your move to buy and sell a stock. When it comes to following a trend, there are a lot of details, such as what the opening price was, the highest price, the lowest price, and the closing price. You will analyze the trend over a period, how long depends on your personal preference. Through your analysis, you'll start to notice a pattern in the trend line. This is the pattern that you'll follow when you decide to take on a stock, see if your strategy will work for the stock, or what strategy to use.

The factors that you'll look at when trend following are:

Price of the Stock

The price of the stock is one of the most important features that you'll pay attention to. This doesn't just mean the price of the stock at that moment, such as what you would pay in order to purchase the stock. Even though the current price is the most important price, you will want to pay attention to all of the prices that you see for every day that you take into your analysis. For example, if you decide to look at the historical context of the last two months, you will look at about 60 days of stock pricing in order to help you find a trend. This means that you'll look at the opening price for each of these days, the closing price, the highest price, and the lowest price. You will want to look at these prices in detail and in general. In a sense, this means that you'll look at the larger image and the smaller pieces that make up the larger image.

Managing Your Money

Money management is thought to be one of the trickiest parts of trading. When it comes to managing your money, you want to make sure that you don't have too much money as it can give you a bigger loss. However, if you have too little money for the stock, then you can't reach the full benefits when you make the trade. This is another time in swing trading when you want to find the best spot in order to make the trade.

One of the biggest tips to help you figure out how much money to put towards a stock is by evaluating the risks associated with the stock. You will be able to do this through any strategy that you'll use and various other factors that are part of your trading plan.

Rules and Guidelines

One of the most important factors to remember when you're looking towards your trend line and thinking of making a trade. These rules are not only the guidelines that you will receive as you start to learn the swing trading technique, they are also the rules that you'll set for yourself. For example, if you decide that your stop-loss price is going to be $10.00 lower than the price you bought the stock from, you will want to make sure that you follow this guideline.

One of the biggest reasons you need to make sure that you're following your guidelines is because the more consistent you're with your trading, the more likely you are to become successful. Furthermore, you'll want to make sure that you follow the guidelines as they will help you to think systematically when it comes to making decisions. While you might find yourself turning back to your trading plan and guidelines consistently as a beginner, the more you follow the same procedures, the more you focus on them as a way in making sure you're following the steps instead of needing them for direct reference on where to go and what to do next. In a sense, trading will start to become more natural to you, which is a great strength when you're analyzing trend lines.

Diversity

Diversity is one of the more popular controversies when it comes to trading. While some traders feel you need to have great diversity, which is a variety of stocks, in your portfolio others feel that this isn't as important. But really, the more serious you want to be with your trading, the more you'll focus on diversity. However, this isn't always true when it comes to investors. But, as stated before, investing and trading are two different career paths in the stock market.

You can look at diversity as what is the right feature for you. You might find that you don't need to have a large diversity because you are a part-time swing trader, or you have a specific target that you focus on. Although, you might also find that the more diversity you have, the better-rounded you feel as a trader. You may see that diversity is helping you learn more about investing in general.

Always Note the Risk

Another important factor to pay attention to when you're looking into trend following is how much risk is involved if you decide to take on the financial instrument you're looking at. When you're looking at the risk, you must always pay attention to your guidelines and your trading plan. These two factors will help you decide if you should take on the stock due to the risk it carries or not. It's important to remember you need to stick to the risk level you are comfortable with. Even if you think that this stock could give you good rewards, this doesn't mean that you should agree to take on the financial instrument if you're uncomfortable with the risk.

This also doesn't mean that you can't increase your risk level as time goes on. You just want to make sure that you build your confidence and comfort level with risk as your risk grows. Furthermore, as you get more knowledgeable with swing trading, it might be a good thing to slowly increase your risk when it comes to taking on stocks. It's always good to grow in many directions as a trader, including with risk.

Trend following tends to be one of the most popular techniques when it comes to trading because it has a high success rate, providing you understand where the trend line is heading. Of course, you should always remember that the stock market can take drastic turns, and no one can truly predict the future. This means, even if you analyze the trend lines to the best degree, you will still have some risk involved as the trend line could differ a bit from what you originally thought.

Using Options as a Strategy

Because you can set up an agreement which gives you the option to buy or sell the stock later, you are technically strategizing the right time to take the next step in the future.

One of the biggest ways to do this is through analyzing the various charts that you see for your stock. You'll focus on the historical charts of the stock as this will give you a timeframe for when you'll want to take the next step.

Options are known to be a great strategy if you're looking for leverage, which is when you increase a return on a trade through borrowed money. It is important that you need to make sure you'll only use this strategy if it will help you to receive more of a profit. In fact, this is one of the most important factors of choosing a strategy. You have to make sure that it's going to help you gain a profit and decrease your risks.

Short Interest

Many experienced traders state that beginners should not take part in the short interest strategy as it tends to be more of a guessing game than other strategies. When you focus on the short interest strategy, you'll compare the number of short shares to the number of floating shares.

This is a great strategy to learn as a swing trader because it can show when the stock market is about to go into bearish conditions, which means that the stock prices will start to go down. Furthermore, short interest can also warn you about short squeezing.

Pay Attention to the Float

One of the best ways that you can tell if a trade is going to help you is through a technique known as float. Essentially, a float is the total number of shares that a trader will find in public sharing. This can become very helpful because, if you have the right size of float, you can see higher profits.

But, this is also the trick when it comes to the float strategy. There tends to be a fine line between having a massive float and having a float that will give you the best profits. The reason why a massive float, which would be too many shares, can cause you to lose capital instead of increasing your profits is because if you have a huge float, the price won't move as quickly. However, if you have a smaller number of shares in your float, then you'll find that the price moves a bit higher, of course this gives you a larger profit. With this said, you also don't want to have too little shares in your float. If this happens, you won't be able to make much of a profit either as this can stop your float from increasing in price.

Breakout and Breakdown Strategies

When you focus on the breakout strategy, you're looking at the history of your stock's trend line in a microscopic fashion. What I mean by this is you will be focusing on what the trend has done over the past few days. When you're looking at the trend line, you'll see every time the price has gone up and down. Stock prices are almost constantly changing throughout the day, which is what the trend line shows. Every now and then, you'll notice in the trend line that you have a several high points and several low points. These high points indicated the highest prices of the stock and the lowest points show the lowest prices.

The biggest difference between the breakout strategy compared to the breakdown strategy is the condition of the market. If you notice that the stock has been going on an upward trend for a while, you'll use the breakout strategy. However, if you notice that the trend shows the price has been decreasing over time, you'll use the breakdown strategy.

Of course, for both strategies, there is that specific spot you need to try in order to gain your best profit. The best spot to make your next move will depend on the pattern of the trend.

News Playing

As you know by now, one of the most important parts of your day is your pre-trading portion. This is one of the first things you will do once you start your day. You'll want to do this before you start trading; however, you'll probably be checking out the stock market so you can see the changes in your stocks and any target stocks that you're watching.

However, one of the most important parts of this part of the day is reading the news that happened over night. This is important because you need to know what news is going to affect what stock, especially if you own the stock. You should always make note that any type of news can affect the pricing of financial instruments. For example, if you read that a company donated a large amount of money towards a nonprofit organization, people might be more likely to invest in that stock. However, if you read any negative news about a company, you'll find the stock price going down because people are selling their shares.

But you need to remember the trick of keeping your emotions out of the stock market. While News Playing is a strategy which is used all across the board when it comes to the stock market, for example all traders and investors use this strategy, it's important to remember that you should never make a decision to sell or take on a stock because of your emotions. I won't go much more into this because I discuss how your emotions can be a risk factor in the stock market in another chapter, but it's also a big part of News Playing that you have to look out for.

You always want to make sure that you think logically when you're planning to buy or sell a stock. Even if you find you hold a stock where the price is dropping due to negative news, you want to make sure you continue to follow your trading plan instead of going on your emotions. Therefore, you should only focus on selling the stock if the price drops to your stop-loss price. You also should not hold on to a stock for longer than you originally planned, even if they are the center of a positive news story. While you can be a little flexible when the price continues to rise, at least in swing trading, you don't want to hold on to the stock for longer than a swing trader should. You have to be aware of the timeframe.

Picking out the right strategy will be one of the most important decisions that you will make when it comes to any investment, but especially when you're dealing with swing trading. It will determine what information you're looking at for the market trends and will ensure that you catch the upward trends at the right time. If you can pick out a good strategy and stick with it for the long-term, you'll see success with swing trading.

Chapter 9:

The Best Qualities to succeed in swing trading

T he goal of this chapter is to orient you in the right direction and provide you with the right mental framework so that with time, your learning can take pace smoothly.

Discipline

Discipline is another habit that trading demands a lot. If you aren't disciplined, you will find it very hard to succeed in this business.

So, what is discipline exactly and how do you cultivate it?

In simple terms, discipline is simply the ability to stick to a certain set of rules or code of conduct. In other words, it's the ability to exercise self-restraint and deny your indulgent behavior in a given situation.

Lack of discipline is a problem that plagues many traders who fail to get consistent results in the markets. It many instances, it is not the lack of knowledge of what to do that is the problem. It is the failure to implement what you know that is often the enemy.

For instance, you are probably aware that you should study instead of going out clubbing because your grades are dependent on it. You are also aware that exercising is good if you want to keep physically fit. Additionally, you may also be fully aware that you're supposed to avoid certain types of meals because they are harmful to your health. But somehow, you keep doing the wrong things.

That is the same case when it comes to trading. You are aware that you should have a stop-loss order in place and stick to it. But somehow you keep moving it around because you believe that the market will always come back. Over time, your loss grows to unmanageable levels.

Likewise, you may already be fully aware that you should stick to one trading system that fits you. Yet, for some reason, you keep hunting for the latest system, the Holy Grail.

It's clear what is wrong here. Simply knowing what to or what not to do isn't enough. You need a set of actions that you need to take in order to keep your discipline intact. Those actions include:

Plan every trade ahead of time

You need to plan every trade and trade the plan.

By this, I mean that you should sit down and invest time in coming up with a set of rules that you should always follow. Your plan should contain the following.

1) The market setup that you are waiting for

2) The rules governing the entry price

3) The rules governing where you should place your stop-loss order

4) The rules governing where you should place your take profit order.

If your plan contains the parts above, then you are all set.

Make sure that you have written them down. Do not plan things in your mind and imagine that all is well. A plan is better written down instead of in your mind. You also need to vow to always stick to your plan no matter what.

Go over your plan at the beginning of every day and before you place any trade. It will improve your discipline over time.

Keep a trading journal

A trading journal is another vital tool to have.

In the same way a personal journal records the events of your life in a certain day, a trading journal is meant to record the events that take place in a typical trading day.

In it, you record everything that happened right before and after you took the trade. Did you follow the plan that you had? Did you stick to the 2% risk management rule? Did you wait for the right set up to form before you acted? Were you tempted to move your stop-loss order or to close out the trade prematurely?

Record everything. Then review it later.

A trading journal helps serve two important purposes. First, it provides a record that you can always revisit and see what you did right at a given point. At the same time, you'll be able to know what you did wrong at a certain point and stay away from it in the future.

Secondly, it keeps you in check in that, if you remember that you're going to have to record your trading in your journal, you'll try your best and avoid deviating from your plan and making a mistake.

It is another tool that helps you develop your discipline.

Keep a physical reminder

A physical reminder in this case means a simple note that you right down.

It's likely that sometimes for some reason, you simply deviate from your plan and make a huge mistake that costs you dearly. We've all had such times.

Maybe you overtraded, maybe you raised your stop loss, maybe you acted prematurely, and maybe you traded a different setup from the one that you vowed to stick to, which resulted in a significant loss to your account.

Instead of just letting it go, which increases the likelihood of you repeating that mistake, simply write it down and stick it somewhere. You could stick it on the wall of your home office or at your trading desk, somewhere where you will always see it.

Doing so will always keep you aware of your past actions and will likely curb your habit of repeating mistakes in the future.

In conclusion, discipline is a must-have for any trader. It doesn't matter how intelligent you think you are right now or how good a track record you have kept in the past. If you don't make an effort of becoming disciplined, then it will only be a matter of time before you learn otherwise. The tools we have looked at will help you figure that out.

Let's now look at the last point in our discussion of trading psychology.

View trading as a game and not a way of making money

Trading in general needs to be an activity that is fun, exciting and financially rewarding.

Yet, for some reason, we tend to overcomplicate it and take the fun away from it. This is probably one of the reasons why many fail so terribly at it. One solution to this is to change your view of the whole activity and begin looking at it as a game of sorts.

When you think of a game, what comes to mind?

Mostly, we associate games with a lot of fun. We also view games to mentally challenge ourselves. In addition to that, we view games as activities that we engage in which have no real consequences in the case of failure.

You can apply the same view in trading.

Pretend that trading is simply a game of points. The points are the money that you invest in it. Your goal in this game is to play and accumulate as many points as you can over time. The nature of the game is that you're going to lose your points some of the time and win likewise.

At some point, when you play and accumulate so many points, you can increase the size of your operations. You can even redeem some of the points into your bank account for use in real life, but that isn't the point.

What matters is that you're simply playing a game that you are enjoying and having fun beating the game as it challenges you to get better. And you will keep playing for as long as you possibly can.

Notice how you feel, aren't you now feeling better? If you have traded before, can you now see how it seems to take away almost all the stress out of trading? Can you now see how it can potentially open an entirely new world for you? What if you chose to live your life as trader bearing this perspective?

Now, compare it to this. You are trading $100,000 account and you were up 20% this month. And you're thinking to yourself, "Wow, I have made so much money I could buy a car with it!" But, suddenly, you come across a downward slope and you lose 10%. Now you start complaining, "I just lost money that I could spend on a holiday vacation." Or you start telling yourself, "Oh my God, that money is equal to my two my two monthly paychecks! How could I have done that?"

Can you see the difference between these two points of view? One allows you to have fun and the other one puts you on an emotional roller-coaster ride. Which one do you think helps you last longer and succeed as a trader?

If you want to enjoy success as trader, you have to change the traditional view of money that the rest of the world holds. You should view trading, not as a way of making money, but simply a game of points that you're playing and having fun with it.

If you do so, you'll enjoy immense success in this business for years to come, all while managing to stay happy and keeping a level head.

View trading as a long-term venture

As with most things in life, trading is a venture that takes time and effort to master and be successful in. As simple as this concept sounds, this is not the first thing that most new traders keep in mind when they first hear and become excited about this business.

To understand this better, let me lay it out for you.

As your browse through the internet, you come across an ad on social media that reads, "Emerson makes $100 a day day-trading from his home. Find out how." Then you think to yourself, "What if I could make $100 a day from home?" "Perhaps I could quit my job." "I've heard of many people who make money from home. Maybe I should try it."

So, you answer the ad.

Then the landing page contains a video describing a trading system in which you could invest as little as $100 and make twice perhaps thrice the same amount every time it gives you a signal.

Then you find endless testimonials from customers who say that it's working and has even made their lives better. Most of them describe financial problems that they had before they began using the system, which are now gone. Then you start thinking, "Maybe this thing is real." And the system sells for only $300! You say, "I could afford that. I have my credit card."

As you pull out the card to make the purchase, you start imagining of the thousands of dollars that you're going to get out of this system. How you'll suddenly start going on vacations in a few days. How you could get a new car, perhaps a new house. Or even pay your mortgage in full.

153

Sound familiar?

Long story cut short, a month after getting this system, you are nowhere near where this system promised it would put you. As a matter of fact, you are $5,000 in debt and no longer trust ads from the internet anymore.

This has happened to countless people the world over and is probably going on now.

Don't get suckered in by the prospect of quick and easy money. Trading is a business just like any other in which you need to put in a lot of hard work, time, money, hope, risk among other things before you can start enjoying its fruits.

Think of it this way. Could you imagine how many years it takes to stay in school in order to emerge as an undergraduate doctor? In case you didn't know, it takes seven. Majoring in other disciplines in medicine takes even longer.

At the same time, think about the years of sleepless nights that a lawyer spends in school studying trying to master the discipline so that he or she can emerge as a top lawyer. Think of the years it took a businessman to build up a business empire. Think about the deals that went bad, the stiff competition, lack of money to pay workers among other business headaches.

Why should it be any easier for you? Why do you think that you should strike 1000%+ return every year just after spending a few weeks learning how to trade?

The point I am trying to make here is this. Dump the 'get rich quick' mindset as fast as you can. If you do, you will have saved yourself a lot of wasted energy and money.

Trading can end up being one of the most rewarding ventures you can find in this world, but in order to succeed in it, you need to develop a long-term view of it and be willing to put in the hard work that is required.

For instance, you need to study books like this one for as long as is necessary. You need to invest your own money in this business. You need to be willing to delay gratification. You need to take risks. You need to network with other people in the business. You need to fight to stay on top of your game. In the end, if you work at it, you will attain success in it just like any other professional.

Start viewing losses as part of the game

If you are one of those people who seems to believe that there is a magical crystal ball, the Holy Grail, that little truthful piece of information that makes a trader win every time, then you had better change your point of view.

155

In the trading business, there is no guarantee of succeeding every time. All we are trying to do as traders is beating the odds. We must accept that losses are going to be part of that process no matter what.

This is one of the reasons why the subject of risk management is so important in this business. If you manage risk in the way we described in the previous chapter, you'll often find that succeeding in this business becomes easier.

It comes down to making more money than you lose.

Winning 100% of the time is statistically impossible. Losses come by even to the best in this business. There is a kind of myth going around that the professionals in Wall Street know something that we don't, something that gives them an edge. That is simply wrong.

The best in this business have learnt the hard way. They have learnt that you cannot eliminate losses in this business. They learnt a long time that the only secret is to manage then in a way that makes you win in the long run. That is what they strive to do every day. You must do the same if you want to succeed.

This brings me to another point; you need to adopt a system, a strategy, that you prefer and that you prefer to work with above anything else. Then you test it with a demo to see how well it performs in the long run. Get a feel of the winners and losers your system gives out. As you do this, you will begin to understand that losers are just a part of this game as is winning and that if you manage them well, then you have little to worry about.

As you do this, you will start developing confidence in your system. One of the worst challenges you'll ultimately run into in this business is that of hitting a losing period (also popularly known as a losing streak). This is a period during which your system seems to be performing poorly with every signal that comes out of it.

If you aren't experienced or well versed in the knowledge that at times this happens in trading, then you're likely to throw in the towel. If, however, you took the time to learn about the challenges that occur in this business, you'll learn that perhaps if you took a break from trading then you could go back again later when conditions get better.

So, starting today, realize that losses in trading will always happen and are part of the game. If they are well managed, there is less reason to worry about them. Stick to the 2% rule of money management and you'll be okay. Realize that you could be right even 50% of the time and still make plenty just like the professionals do.

Keep trading as a part time activity

Another successful trick that can help you turning trading into a successful venture is that of keeping it as a part time activity.

It's very difficult to trade successfully if you are in a position of trying to make a living out of it. Sure, there are professional traders who trade for a living, but most of them are getting a regular paycheck from the firm that employs them. The proceeds from their trading only gets paid in the form of bonuses. This is how Wall Street works for the most part.

Big time professionals in trading are the hedge fund managers and other professional money managers. These people charge professional management fees from the people who invest with them, if their performance is at its peak.

If you look at the big picture, these professionals are not depending on the money they are making from their trading even if they are earning it. This is perhaps why they are so good at the game.

The reason is simple. The best trading decisions are made when you're in position where you don't need the money.

When you're constantly under pressure of things such as, "How will I pay my rent this month?" or "How will I pay my daughter's school fees?" you are likely to make some very bad trading decisions. You're more likely to act such as trading excessively or placing trades when action is not warranted, all in a desperate attempt to make some money.

So how do you deal with that?

Get a day job. Find something else that you can always do on the side that will help keep things in order financially and then trade part time. As we discussed before, you can use swing trading strategies even if you're currently employed. Analysis only takes a few minutes per day and this is something most of us can deal with.

You can even decide to trade when you get out of work. Markets such as the FOREX market trade 24 hours a day, and this guarantees every person in the world that each person can at least find some time to trade that market. You can use this aspect to your advantage.

Getting a day job and trading part time helps in several ways. Firstly, it helps you take care of your bills and other financial responsibilities without putting a strain on your trading.

Secondly, it helps grow your account financially. This is especially true if you intend to use trading as a way of investing in order to grow rich. You can always put aside some money every month so that your account grows, and you can trade more.

Thirdly, it takes away the stress from trading. Let's face it, trading can be very challenging. When you're dealing with losing and making money, then stress can build up very quickly. It gets worse if you're thinking of using the money to maintain a decent living.

When you have something taking care of your financial responsibilities, then you can relax. When this happens, then you'll think clearly. You'll be patient enough to wait for the right opportunities to trade. If you make decisions from a position like this, then over time, your account only will soar.

Fear

At the point when the market quickly moves against our trade, you may see a prompt rise in your nervousness. Prepared traders are utilized to this since it's very occasional that a trader will wind up in a real predicament or top of any trade to make an entry. They anticipate a move against them for a short measure of time. When is it time to leave the trade, on the off chance that it proceeds with its turn against you?

It isn't that feeling you get when somebody hops out and alarms you. It isn't that feeling like nearly getting hit by a vehicle. Nor is it the inclination that you have when viewing a terrifying motion picture.

Often, fear in the market is a subtler encounter. You will have a hard time remembering it as fear necessarily because your mind will be gotten up to speed at the time. You'll be caught up with attempting to settle on a significant decision and discerning the future remorseful distastefulness you'll understand whether the wrong choice is made.

After a decision is made and you're finished celebrating your most recent triumph or lamenting the disappointment of your choice, venture back and give yourself a legitimate, non-stooping, non-self-indulging analysis. You will find that fear had gone into the condition of a proper conclusion.

Continuously know about this emotion. You have never given it a chance to choose your destiny. The best way to overcome it is to plan and adhere to that plan. Plan your entry, your leave, your target(s). Make a point to have elective procedures if there should arise an occurrence of various situations that could become possibly the most important factor with your trade.

In finding out about fear and greed in the market, I have seen that something was missing in those works. Patience is never referenced. Patience can amplify fear and greed.

Since we are discussing fear, we should take a gander at how patience impacts fear inside the trade. Situation:

Your trade is moving against you. You are losing money. You feel that unfilled premonition and slight frenzy. So, if you give the situation a lot of patience, you could be in for more profound losses. But, if you have too little patience, you could leave the trade rashly and miss out on much-invited additions.

So, what do you do? Now in the diversion, it's a hurl up. Try not to whip yourself too severely on the off chance that you settle on the wrong decision yet ensure you learn from this experience. The exercise in learning is to plan BEFORE you click that catch that gets you into the trade in any case. Many prepared traders fall into the snare of neglecting to plan correctly as well. They get arrogant, yet the market will tell them soon enough of their failings.

Trading ought to exhaust. In case you need the rush of the rollercoaster ride of 'money related emotion,' go betting. If you need to prevail as a trader, plan your trade and trade your plan - keep it exhausting.

Just trade what you can bear to lose. Make sure beyond a shadow of a doubt that the money you use to trade is intellectual, disposable capital. If you wind up in an 'unquestionable requirement win' trade, your decision-production capacities will be incredibly frustrated. This, along with patience, will intensify your sentiments of fear and greed.

Greed

You make an incredible entry. You have perused to give the great sections a chance to ride while you cut the terrible passages off. Greed is a piece of amusement. You need to ensure that you snatch all that you can because the following trade can make you lose more than you would hope to lose. You would prefer not to leave any money on the table - people, this is greed. Greed can turn into fear all around rapidly.

Greed, like fear, is additionally an inconspicuous emotion with regards to trading the markets. It is likely subtler than fear. Nobody likes to consider themselves being greedy. Furthermore, it's presumably evident that you aren't greedy at everything except rather greed can assume a ground-breaking job in your trades. It won't resemble the greed of Mr. Penny pincher. Sweat-soaked palms, a little spot of slobber and a somewhat stern face will likely not be on your trades' motivation. More probable, without a plan, you'll hold tight to trade excessively long or hop in at the wrong minute to satisfy your dream of profiting. Trading verifies that fear and greed exists. This is key because you'll need to stop your losses while giving your additions a chance to keep running the extent that they can. This gives fertile ground to greed and fear to develop.

When greed has dominated, and you commit your error, greed can turn to fear in all respects rapidly. A stock trader can encounter fear and greed a few times inside one trading day. I have seen greed turn to fear at that point and then back to greed again inside seconds. Try not to ride this sloping ride. Make sure to do your best to dispose of the emotion by planning. The more emotional you become, the more probable you are to commit an error.

We should take this unusual to make a point. Specialists are not permitted (by and large) to perform a medical procedure on a friend or family member. Relatives and dear companions must look for assistance from another specialist. Why? The specialist is emotionally included, connected to the patient. That is an issue since emotion fits committing errors. The equivalent is valid for trading the markets.

Where does patience become possibly the most crucial factor with greed? Patience collaborates with. Similarly, it does with fear. It enhances the emotion. If you have a lot of patience with trade and become greedy, you can lose a considerable segment of your increases or finish up with a loss on a trade that was performing incredibly. You should leave when your plan directs that you exit. You could likewise go into a trade rashly. A trade you ought to have avoided in any case.

The accompanying should look extremely well-known to you from the Fear data.

Continuously know about this emotion. You have never given it a chance to choose your destiny. The best way to defeat it is to plan and adhere to that plan. Plan your entry, your leave, your target(s). Make a point to have elective procedures if there should be an occurrence of various situations that could become possibly the most important factor with your trade.

Trading ought to exhaust. If you need the fervor and rush of the rollercoaster ride of 'budgetary emotion', go betting. On the off chance that you need to prevail as a trader, plan your trade and trade your plan - keep it exhausting.

Just trade what you can stand to lose. Make sure beyond a shadow of a doubt that the money you use to trade is intellectual, disposable capital. On the off chance that you wind up in an 'unquestionable requirement win' trade, your decision-production capacities will be extraordinarily impeded. This, along with patience, will intensify your sentiments of fear and greed.

So, to sum up, "Patience enhances fear and greed." The absence of patience will make you enter or leave a trade that you ought to have avoided in any case. The excess of patience, will make you exit, enter or remain in a trade that you ought to have left.

Chapter 10:

How much influence does the mind have in swing trading

You have your trading strategy and have been persistently trying and refining it to the point where you're incredibly certain about it, and as a rule, things have begun meeting up for you and your trading. You have a watchlist brimming with exceptionally promising setups, and you're feeling like this is your time to start seeing a few outcomes truly. One of the structures begins to give you a buy flag, so you take it and make your entry. Everything appears to be impeccable, and you're envisioning ringing the register when your objectives are hit, however instead the activity turns around on you and hits your stop loss, so being a disciplined trader, you get out for insignificant harm. Nothing amiss with that, we realize that few out of every odd trade is getting down to business out, so everything we can do is limit the washouts and given the victors a chance to run. Sounds excellent, except the stock you just abandoned inverts once more and goes onto doing precisely what you thought it would do at first, to say the very least. Ouch, that sort of stings.

So now we have a fresh start again however that last trade isn't sitting excessively well with you, and you're genuinely lamenting getting ceased out like a blockhead, to watch it take off without you. You don't freeze, however, and after some additionally pausing, another setup begins to trigger an entry. You take the flag and get long the stock, and only like the past trade, this one starts to conflict with you. Be that as it may, this time you choose to fudge your principles a bit, and as opposed to safeguarding here, you decide to add to your position, which genuinely was never part of the plan in any case. The memory of that earlier trade shaking you out is still crisp, so this time you believe you'll be shrewd and not freeze, and in certainty utilize this plunge further bolstering your good fortune. So, what occurs? Of course, the stock continues sinking, and you end up turning a little loss into a lot bigger one when you at long last conceded thrashing.

Currently you're staying there stewing, and the questions are beginning to crawl into your brain. You convince yourself to get pull out there; however, at this point, your outlook isn't almost what it ought to be. You're squeezing the issue, and where it counts, you need to get some retribution and recover your money. You're endeavoring to sit tight for another setup that meets your criteria to show, however meanwhile you see something that is getting your attention. It's anything but a trade you typically would take. However, you see there's the potential for some real upside. "Man, if that thing breaks out, it's going to result in no doubt!", You contemplate internally. So, of course, you bounce into that risky trade, subliminally believing it will refute those last two failures, and like some cruel joke, its accidents and you assume one more huge loss.

Presently you're a stage far from being absolute wreckage. You start to question your system. You begin to challenge yourself. In case your family or companions have been anything short of steady, their expressions of alert will be stuck on rehash in your cerebrum now. After a lot of souls looking, you choose to get retreat thereby and by, and stay consistent with the system that you know, when executed legitimately, will give you positive outcomes over an all-encompassing timeframe. Presently out of the blue you spot two setups on your watchlist that meet your criteria are appearing to trigger sections, yet your capital is lower than typical and can either take a full estimated position in it's possible that one or make a moderately sized position in both. You conclude that one looks more pleasant than the other, and you like your odds (of hitting a decent payday) better by taking a full estimated position in that one. Generally, your position gets halted out, and the other one goes onto breaking out and running more earnestly than you've seen anything kept running in weeks. Unmistakably the stock divine beings hate you, and you choose you should not be a trader. You're a flat-out wreck, and you're prepared to surrender, and this is the place numerous individuals do yield.

It's stunning how rapidly your mentality can change around here. You must keep up a specific level of consistent certainty, while never giving it a chance to turn into arrogance. Arrogance prompts defying your guidelines and risking that you planned on taking, and you would prefer not to get captured in a torrential slide of awful trades. Pride is one outrageous, yet the other is having no certainty, and that is similarly as awful. You need to adjust the two and remain directly in the center. You need confidence, yet to dependably know about how rapidly a poor decision can cost you a great deal of money.

Perhaps the situation doesn't relate to you. However practically every trader can identify with this kind of stuff, where you crave all that you do is the exact inverse of what you ought to have done, and this can prompt some epic crumples in certainty and account estimate. Take a gander at the precedents once more, and if the emotional viewpoint had been monitored, that situation wouldn't have been so obliterating. The initial two trades would have been little washouts, yet instead than other trade was a lot bigger on account of not safeguarding at the correct time and, adding to the losing position. The third trade didn't meet the criteria of the system, and that was a retribution trade, so that ought to never have occurred. To the extent the last two trades, since the two of them fit the system, the two of them ought to have been taken. Better believe it, the position would have been little, yet you would've had the capacity to get that one that wound up running, which likely could have compensated for that string of small losses. At the very least you'd be scarcely in the red. However, the fact of the matter is you wouldn't be any place near exploding your account and having a psychological breakdown. The system didn't breakdown; the trader did.

Swing Trading and the Psychology of the Crowd

This predictability of the crowd is what causes stocks to move up and down.

As a stock's price moves up, with buyers stepping in, this creates a situation where the increasing price encourages further buyers as traders and investors pile in, not wishing to miss out on the market move. This is the psychology of greed, fear, and hope, literally forcing investors to buy in reaction to what others are doing and in tandem with what others are doing.

However, each move will eventually run out of steam as those that bought stock early seek to realize profits and sell out. When this happens, the stock forms a peak and reverses direction. This causes greater numbers of investors to sell, providing momentum to the downside until the stock is deemed to have fallen far enough.

It is this action of the crowd which gives stocks lines of resistance and support, and which gives the swing trader one of their greatest trading opportunities – but only if trading discipline is maintained. Traders who fail to trade with discipline and follow their emotions will always lose money in the longer term.

Swing traders reference chart patterns to make their trade decisions, so it's worth looking at a chart to see how different types of traders act in markets which also helps to identify how psychology affects these different types of trader.

Common Mistakes Beginners Make

Whether you are a beginner or expert swing trader, you will find yourself making mistakes. However, mistakes are more commonly made when you're a beginner. Mistakes are going to happen, and no one knows this better than experts. Therefore, many of them have shared their mistakes with the hope that beginners will remember the mistakes and, therefore, do what they can to avoid them.

You Have Unrealistic Expectations

There are many traders who come into the stock market world with a lot of unrealistic expectations. There are several reasons for this. For example, some might believe that trading is a career which will quickly make them rich while other people might believe that it's an easy work-from-home type job. While you can work from home when you become a swing trader, the job is not as easy as many people believe. In fact, it can be a very stressful job with a lot of factors involved from research to your post-trading analysis at the end of your workday.

In fact, when people have unrealistic expectations, it can cause a lot of problems. These problems have led many beginners to believe that they could not become a successful trader. While they didn't all quit their new career, many did. It's important to remember that you

171

should never give up on your trading career too quickly, even if you feel that you barely know anything about trading, or you realize that trading is different than what you initially thought. You should continue to research and learn about swing trading as you might like it once you get through the first few months.

If you find yourself having unrealistic expectations, it's important to realize there is nothing wrong with this. In fact, you should be proud that you have noted your unrealistic expectations and can now work to change them into more realistic expectations. Furthermore, if you think about previous careers you have held, you have probably gone into your new job with unrealistic expectations. This is common when it comes to people starting new positions. One of the biggest reasons for this is because people often believe that they can take on more than they can when they receive a new job or even a promotion. There is always a settlement period where people start to see the reality of their new positions. During this time, they are not only learning what they can do but also what they need to work a little more on.

You Don't Follow Your Pre-Trading Analysis

I have already mentioned how important following your pre-trading analysis is. However, there are many people who start to feel that they don't need to take the time to do this for various reasons. Sometimes the reason is as simple as people running late and just don't want to take the time when the stock market is opening. Of course, other reasons tend to follow more in the mindset that they understand how trading works and, therefore, don't need to take part in these activities anymore.

While you might feel that there is a lot of research to complete as you get your day started, you still need to make sure to take the time to check out the information. You need to make sure that you completely understand what is going on in the stock market world from the news to the changes that occurred overnight.

Of course, there have been many traders who admitted to not always following through with their pre-trading analysis. They have stated that on these days they noted they didn't perform as well. Maybe, they made more mistakes because they weren't briefed on the changes that the stock market made overnight or the news about a company that they held a share for. They also admitted that it made them feel like they were out of the loop in general. The stock market is constantly changing, which means you need to keep up with these changes and change with the market. If you don't take the time to do this, you will quickly fall behind.

You Don't Follow Through with Your Post-Trading Analysis

You can also quickly fall behind in the stock market world if you don't complete your post-trading analysis after the stock market closes every day. This is a very important part of your day because it will help you become a successful trader. It is important to

173

remember that you will not become successful overnight. In fact, it takes traders years to reach the level of success that they imagine themselves reaching. This is because it takes a lot of time and practice with the stock market to not only understand it but learn all the details and tricks of the trade.

This is very important and could also be something that you change over time. For example, you might start recording the times that you made the trades during the day. However, as you continue to analyze your post-trades over the last few months, you find out that writing down the time isn't doing anything to help you grow. In fact, you might start to see this as a worthless number. If you reach this point, you have two options. First, you can continue to write down the time because you might need this information one day. Second, you could decide to stop writing the time down. One thing to remember if you start to think about skipping the time is that you never know when you're going to need certain information in the future. While a statistic might not be helpful today, it could be helpful in a couple months.

This is one of those times where you must remember that you're still learning all the details about swing trading. Even if you're writing down information after working as a swing trader for six months and begin to believe some of the statistics are meaningless, you should still continue to write them down. First, it is always important to remain consistent as a trader. Second, because you're learning every day, you might come across a more experienced swing trader or other information that will explain to you why this meaningless statistic is actually meaningful. When this happens, you'll be grateful that you continued to write down the numbers instead of ignoring them.

You are Not Consistent

Now that I have mentioned consistency, it seems to be a good time to mention that inconsistency seems to be a common mistake that beginner traders make. Of course, there can be a variety of reasons for this, maybe they don't remember all the steps they have to follow or they start to feel more confident in their abilities. While feeling confident is good, this shouldn't mean that you start to take your job less seriously or feel that you can skip some steps because you believe you have a better hold of what swing trading is.

You want to create a theme in your swing trading career that helps you remain consistent. Because swing trading can become a stressful career, consistency will help you maintain a healthy mental balance. Furthermore, you will be more likely to remember what you need to do and when. Of course, you'll always have a trading plan or business plan to help you with these steps, it's important that you know these steps as well as you know the meaning of swing trading.

Another reason remaining consistent can help is through giving you a healthier professional and personal life balance. While some people feel that they can connect the two, more people feel that they need to create a balance in order to remain happy and content in the personal and business life. Being consistent in your job can help with this because you're more likely to follow the hours that you decide to use for your workday. For example, if you are a full-time swing trader in New York City. You might work from about 9:00 am to around 4:30 pm Monday through Friday. Even if you work at home, you want to keep these hours because this will help tell you that the hours outside of this time are reserved for your personal life.

You Don't Pay Attention to Your Mental Health

Your mental health is just as important as your physical health. However, people tend to pay less attention to their mental health. For example, when you're feeling depressed you don't often take the day off in order to get better like you would if you had a bad cold or the flu. While there are several reasons to why people tend to push their mental health aside, it's something that you need to make sure you take care of. Not only is this important for everyone, but it's important for a swing trader due to many reasons.

First, swing traders need to remain in the right mindset. Because I have discussed the right mindset previously, I am not going to go too much into that. However, I will take time to note that your mental health heavily depends on being able to reach the right mindset. For example, if you're trying to reach the right mindset, you need to be able to reach a level of confidence in yourself. If you are constantly putting yourself down for every mistake you make or you become overly critical of yourself, you will not be able to reach this right mindset. Therefore, mental health and correct mindset go hand in hand for success.

Other than making you believe that you can become a successful day trader, being mentally healthy can also help you keep from being stressed. It's important to make sure that you don't get too stressed as a trader because this can lead you into a variety of other issues from lack of confidence to making more mistakes. On top of that, becoming too stressed can cause you to make decisions based on an emotion. Stress is an emotion which often brings forth other emotions. As stated before, you want to make sure that you do not make decisions based on your emotions because you'll be more likely to make a mistake or jump too quickly when you see the price of a stock fall.

Trading with money you can't bear to lose.

One of the best obstructions to active trading is utilizing the money that you indeed can't bear to lose. Instances of this would be money that should be used to pay the home loan, bills or your tyke's school educational cost. This is sometimes alluded to as "trading with frightened money," and there is an excellent purpose behind that. Eventually what happens is that when somebody knows in the back of their mind that they are risking the lease money, they trade out of dread and emotion versus rationale and no emotion.

If you are in this circumstance, I exceedingly suggest that you quit trading until you earn enough to put into an account that you genuinely can stand to lose without causing major budgetary mishaps. You can begin with as meager as $2000 and trade stocks under $30.

Spending profits before you make them.

Nothing is more energizing at that point getting into a trade that takes off and places you into an exceedingly favorable circumstance. This can cause severe issues in any case, since this sort of trade places you in an exceedingly euphoric state and prompts daydreaming about the huge profits still to come. You state, "Wow I'm now up 15% in two days; I'll be up half in a week and likely twofold my money in no time!" Then the following thing that happens is you are settling on the extraordinary new vehicle you're going to buy or maybe telling your supervisor that he can stick it... Well, you get the thought!

The genuine issue happens as you become involved with the daydream and desires. This makes you not be set up to get out as the market sells off and gobbles up your profits since you have persuaded yourself regarding the possible result and will preclude the truth from claiming the circumstance.

The straightforward solution for this is to know where and how you will take profits once you enter the trade. Additionally, understand that the market will go up as long as it needs and not how high you figure it ought to go.

Shaping a feeling.

I'm here to reveal to you that the market does not care at all about you or your sentiments. Regardless of whether they depend on meticulous research or from a "Money Street Guru," it doesn't make a difference!

Possibly your assessment on market direction for the long term is right. However, it doesn't imply that in the short-term, things can't move against you. Keep in mind that there are a huge number of traders out there who likewise have a conclusion. It is all these distinctive sentiments that can cause incredible variances in cost on some random day or week paying little heed to your viewpoint.

Not adhering to your plan

A primary wellspring of inconvenience arises when a trader begins to go astray from their strategy. Possibly for seven days, they will trade as per one lot of principles and the following use something extraordinary.

This flying by the seat of the jeans dependably winds up exploded backward. This is because the trader can never be sure what is working and what is most certainly not.

You should never go amiss from your system once you begin. For whatever length of time that it is a decent one statistically, there is positively no motivation to transform it. The best approach to profit from it is to trade it again and again to abuse the edge it gives you.

One thing to likewise know about is that a trader is most powerless against exchanging approaches after a couple of losses. In this way, give uncommon consideration at these times.

Not realizing how to escape a losing trade.

It's astonishing what number of individuals I have conversed with who don't have any reasonable departure plan for escaping a terrible trade. By and by they trust, implore wish and justify their position. The least demanding approach to shield an awful trade from going downright terrible is to determine before you get in, where you will get out. You can utilize a dollar sum or at some objective point, for example, the low of the past 15-minute bar.

Make beyond any doubt you don't get the "dazed deer in the headlights disorder". This is the place you see the stock tumble to your stop-loss indicates. However, you're unfit to make a move.

Having a sense of self.

I have seen various people enter the trading diversion that was incredibly fruitful in different business adventures. Given this, they had a genuinely substantial inner self and figured they couldn't fall flat. Their self-images turned into their defeat since they couldn't deal except that they weren't right and would not ransom of awful trades.

Indeed, whoever or wherever you originated from does not concern the markets. All the appeal, forces of influence, number of confirmations on the divider or business insightful won't move the market when you're incorrect.

Chapter 11:

Principles of trading

B efore I discuss various strategies that can be used to swing trade, let's look at the basic guiding principles that I build these strategies on. They are as follows:

Keep it Simple

You may have heard of the term "paralysis by analysis". This happens when you analyze something to the point where you cannot decide. Some swing traders overcomplicate their analysis of a security by using multiple indicators all of which must line up for them to enter a trade. In real life, everything does not often line up perfectly and you should go with what you feel is right.

You do not need to use all of them to be a successful swing trader. Once you find 1 or 2 that work well for you, you should then stick with those. If you decide to use a few different tools that all need to align, it will likely mean that you're not going to be trading very often. That is not necessarily a bad thing though. It is better to sit on your hands and wait for a good trade versus jumping in and out of marginal trade setups and slowly lose your money. The only one who wins in that case is your broker, as they collect fees for all your trades (the successful ones and the losing one's).

Find several indicators that work well for you and focus on using them. Don't trade often, but trade smart, by knowing why you're entering a trade and, most importantly, knowing your risk-to-reward ratio and exit price points. As you gain more experience in swing trading, you'll be able to better recognize trades that are going to work out even if everything is not perfectly aligned.

Having said this, when you do happen to find a number of indicators that are all aligned with the trade you're considering taking, it can certainly provide some level of confidence that you have a potentially profitable trade.

Treat your Swing Trading Activity Like a Serious Business

Should you decide that swing trading is suitable for you, and that it's able to fit into your life along with all of your other interests and responsibilities, then you need to treat this activity as a very serious business. It will require an investment of time and effort, which hopefully will lead to some very good rewards.

Have a designated area where you do your research and keep all of your records. You are essentially becoming a professional money manager for yourself, so you should always keep your work organized . Everything you do with your business should be oriented toward making sure you are a success. If you feel like a professional, then you are more apt to trade like one.

Develop a Work Plan

Have a work plan and stick with it. Your work plan should include checking the market at the open and before the close. During this time, you should monitor your positions, set alerts and possibly enter orders at target levels that you think might get filled during the trading day.

I also recommend that you review your portfolio and market performance every night from Sunday to Thursday to ensure your assumptions about your positions and portfolio are still valid. On the weekend, you should try to do a more thorough review.

It is important to establish a work plan and keep it consistent. By keeping your work plan relatively consistent, you can measure your performance without introducing additional variables. Measuring your performance allows you to find areas to improve and make changes as you see fit.

Actively Manage your Risk-to-reward Ratio, Focus on the Entry

As a swing trader, your first and most important tool is your capital or cash. As I have said before, without cash you cannot be a trader. Following your rules on these points will prevent you from quickly losing all your capital. You will be wrong on your trades some of the time and you need to make sure you live to trade another day.

Just planning and knowing your stop-loss and profitable exits are not enough for swing trading. Your entry becomes the next important step in your trade. You have already determined your stop-loss point and your target price(s) for a profitable exit. However, you calculated the risk-to-reward ratio based on an assumed entry price point.

Let's assume you found a good setup during a scan in the evening after the market has closed. The security closed the day at $10.50 and you see an upside to $12.00 with support at $10.00 where you would stop out. Therefore, you have a potential $0.50 loss compared to a $1.50 gain to the upside. That is a 1 to 3 risk-to-reward ratio, which is very good, and you're ready to pull the trigger and place a buy order in the morning. The market opens the next morning and the security you're ready to buy opens up at $11.00. What do you do? The novice trader is already invested mentally in the trade, so they buy. Unfortunately for them, their risk-to-reward is now 1 to 1 with the downside to $10.00 and upside to $12.00. This is no longer a good trade at that entry point.

The rational trader reassesses the situation. They may put a buy order in at $10.50, hoping to catch the entry they wanted on the security during the normal daily price gyrations in the market. This will give them the risk-to-reward ratio that they need to make a good swing trade. If they do not get a fill, then they need to reassess again, and maybe move on to finding another trade with a more appropriate risk-to-reward ratio.

The bottom line is don't get emotional and chase a trade. The "fear of missing out" can motivate you to make a bad trade and you should be aware of this when picking your entry price on a trade.

Measure your Results and Adjust Accordingly

As a trader, you must track your results to measure your performance. Nothing gets improved that does not get measured first. Every trader should use a tool to record the different aspects of each trade, from initial assessment through to the risk-to-reward expected, the entry point, and, finally, the exit. The tool can be a spreadsheet, it can be done on paper or it can be web-based. It does not matter how you do it if the process allows you to track the details of each trade as well as your performance.

Once you have your trades recorded in detail, you can go back at any time and review how the trade worked. You can compare your performance on using the different indicators, i.e., is one working particularly well versus the others that you use? Are you getting good entry points on your trades or do you need to exercise more patience? Are your exits working or are you consistently exiting a trade too early and not getting all the money you could on a profitable trade? Are you respecting your stops?

Having all this information to review will help you adjust your trading process and plan accordingly to maximize your performance without letting emotion enter your decision-making.

Establish Your Business Plan

Because you should treat trading like a profession, it's essential you follow several steps you would use when starting your own business. First, you'll want to make sure you create a business or trading plan. This is a plan which will discuss all the details about your style as a trader. You'll discuss your enter strategy, exit strategy, your pre-trading analysis, and your post-trading analysis.

Your business plan is going to be your comprehensive guide that will help you with your decisions as a swing trader. These are not only important because every business should have one but because they can help you make the best decision when you come across one to take on or sell a financial instrument. No matter how well you have researched swing trading or how long you have been a swing trader, when you're faced with a decision you can easily struggle to come up with a solution. This is when your trading plan will come in handy. You'll focus on every aspect that goes with swing trading, including tips to help you focus on making the right decision and why.

It is worthwhile to evaluate your trading plan often. In fact, many traders state you should read through your trading plan during your pre-trading analysis. Other traders state that you should at least read through your plan and make any changes, if necessary, on a weekly basis. Whatever you decide to do, you want to make sure that you know your trading plan as well as you know anything else in trading.

Even though you'll be reading the plan often, you still want to make sure you have memorized the plan as this will help you when you face a difficult decision.

Why You Need a Trading Plan?

Your trading plan has several advantages. First, it will help you make decisions when you're focusing on a trade. While you might feel that these decisions should be easy, there is a lot of analyzing and details that go into planning to take on a financial instrument. This means that when you're faced with a decision that you need to make within a minute or two, you can often become stressed or worried about your decision. Of course, this isn't something you want to do when it comes to trading as then you might make the decision with your emotions, which definitely isn't something you want to do as a trader. If you find yourself in this position, you can turn to your trading plan. This plan will walk you through your decision, so you're less likely to make any mistakes.

Set Your Schedule and Stick to It

First, you will want to decide if you're going to become a part-time or full-time swing trader. This will let you know how much time to set aside for your trading career. For example, if you are part-time, you might think about focusing on trading a couple of days during the week or trade in the mornings. However, if you are a full-time trader, you'll probably want to stay close to your computer during the hours the stock market is open. Below are the pieces of your schedule you should make sure to include no matter how often you trade during the week.

Pre-Trading Analysis

You will want to make sure to include time for your pre-trading analysis, which is a part of your trading plan. This analysis typically takes place before the stock market opens; however, some traders will use the first half hour as their analysis time. For instance, if you want to make sure your analysis is complete by the time the stock market opens, you'll want to make sure you're done with this part of your day by 9:30 Eastern time. This could mean that you start your day at 5:45 am or 6:00 am as it's a good idea to have at least a half hour for your pre-trading analysis. However, many traders state that beginners should allow themselves a bit more time because they are still learning the whole trading system. Therefore, it could take them more time to analyze the changes that occurred in the foreign stock market or the United States stock market overnight. On top of this, they might take more time reading the news.

The Market

Of course, you'll want to make sure that your schedule includes the on goings of the stock market. For example, you'll want to note that from about 9:30 am to around 10:00 am, the market is in volatile mode. This means that there are a lot of changes occurring in the market which makes it unstable. When the market is unstable, you typically don't want to make any purchases or sales. Most people tend to just sit back and watch the market or spend their time reading the news or doing some research.

Another time to note about the stock market is that from about 11:15 am to around 2:00 pm is when the market seems to have the lowest amount of activity. Many traders refer to this time as the stock market's lunch time. Before 11:00 am, many traders will end their day as they are only part-time. However, those who are full-time might continue to research or look for stocks until their lunch time.

Starting around 2:30 pm, the stock market will begin to pick up again. When this happens, you'll start to see activity and, if you're planning on making a sale or trade, you'll most likely start looking into that. This activity continues until the stock market closes around 4:00 pm.

Post-Trading Analysis

Post-trading analysis is just as important as pre-trading analysis. You want to make sure to make time for this every day and it will occur after you have completed your day. During your post trade analysis, you'll reflect on your day and you can do this through a trading journal or by taking screenshots of your charts for any trades you made that day.

If you use a trading journal, you'll want to make sure to note every detail you feel is necessary about the day. This not only includes any financial instruments you bought or sold but also why. You will want to focus on why you made the decision, what strategy you used, what factors contributed to this decision, you'll want to discuss if you were distracted, what device you used (computer, phone, etc.), your capital gain or loss, and anything else. It is important to write down as much as you feel you'll need to so when you can get a sense of where your strengths and weaknesses are. On top of this, you'll be able to get to know yourself as a trader.

If you decide to take screenshots of your charts, you'll want to make sure to make notes within your charts. You will want to find a spot where you won't become distracted and can still read the chart easily. You will want to make the same type of notes you do in your trading journal. Of course, you could always take screenshots of charts and keep a trading journal. How you do your analysis is up to you.

Take Your New Career Seriously but Not Too Seriously

Before you get into swing trading, whether you're going to focus on it halftime or full-time, you want to make sure that you are 100% committed to the career. It is very crucial that you don't feel like this is something you just want to try because you're bored or want to see if you can make some extra money every month. However, if you do feel this way, it's best to start up part-time and go from there.

At the same time, you need to make sure that you don't fall into the trap of taking your job too seriously. While this might sound odd, it

191

can happen and has happened to many people within their jobs. Typically, when people start taking their job too seriously, they start to let it consume their life and there is very little professional and personal life balance. In fact, what happens is people tend to put all their time and energy into their job that they reach a state of exhaustion.

Becoming exhausted from trading can happen to anyone, and it's a fairly common trait, especially for beginners. Part of this reason is because they don't understand how demanding trading really is. Therefore, when they first get into the business, they have not dedicated enough time for what they wanted to do. Of course, this can be easily fixed by creating more time for trading or taking on less stocks. But, at the same time, they could reach a state of exhaustion before they realize they took on too much.

How to Tell When You're Heading Towards a Burnout?

Becoming burned-out from you job can happen to anyone. In fact, most people feel that they reach a stage of burnout at least once throughout their professional career. It is beneficial to note that if you start to feel burnt-out, it is best to take a step back or a break. If you continue to work at the pace you're going and become too exhausted, you can easily start to cause other work-related problems. For example, you can start performing poorly. When it comes to swing trading, you might find yourself making more mistakes and unable to read and analyze charts that you used to be able to understand easily.

Many people reach a state of burnout simply because they feel their job is too stressful. In fact, stress is the main factor of becoming burned-out. This is a common problem for many people in the trading community because, even swing trading, can be demanding.

There are many basic signs for a person who is starting to become burnt-out from their job.

You have lost your motivation for your job.

One of the biggest signs that you're nearing or becoming burnt-out is you has lost motivation for your job. This can happen to anyone and in any field, not just trading. In fact, you might have already felt this way in a previous job. When you lose motivation, you really begin to feel that you can't do the tasks that you once used to do. You might feel that you're too tired to perform the tasks (exhaustion is another sign of being burned-out). You might also feel that the tasks aren't worth your time or find yourself procrastinating.

You feel a lot of negative emotions.

Another sign that you are becoming burned-out is you feel more negatively towards your job than positively. You might find that you're easily irritated by your co-workers or even feel that you just want to be left alone. You might find yourself becoming easily frustrated at the simplest tasks you need to complete. Of course, you'll want to remember that people generally feel a bit negative about parts of their job from time to time. If you find yourself feeling negatively occasionally, you might not be burnt-out. But if you notice that you're more negative than you typically are, especially if you begin to become concerned over your mental health, then you are most likely burnout.

Your job performance is suffering.

One of the biggest ways to notice that you're burnt-out is by looking at your previous job performance and comparing it to your current performance. If you found your performance is sloppier and you're not putting as much effort into your job duties, then you have most likely become burned-out.

Always thinking about work, even when you're not working.

While people usually think about the things they need to do at work when they are not on the clock, if you find yourself doing this often you could easily be at the burnt-out stage. In fact, part of the reason you might feel bad is because you think of your job when you should be focusing on other things to give yourself a better balance between work and home.

This is one downside when it comes to working from home. People who are used to working in an office and then start to work from home can often find themselves working longer hours or thinking about work more. One reason for this is because it's more convenient for them to get to their office as it might just be down the hall. Furthermore, if you are a trader, you might trade through your desktop, which you use throughout your day for various reasons. Therefore, it's important to make sure you have some type of work schedule that you stick to when you work from home.

Your mental health is starting to decline.

Your mental health is one of the most important factors of your life. It's just as significant as your physical health. In fact, it's been proven through scientific studies that if you're struggling with your mental health, you can become sick more often. Because your health is so important, you must make sure to keep your mental health as healthy as possible. So, you should watch for any signs of feeling burned-out so that your mental health doesn't start to decline.

Once you start to notice yourself struggling with your mental health, you can quickly run into other concerns, such as anxiety and depression. You start to take less care of yourself. For example, you might feel that you don't have to eat healthy when you typically watch what you eat. You might also stop exercising as you just don't feel like it anymore. It is vital to note that if you start to feel this way, you should take a break from your job as quickly as possible. Even taking a couple of days or a week off can help you feel better about yourself and set your motivation back on track.

Conclusion

At the point when utilized forcefully swing trading is an astounding strategy used by numerous traders crosswise over different diverse markets. As usual, one must recollect that swing trading is just a single strategy and ought to be used only when suitably comprehended. Like any trading strategies swing trading can be hazardous and moderate strategies can transform into day trading strategies rapidly. If you plan to employ a swing trading strategy, guarantee that you completely comprehend the dangers. So try to ensure you build up a strategy that will most likely enable you to produce highest rate returns on your positions.

You should also understand what simulation trading is and how important it is to make sure you complete this type of trading before you start trading for money. You should also not only understand risks which are associated in swing trading but also have an idea on how to decrease these risks once you start swing trading. Of course, this is one reason you want to make sure to practice simulation trading at first. As stated before, simulation trading will help you make sure that you understand the risks and the strategies which are associated with swing trading.

Good luck.

FOREX TRADING:

Table of Contents

Introduction

FOREX trading is one of the most exciting ways that you can build your own wealth and independent income. It can be fast-paced and exciting; however, there is a FOREX trading strategy for nearly every type of mindset. In this book, which is intended for beginners, we are going to explain in basic and easily understandable terms what FOREX is all about. You are going to learn how currencies are traded, where they are traded, as well as how you can get involved with FOREX trading.

We will discuss the amount of money that you need to get started, as well as how much you can realistically expect to make. You will learn how the markets work and the different approaches to trading that can be used and fit with any lifestyle. We'll explain how you can trade part-time with relatively low risk, or if you want to become a full-time trader that earns fast profits, we'll discuss that, too.

Online trading is subject to numerous risks, but it also has excellent advantages. Knowing the basics and the trading strategies to follow is fundamental. It is easy to make mistakes; the reasons are always the same: inexperience, emotionality, policy of a strategy.

The difficulties are many, and this must make it clear how important it is to have a good knowledge of the markets, analysis techniques and reading charts. It is from the result of these studies that a strategy can be developed that can perform operations at the right time and limit losses by using suitable tools.

Trading FOREX means you need perseverance, study, and self-discipline so you can avoid the mistakes that beginners usually make.

But there are many strategies that are unique to FOREX, that result from the unique properties of the market and the assets being traded, and how they are being traded. We will be discussing those throughout the book, so that you can figure out the style that would be the best fit for your personality and the level of pressure and risk you are willing to accept.

There are also many different styles of trading that can be adjusted, depending on the time commitment that you are willing or able to put into your trading.

Many people are turning to trade in order to generate their income, invest in their future, or simply give themselves extra cash for the month. Whatever your reason is for getting into trading, you'll learn four different types of trading strategies within the contents of this book.

To become a successful trader, you need to continue your education, studying in more detail the type of strategy you want to focus on. This means you have to read more books, research online, join at least one online community and begin talking to a mentor or to more experienced traders who are willing to guide you. Even though the market is competitive, people still want to help one another and make sure they have the best possible experience.

Remember, good discipline and money management are key to being a good trader. Also, not allowing your emotions to run away with you when it is time to make a trade, or when you have heard some news is also imperative. Try as hard as possible to be logical and thorough when it comes to your trading practices, and with time you could be making a 6-figure salary from the comfort of your home.

This book is the best guide to foreign exchange trading. The structure of the book goes from shallow to deep, and the chapters complement each other, forming a basically complete system of foreign exchange transactions. "Practice-Practicality" is the feature of this book. I believe you, as a "novice", will have a clear and complete understanding of foreign exchange trading after reading this book, thus eliminating your fear of it. Of course, foreign exchange traders with certain experience can also learn a lot from this book.

Chapter 1:

What Is FOREX Trading?

T he FOREX market can be imagined from two different points of view. The first image is certainly positive, that is the vision of a financial market that is able to offer anyone the possibility of easily making profits: an opportunity to round up one's salary or even to transform investment into a real work. The second image is negative. The FOREX can indeed be seen as a money-eating system, illusory and bankrupt.

In reality, both visions are wrong. In fact, FOREX is a system that allows for gains in the medium-long term, but only for those who decide to implement a strategy correctly, dedicating both money and time to the market. In fact, trading is complicated and difficult, but not random activity. This concept is very important as it means that any fluctuation could be anticipated correctly by investors. However, there are a number of theories and tools that can simplify their tasks. But even these tools require time and money to function properly and send the right signals to the trader.

The brokers, with the advent of the internet, have made different platforms available to their users. They have some fundamental indicators and oscillators and translate the oscillatory movements of the market on the charts, so as to simplify their reading.

However, it is necessary to always consider the risks associated with the trading activity. In fact, investments in the financial market offer as many profits as losses. It is impossible to eliminate the negative components, which may be due to incorrect strategies, lateral phases of the market and normal competition present in FOREX. The losses, therefore, must be received according to a positive vision, accepting them as much as the profits. It is true that there are few traders who succeed in making profits in the long run, but it is also true that few investors enter the market in a rational manner, without being carried away by revenge or by the will to carry out simple attempts to become rich.

Once the strategy has been implemented, it is necessary to follow it assiduously, unless it presents some gaps and requires instrumental corrections.

The concept is to "play" responsibly, that is to invest one's capital with the knowledge that success and failure rates can be almost similar. In fact, the first objective must be to develop a strategy capable of minimizing the risks of the trader.

Currency pairs and pips

As we know, the basic of the FOREX market is buying and selling currencies. Trading is always by pair of currencies. We have base currency and the other side is counter currency. We need to know the information of how much the exchange rate.

For example, EUR/USD has the quote 1.24. That means 1 EUR is worth $1.24. EUR is base currency. USD is counter currency. That is how FOREX market works. The currency pair is necessary to form for the traders to do transaction. These are some prominent currency pairs that traders always focus on.

Majors

EUR/USD

The Euro and U.S. Dollar currency pair is the most popular and widely traded of the majors. The Euro was introduced in 1999, and it's a relatively strong currency that represents all the major countries in Europe that are part of the European Union. Although Brexit is dominating recent headlines, even with Britain as a part of the European Union, it has maintained its own currency, the Great British Pound. Hence, the Euro is the currency used by members of the EU on the continent.

When it comes to this currency pair, you are going to want to watch moves by the European Central Bank or ECB, and also the U.S. Federal Reserve. Of course, in any of the majors, you are going to be looking at moves by the U.S. Federal Reserve.

The biggest strength of this currency pair from the perspective of a small retail trader is that it is a highly liquid financial asset that often has substantial volatility. In recent years, the volatility and the magnitude of moves (on average) have decreased somewhat, but it's still a rather strong average pip movement of 200 pips. Since this currency pair is so liquid, getting in and out of trades fast is not going to be an issue. This currency pair is certainly a good choice for beginners, or for a trader of any level.

USD/JPY

This is the U.S. Dollar and Japanese Yen currency pair. Japan isn't quite the monolith that it was in the 1980s when everyone thought that Japan would take over the entire world economically, but Japan still maintains a large and powerful economy dominated by well-known companies like Toyota, Subaru, and Sony, among others. One factor that is important when considering this currency pair is the fact that Japan remains one of the world's largest exporting nations. This means that it's a frequently traded and highly liquid currency because all that exporting means that people have to convert dollars into Yens and vice versa all the time. The interest rate is low, which also makes this currency pair more attractive for holding over longer time periods.

GBP/USD

As we mentioned above, despite being a long-time member of the European Union, Great Britain held onto its own currency rather than adopt the Euro in 1999. Now that Britain may exit the European Union, for good or for worse, this probably means that the Great British Pound is here to stay for the foreseeable future. We noted earlier in the book that this was once (and sometimes still is) referred to as the cable, as currency trading between the United States and Great Britain went on via electronic cable under the Atlantic Ocean starting in the late 19th century. Brexit may introduce a lot of volatility in this currency pair, and in fact, in any currency pair involving GBP, so traders may want to pay attention to it at least for the near future. Even after Brexit is finalized, if it ever actually is, then there is likely to be some extra volatility introduced into the price movements of GBP currency pairs. Whether that is in favor of the GBP or against it, that is not a question that is relevant to the FOREX trader. You are not favoring one currency over another because you like it, you are picking currencies based on what works in a given trade.

USD/CHF

CHF is the ticker symbol (to use a stock analogy) for the Swiss Franc. Switzerland is another country maintaining its own currency, and given Switzerland's strong banking presence, it's an important currency despite the relatively small size of the country and its economy. Traders consider the Swiss Franc to be an important currency during times of economic trouble or international crisis. When there are international problems, in most cases, the Swiss Franc can be expected to increase against the U.S. Dollar because the demand for the Franc rises as people look for a relatively safe place to put their money in. So, if there is an economic crisis that you happen to experience, remember this and bet on the Swiss Franc against the dollar. In times of uncertainty, economic downturn, or crisis, the Swiss Franc may also do well against several other currencies such as the Japanese Yen. The USD/CHF pair sometimes goes by the nickname, "Swissie."

USD/CAD

Although Canada has a relatively small population compared to the European Union, Japan, and the United States, its economy enjoys outsized importance because it shares a border with the United States, and a large amount of trade goes on between the two countries. Canada has a lot of natural resources that it exports, such as oil, natural gas, and timber, which again helps it to maintain an outsized level of importance in the world of economics and in currency trading. Due to its direct relationship with the United States, the USD/CAD currency pair can be a good trade, even though it doesn't play as large a role in the markets as the EUR/USD currency pair does. When relations between Canada and the United States are good, volatility can decrease for this currency pair. When there are some difficulties, this can lead to increased volatility making it more attractive to trade. Canada has large exports of coal, raw aluminum, iron ore, gold, and copper ore. So, to get a feel for how the movement of the Canadian dollar may be trending with respect to other currencies, you might want to see if the prices of these commodities are rising or falling. Since Canada is exporting these materials, this generally means that rising commodity prices are good for Canadian currency.

AUD/USD

Australia is a diverse and highly modern economy, but like Canada, its economic fortunes are often influenced very heavily by the export of natural resources. When it comes to Australia, you will want to pay attention to iron ore and rare earth metals, along with coal. When commodity prices are rising, the fortunes of Australia are often rising with it, but when they are declining, the fortunes of Australia are probably going down as well. When you are trading any currency pair involving the Australian dollar, you'll want to look at the prices of various commodities, but especially coal and iron ore, to see how they are going. Australia also exports large amounts of gold, petroleum, and wheat. So favorable pricing moves for these commodities may put the Australian dollar in a position to rise against other currencies.

NZD/USD

The last of the majors is the currency pair between the New Zealand Dollar and the U.S. Dollar. The New Zealand economy isn't as large as the others we've considered, and it's highly dependent on tourism and the export of agricultural products. It is a leading exporter of dairy products as well as lamb and other meats. If dairy prices are rising on commodities markets, this can bode well for any currency pair involving the NZD.

Crosses

If the USD is not in the currency pair, these are called crosses. There are crosses for each of the currencies from major economies, such as the Euro or the Japanese Yen. The majors enjoy the highest trading volume and are therefore the most liquid currency pairs that you can trade, but there are several crosses that also have high trading volume, and so can be good to trade as well.

First, let's look at some of the Euro crosses:

- EUR/JPY: As you might imagine, there is a lot of trade that goes on between these two major economies. As a result, this can be a good currency pair to trade. When exports are in favor, Japan might have an edge, in particular when electronic components are considered.

- EUR/CHF: This is the Euro and Swiss Franc cross pair. The thing to look for here is the overall economic situation and whether there are any international tensions. Generally speaking, if people are looking for a safe refuge for their money, the Swiss Franc is going to be it. So, when times are tough, you might look for increased volatility with this currency pair, and you might also look for the Swiss Franc to be rising in value against the Euro.

- EUR/GBP: This is certainly a currency pair to watch with the pending Brexit move, no matter how it turns out. If the situation is viewed favorably in terms of the European Union, then certainly, the Euro is going to rise in value against the Great British Pound. In the near future, at least, the Great British Pound is probably going to be declining in value against several major currencies, although over time, this will probably stabilize, and once things settle down, the Great British Pound is probably going to be rising in value. But for now, look for it to be the weaker member of a currency pair with another major country.

- AUD: The Australian dollar is also a good cross to look at when trading with the Japanese Yen, New Zealand Dollar, Euro, Canadian Dollar, and even against the Chinese Yuan. The main thing to look at when it comes to the Australian Dollar is to look at what Australia exports and who is importing from it. When commodity prices are rising, this is something that is going to favor the Australian Dollar against the currencies of those countries that are importing large amounts of raw materials from Australia. China is a big consideration here.

- Japanese Yen: Any cross pair involving JPY is going to be important. The key data point for Japan is to remember that Japan has few (if any) natural resources, but it's going to be importing a large number of commodities since it has a thriving export business of major manufactured goods like automobiles. Therefore, rising commodity prices may be something that hurts Japanese currency, while falling commodity prices might help it, as that means the steel in Toyotas and Nissan cars are going to cost Japanese companies less, and lead to increased sales worldwide.

Exotic Currency Pairs

Exotic currency pairs are generally going to include currencies from countries that we have not yet discussed. These are currencies that are not traded nearly as much, but many exotic currencies are going to be associated with developing countries. Examples can include countries like Mexico, Thailand, and Brazil. Some currencies that fall in the exotic category have manipulated or fixed exchange rates, making trading them problematic. The biggest weakness with exotic currencies is that they tend to have small trading volumes. Professional FOREX traders are generally not spending their time focusing on exotic currency pairs.

Some exotics like the Mexican Peso are more stable than others, such as the Iraqi dinar. But the biggest weakness for any exotic currency is that they are not highly desired by traders, and as a result, you might find yourself stuck in trade far longer than you want to be.

The economies of many exotic currencies are also unstable and subject to more political upheaval than the economies of most major countries. This means that volatility can suddenly be sent soaring on some political event. Rapid depreciation can often be seen with exotic currencies, and while this can offer an opportunity to bet against the currency, remember that getting out of a trade is something that can always be an issue. So, there are two main weaknesses that you need to consider when thinking about trading exotics – instability and low levels of liquidity.

However, there are some reasons that traders will find trading exotic currency pairs to be worth their while. The first aspect is that they move a lot. If you put the time in to study the charts of exotic currency pairs, you are going to find that they can move by large amounts, and then the price movement will come to a grinding halt. The movements can be extremely large – even on the order of thousands of pips, making it possible for traders to get large profits if they are able to get into the trade at the right time, and able to sell their position before the price goes down again.

One factor that influences exotic currency pairs is that they are only traded by a relatively small number of banks, whereas the U.S. Dollar is going to be traded by all banks. So, this is something that can work for or against you. When there is a price movement of the exotic currency pair, it is going to be quite large. Since there are not large numbers of institutions or traders (relatively speaking) trading the exotic currency pair, this means that it's not easy to reverse a trend in price that happens when banks make their moves on these currency pairs. If you are following a trend trading strategy (see future chapter), then exotic currency pairs might be something to look into. But again, the biggest problem with exotic currency pairs is that at some point you need to get out of the trade – and it might be difficult to find someone to take the opposite side of the trade so that you can close out your position.

One exception to the rule might be exotic currencies that are paired with the U.S. Dollar. For example, one of the favorites in this regard is the U.S. Dollar and the Mexican Peso. The United States and Mexico are involved in a significant amount of trade, and so this currency pair is going to have more liquidity than many other exotics. However, it's a currency pair that is often going to have large moves in price, which can either be sudden moves that can result in large profits or solid trending. Either way, it's an exotic currency pair that is a middle ground because of the large amount of trade between the two countries coupled with the fact that people are always looking for U.S. Dollars in countries with developing economies, because their currency is not as stable and trustworthy, while the dollar, for all its faults, fills these roles. So, there may be exotic currencies that could be worth trading, but you must do some research before just jumping in.

PIPS

If you get into FOREX trading, the concept of a pip is one of the most important that you will come across. Essentially, a pip is a measure of a price change in a currency pair, and it can be considered the most significant measure to make. Small pips mean big money when you are trading lots of currency. So, it is crucial to understand a pip. We might begin by asking what does this phrase mean. It is nothing more than an acronym, and you must familiarize yourself with what it stands for.

PIP means percentage in point. It can also mean the price interest point, but most people think of it in terms of percentage in point. In truth, most traders probably don't think about the formal definition, but they know how to work with pips and what the meaning is, when looking at prices of currency pairs.

To understand how to use pips on a practical level, you must look at how currency pair prices are quoted. Most currency pairs are quoted to five decimal places. It used to be four decimal places, but this has changed in recent years. One pip is a one-point change in the fourth decimal place. Let's suppose that the EUR/USD pair is quoted as:

1.14671

This is not a real value; I have made this up for illustration purposes. The number to note is number 7, which lies in the fourth decimal place. This is the pip. If this value were to change to:

1.14681

Then there has been a 1 pip move for the EUR/USD currency pair. We can practice some more. If the price moves to:

1.14781

It has changed in price by 0.00100. That is, the price went up by 10 pips. Now suppose that it changes to:

1.14731

If you take the difference, you get 0.00050 – that is, the price has dropped by five pips.

You are already becoming an expert at FOREX trading. But you will notice that we have added a fifth number. The firth number is called the "pipette." Sometimes, the pipette is shown in a smaller font. Generally, the pipette is not all that important. You can do well in FOREX trading without worrying about pipettes. It is such a small number that it hardly matters for anything, but at least you know that it is there and what it is called. So, if someone calls you and says that the GBP/JPY pair moved by 1 pipette, you know that the 5th decimal place has increased in value by one. But does it mean anything to the trader, as far as gaining or losing money? Not really.

Choosing Currencies to Trade

The strategies or method for trading is necessary. However, the traders need to know how to pick what currency pairs to trade. If you pick the wrong one, you will not make profit even if you have the perfect strategies in the world.

Each currency is representing the primary sector of each economy. When you trade for a currency pair, you need to collect information to understand the two economies and how they are related in many aspects. That will be complex as well.

New traders should just focus on the currency pairs that have steadiness and decent spreads. The liquidity is also important. The volatility is needed but only the new traders can proactively participate. These are essential keys to pick the currency pairs for trading if you are new in the FOREX market.

All the good choices in the FOREX market often include the US dollar because it is the most popular currency in the world. It is still going strong and stable. When traders do it to pair with other currencies, it will give them more benefits.

The traders should also watch out for the factors such as economy, political issues and so on in any currency. The right strategies are necessary too because you trade with the two currencies with the different economies.

Concepts of FOREX trading

You have to understand that the FOREX market works in a simultaneous buying and selling fashion. This means that if you want to buy one currency, you will have to sell the one you have at the same time. This is easy to understand if you have, for example, physical Euros, and walk into a Bank and exchange for physical Dollars. You sell your Euros and purchased Dollars. One transaction that includes buy and sell.

But in the FOREX world, we trade FOREX symbols called "pairs." So, when you are buying one currency, you will automatically be selling another. In the simple example mentioned above, you traded the pair EUR/USD. In a trading platform, you use this symbol if you want to buy Euros (in Dollars) or Dollars (in Euros). All pairs or symbols have the same principle. If you "buy the symbol" you are buying the first currency if you "sell the symbol" you are buying the second currency. You must get used to this concept in order to trade in FOREX. You will have to calculate the basis points of the currencies based on their difference. That you can calculate by looking at the trending rates of the two currencies. The basis points refer to a measure of the interest or any percentages that you need to calculate before you go ahead with a deal. You will be able to calculate your gain by doing so.

Rate of return

The rate of return in the FOREX market is quite large. This means that you can remain with a big profit or a big loss depending on your investment. There have been cases of people making millions by just investing a few hundred or thousand dollars. This is possible if you know to invest in the market the right way. Let's say you invest $10 in the market and it gives you a return of $1000. That is highly possible in the currency market. However, if you get it wrong, then you might end up losing a lot of money. The currency market is extremely volatile, and you must remain abreast of the difference in values of the currencies. The idea is to look for currencies that are momentarily undervalued, that way, you can expect a big change in value to finally close the transaction at your desired profit. If at any time you feel that the prices of the currencies are going to cause you a loss, then you must sell them off.

Dual benefits

The FOREX market offers you dual benefits when you invest in the market. It is better known as the Currency Carry Trade. The Currency Carry Trade is one where the person stands to benefit in two ways. Let's look at an example. Let's say a Chinese trader exchanges 5000 Yuan for dollars and buys a bond with the dollars' worth. The trader will receive an interest of 5% on the bond provided the rate of exchange between the two countries remains the same. If it does, then the trader will stand to gain a profit of 50% owing to the difference in the currency values. This is an added benefit to the fact that the trader will also be able to avail a profit from selling the bond later. Here, you have to understand that the exchange rate between the two should remain the same otherwise the trader will lose money. This risk is quite high with currencies whose rates are volatile. You will not be able to predict the difference in rates, and by the time you withdraw from it, you will probably have lost quite some money. The difference in the rates usually occurs over a period of years and will not be within a short period of time.

OTC

Unlike the regular Stock Market (that deals with regulated Financial Instruments), FOREX is always traded OTC (over the counter). This means that the currencies are not considered "financial instruments" in most countries and are not regulated as such. Banks and Brokers trade currencies via an Electronic Communication Network (ECN). A medium that is different from a stock market exchange like NYSE or AMEX. A dealer will be responsible for the trade, and there will be no centralized control over the trade. It is the same way penny stocks and bonds are exchanged. You will have to do some homework on how you can start trading in your local market as the method differs from country to country. You have to look at dealers that will help you get these currencies. All Banks and Brokers, authorized to exchange, are connected to this network. In essence, you need an authorized bank or broker to handle your orders via the internet.

These form the different basic concepts of FOREX that you have to understand if you wish to trade in it. They will act as your guide when you partake in FOREX trading.

Buying and Selling

As we already discussed on Page 19. The fact that the FOREX market works in a simultaneous buying and selling fashion is an important aspect to pay attention to. So, if you buy one currency you sell another. Just like how you would go to a bank to exchange Euros for Dollars in a single transaction.

But in the FOREX world, we trade FOREX symbols called "pairs." So, when you are buying one currency, you will automatically be selling another. In a trading platform, you use this symbol to buy Euros (in Dollars) or Dollars (in Euros). All pairs or symbols have the same principle. If you "buy the symbol" you are buying the first currency if you "sell the symbol" you are buying the second currency. You should get used to this concept. You are going to calculate the basis points of the currencies based on differences. You calculate that by observing the trending rates of the two currencies. The basis points refer to a measure of the interest or percentages that need to be calculated before you go ahead with a deal. This way you can calculate your gain.

The spread is something that is important to pay attention to. First lets us say what will happen if you enter a trade by various methods. Well, actually there are only two ways that you can enter the FOREX trade. The first method that can be used is buying the currency pair. If you buy the currency pair, then you are going to start the trade-up by a small amount, because the buy quote on the right-hand side is always a little bit higher than the sell quote on the left side.

SWAPS

Another concept that you have to become familiar with when it comes to FOREX trading involves what are called swaps. A swap is involved with the payment of interest rates. When you hold currency, that means that you can earn interest on the currency. Well, to be honest, it depends on the situation. You need to know the interest rates in each country of the currency pair in order to determine whether you will earn interest. Consider the following currency pair, for the sake of our discussion here:

Currency-Value Fluctuations

There are internal-market reasons and external reasons for a currency's value changes. Internally, one country's currency can increase while another currency you hold decreases. These fluctuations are often dependent on how many people are buying and selling the currency. For example, if the yen isn't strong, then more people will purchase the yen, which makes the value increase. This could show a decrease in the American dollar in comparison to the yen because traders are using the American dollar to purchase yen. In other words, the more people purchase currency, the stronger it is value. The more people sell a currency, the lower its value.

External factors can be anything from politics to other events going on within the country. These are things that traders cannot control, but you should always be aware of them. Because of this, many traders will spend at least half an hour every morning going through the news in order to get an idea of what the market is going to look like that day. Doing this will allow you to know if you should purchase a currency or trade one within your portfolio.

FOREX Session Times

If New York City is the city that never sleeps, then the F market is the market that doesn't sleep. This contrasts with th market which is usually open for eight hours per day and the down. After-hours trading exists, but this is a fraction of wha place during the market session. The closure of the stock brings many risks with it, most notably gaps.

When the market closes for a long time, there is a far greater of the next day's price not opening at the previous closing This is because opinions change overnight, and new develo come to light. The longer you switch 'off' a market, the gre chance of an overnight price gap.

With FOREX, this doesn't happen. The market is continuo thus the only gaps occur when Sydney/Auckland opens on N morning (local time). While the market is open all day, you not make the mistake of thinking that volumes are constan with liquidity and spreads. These keep changing throughout and depending on the session, liquidity changes for a pair.

The FOREX market has roughly four sessions each, wi session indicating when a major financial center is online. T to open is Auckland, but the FOREX day is considered op AM Sydney local time. Next, Tokyo opens at 9 AM loc followed by London at 8 AM and then New York at 8 A

224

time. Table one provides the open and close times, converted for time zones.

Session Name	EST Time
Sydney 7 AM-4 PM local	5 PM-2 AM
Tokyo 9 AM-6 PM local	8 PM-5 AM
London 8 AM-5 PM local	3 AM-12 PM
New York 8 AM-5 PM local	8 AM-5 PM

This time zone hopping will take some getting used to, but once you have traded for a few weeks, you'll know which center is open and which is closed. I would like to draw your attention to two facts. First, as you can see, Sydney opens almost as soon as New York closes. Next, you will see that the sessions overlap with one another, with Sydney and Tokyo having the greatest overlap.

Tokyo and London overlap for two hours, and London and New York overlap for four hours. These four hours are the most heavily traded portions of the day. You have the two biggest financial centers in the world slugging it out at the same time. The London and Tokyo overlap also sees significant volume increases, not least because London is the last European financial center to come online.

During that overlap, you have all of continental Europe and all the financial centers of Asia online, including Hong Kong and Singapore. Post the New York close, volumes dip drastically since you have just Oceania online. The Aussie and kiwi pairs see good volume, but the rest of the FOREX world is asleep. San Francisco is online for a while, but it really isn't comparable to New York in terms of volume.

Knowing the way, the FOREX calendar works is crucial to your success. The times you choose to trade will determine the pairs you wish to trade. In addition, it will also determine the style of trading you choose. For example, if you live in the Midwest, you're an hour behind New York. Usually, people need to be at work by 9 AM.

So, if you were to wake up early at say 6 AM, you can analyze the market and enter positions between 7-8 AM. You probably cannot day trade (I'll explain this later), but swing trading is a great option for you if you use the four-hour charts (again, I'll explain later). You leave for work and return at 5 PM. New York has closed but you can assess how your trading day went from 6-7 PM and enter more positions between 7-9 PM when Tokyo is online. You go to bed and wake up the next day at 6 AM and repeat the process all over again.

When trading like this, it makes sense for you to trade the Aussie, kiwi, and yen pairs. Trading European crosses is not going to do much for you since you'll be operating during times when these just aren't active. Of course, the EURUSD will be active, but it doesn't make sense to trade the euro outside of eurozone hours, does it?

You can see the flexibility that FOREX trading offers you. The stock markets are operational exactly when you're at work and thus, don't leave you much time for trading. This problem is solved for you with FOREX. The best times and pairs to trade depends entirely on your situation. Liquidity during market hours is never an issue unless you're trading exotics, and you're always going to get good prices.

FOREX Trading Terminology

There are a lot of terms used that are new to a trader who is just starting off and are vocabularies to them. It would do well to an aspiring trader to acquaint themselves with the new terms and understand the meaning behind them and how to use them appropriately when trading. This will prove essential to avoid miscomprehension of certain concepts when trading. To new traders, the terms may be a little bit difficult and have a completely different meaning than the expected one from its word-formation. The following words discussed below are some of the new vocabularies that will be encountered by a new trader, which are common in the language of trading.

- **A pip.** A pip is the lowest measure of the value of movement of currency under observation. The term pip is, however, an abbreviation of the term-percentage in point. A pip, as the

227

lowest measurable value of the movement that the currency makes, always measures ad 1% of the currency that a trader wants to exchange. When in the FOREX market a currency increases or decreases by a single pip, the inference has the meaning that the currency either increased or decreased by 1%. A great example is when the market analysis tools show that the US dollar has increased by a pip. This is to mean that the US dollar has increased in its value by $0.0001.

- **The base currency.** The base currency is the type of currency that a trader has and is currently holding. The base currency is likely the currency of the country that you're from. If a trader is from the US, his or her base currency will be the US dollar. If the trader is from the UK, the base currency of the trader will be the pound. The base currencies of traders therefore different across many traders around the globe due to different geographical differences.

- **The asking price.** The asking price is a term that is used to refer to the amount of money that your broker firm will demand from or will ask from you when you are making a trade. A broker always demands this price, or this amount of money when they are accepting the pair of currencies to be traded from you. The price is for buying the quote that you've made of the pair of currencies. A note to be made is that the asking price; made by the brokerage firms, is always higher than the bid price, as will be discussed immediately below.

- **Bid price.** The bid price is mostly used in reference to the brokerage firms, where it is the amount of money that the brokers will be willing to buy or to bid the base currency that you are currently holding. The broker firm sets the bid price according to their ability to bid on the base currency that has.

- **Quote currency.** The quote currency, unlike the base currency, is the currency that a trader wants and is willing to purchase, in exchange for his or her base currency. If a trader wants to exchange US dollars to get South African Rand, the currency of South Africa; the Rand is the quote currency. It is always stroked against the base currency when trading and when the currencies are made into pairs.

- **The spread.** This is the commission that the broker firm receives from being a platform where FOREX trading can take place. When referred to, the spread means the difference in value between the bid price made by the broker and the asking price, also quoted by the broker.

These are but a few but the major terms that are used in the FOREX trading world. Knowing this alone will not be enough, you should be familiar with more words and phrases that can be found in books concerning FOREX trading.

Chapter 2:

The Basics of FOREX

FOREX is considered the largest financial market in the world. This statement is confirmed by the enormous amount of trade volumes that are exchanged daily within it. FOREX is also the only market in the world to remain open uninterruptedly for five days a week, allowing traders to make their investments at any time of day or night.

The term FOREX is derived from the union of two words, namely Foreign and Exchange, which allow it to be identified as the foreign currency market. Precisely for this reason, it is easy to imagine FOREX as the most frenetic market on the entire planet, which at the same time allows traders who decide to invest in it to make greater gains.

To be able to make the trading activity advantageous, however, it is necessary to devote time and money to study FOREX and the currencies traded in it, but also to engage in order to implement an investment strategy that allows profits to be made in the medium and long term.

Naturally, as an investment activity, every trader has to study and contemplate the percentage of risk. No strategy, not even that considered almost perfect will be able to guarantee the complete elimination of losses, which however will have to be reduced in such a way as to optimize the relationship between yield and risk. To think of relying totally on chance, on the other hand, is the worst idea an investor who wants to be successful can have.

The fluctuations, albeit minimal and centesimal, relative to the currency trading carried out in the FOREX, are not in fact given by chance but are the result of a series of mechanisms and events that the trader must be able to understand. A profit will be made when a trader succeeds in correctly anticipating a future oscillation. Naturally, this profit will increase proportionally to the percentage of risk present in the operation carried out.

It is obvious that each trader will have to implement a strategy based on the objectives he or she aims to achieve. People have different risk appetite and this feature also affects the world of trading.

But there are so many other differences that distinguish one trader from another. For example, in the financial market, investments can be made in a very short time, even within a day, or in a very long time: the choice of the type of trading to opt for will depend on the balance that the trader will be able to give to the relationship between rationality and will to make profits as fast as possible.

Setting Up Your Own Trading Account

Once you've decided to trade FOREX and you've gathered some funds together than can be used, the next step in the process is to open a trading account. In order to do this, you will find a broker or dealer that is suitable for your needs. You'll want to find an established and trustworthy dealer that is in your home country. In the United States, many well-known and established stockbrokers such as TD Ameritrade also offer FOREX trading. The comfort of being able to trade using a broker like this is that you know it's reliable and that you can trust them. However, there are many other options.

Opening an account for FOREX trading is a little more involved than opening a stock trading account, due to the possibilities (real or imagined by authorities) of money laundering. Because of this, broker-dealers are a little more careful about verifying your identity and so forth, but it's not really a big deal to worry about.

Factors to Consider When Opening a Trading Account

There are many things that need to be considered when opening a FOREX trading account. The first thing you are going to want to look at is simple ease of use and convenience. These days, many people want to be able to trade using a mobile device such as an iPhone or tablet. Doing so with website-only access can be a bit cumbersome; therefore, many people are searching out dealers that also have mobile apps they can use to execute trades.

Of course, having flexibility is important, too. So, traders are also going to be interested in a company that has a desktop, as well as a mobile platform. Most established broker-dealers have both, although, in recent years, there have been some mobile-only stockbrokers emerging. The point is, as a FOREX trader, you want to have unfettered access to your account at all times, and you may need to access it on a desktop computer when mobile access is not available for one reason or another.

Another factor that is important is the tools that are made available. Charting is an all-important tool for FOREX traders. You need to be able to see price movements in the blink of an eye and be able to recognize trend reversals. So, while it sounds basic, you'll want to make sure that your dealer has built-in charts that can be used for the purposes of at least a simple analysis. But, generally, the more tools that are available to the trader, the better.

When looking at charts, a line graph is nice, and it shows you the overall price movement and trend, but it does not convey the level of information that a trader needs to have access to. So, you will want to make sure that any broker-dealer that you select also has the ability to make candlestick charts. As we will see later, candlestick charts are important to use in order to determine the trends underlying the current pricing on the charts, and they also play a central role in determining when there is about to be a price reversal. These price or trend reversals (that is, when a rising price is about to become a falling price or vice-versa), are important for traders when determining when to buy or sell currency pairs.

Another tool that your broker needs to make available are technical indicators. You are going to want to be at least able to use moving averages, and also tools like Bollinger bands and the relative strength indicator. Don't worry if you aren't familiar with these tools right now, the important point here is that you have a platform that makes them available. You might not even use all of them in your trading activities, but you should have them there just in case you need them.

The Basics First

Of course, in any business, whether it's a used car dealer or a FOREX broker, one of the first things that come to mind is how long has the company been operating. Of course, new companies are rising all the time, and so this is not a make or break factor. In fact, in recent years, many new stockbrokers have come into existence that has become very popular over a short time period, such as Robin Hood.

Usually, a company that has been in business for a long time period is one that inspires more confidence. You can be assured that the company has some chance of weathering major economic downturns and other events if it has been in business for more than ten years. Some companies, like TD Ameritrade, have been in business for much longer, something that gives us some confidence that the company is mature and stable.

Remember – you are going to be putting your money into an account that is managed by the company. Of course, if the company failed, you could just go trade FOREX somewhere else. But what you want to avoid is a situation where the company fails, and you've got $10,000 in your account, and then you have trouble getting it back. While the FDIC insures up to $250,000 in a bank account, you may find that any money you put in a FOREX trading account isn't protected. This leads us to the point where looking for established brokers is the preferred route when setting up a new trading account.

Second, you might be interested in the size of the company. Again, this obviously cannot be a hard and fast rule. All companies start somewhere, and many of today's largest corporations like Apple were once operated by two or three individuals in someone's garage. However, mostly, a company that has a larger size is going to be one that is preferred to a new startup that only has five employees.

If the company is publicly traded, this is another good sign that it's a brokerage that is – generally speaking – reliable and trustworthy. Of course, we can point to many old, well-established, and large, publicly traded financial companies that have gone bust in the past. Three of the most famous examples include Lehman Brothers, Bear-Stearns, and Merrill Lynch. These companies were all household names, they were older and mature companies with large numbers of employees, and they were publicly traded. They all did go bust during the 2008 financial crisis. So, there are no guarantees in life, but you do have to play odds. And when it comes to probabilities, a company that is publicly traded is a more stable company.

Regulation

Although we prefer a lighter regulatory touch as FOREX traders, you do want some regulation; otherwise, you might be taken in by fly-by-night operators that have fancy looking websites. These days it's very easy to create a flashy and professional looking website that can entice people to sign over their money. The website might be based overseas and lack the usual protections that an American based company would offer for investors. A trader is better off going with a domain where there is some regulatory touch. The best locations for this are the United States, the United Kingdom, Australia, New Zealand, and Canada.

Creating Your Currency Trading Account

Opening a FOREX trading account, for the most part, is no different than anything else you do online. You are going to have basic forms to fill out that asks you general information such as your name, address, and phone number. Other contact information like your email address will probably be required.

236

To start off, rather than just creating an account, you are going to be required to apply for an account. Remember that FOREX trading is considered risky by the authorities in the sense that currency trading could be used for money laundering. So a few hoops are in place that you have to jump through in order to demonstrate that you are who you say you are so that they have some reasonable level of confidence that you are not using FOREX trading for this purpose. There are two main things that you must verify in order to pass the application – the first is that you are a citizen of the country that you are claiming. Second, you are going to have to offer some level of proof of residence—that is, you actually live at the location that you are giving to the broker as your address.

This simply means that you are going to have to upload some documentation. The specifics may vary from broker to broker, but you may be required to send in copies of such items as your driver's license and a current utility bill.

Once this documentation has been sent in, the broker-dealer will review it and get back to you. Assuming that your application is legitimate, the broker will probably approve your application over a time period of 1-3 days. Most applications are approved in about 2 days of time.

Connecting a Bank Account

Once the application is approved, you are nearly ready to go. The final step in the process is to connect a bank account so that you can move funds into an account that your broker sets up for you. And of course, wishing you successful trading, we will want to be able to quickly move profits to a bank account we use so that we can enjoy the fruits of our labors. In order to get started, you will have to wire funds to your broker. As we noted earlier, some brokers might require a minimum deposit. It could be $500 or $1,000. Check with specific brokers or dealers that you are interested in and find out what the specifics are for each particular brokerage.

Once the bank account is connected, the money will move by wire transfer into your account with the brokerage. At this point, you're able to begin trading.

Trading Platform

Many FOREX dealers will have their own trading platform, but others will be using Meta Trader 4, which is a trading software designed for FOREX markets. Meta trader was first introduced to the FOREX community back in 2005. The software is immensely popular among FOREX traders, and it's available through many FOREX dealers and brokers.

Meta Trader 4 includes a server component that is run by the broker. Client software is run by traders on their own desktop machines. More recently, you can download mobile apps to your smartphone or tablet in order to run the platform. The platforms will allow you to pick currency pairs, view charts and indicators at a glance, and place your trades. It's a very easy platform to use that most people can pick up nearly instantly.

While there are other trading platforms available, one of the benefits of Meta Trader is the ability of traders to write scripts and even build robots using the platform. This powerful capability enables small, retail traders to automate large parts of their trading activity and to engage in faster computer-controlled trades. This can help traders to earn larger profits by moving in and out of currency positions quickly.

The important part of a trading platform is to be able to look at charts to spot pricing trends. Depending on what type of strategy you adopt for trading, you will be interested in using these charts – often in real-time – to decide when to place your trades. If your broker is not using meta trader 4, then you are going to want to make sure that whatever software they are using, including if it's in-house developed software, allows the capabilities that you must have so that you can not only make trades quickly but that they are also informed trades.

How to Start

Whenever you start trading, you want to ensure you follow certain steps for success.

First, you always want to do your research. You want to learn as much as possible. This means you will read books, join FOREX trading forums, find a trusted broker, and anything else you feel is necessary. Once you feel like you know FOREX trading like the back of your hand, you will be able to move on.

Second, ensure you understand the language. FOREX trading has its own language. Take your time to learn these terms, and if you have questions, find another trader to discuss your concerns with.

Third, you want to find your trusted broker. This person will help you make decisions and explain the world of investing to you. Take your time to find the best broker for you. Your broker will help you set up an account.

Fourth, take the time to analyze the FOREX market. Learn about the charts and what they mean. Look back in the history of some currencies so you can gain a better understanding of trading. For example, charts can help you analyze the best time for trading and which currencies are best within the market and help you find the best currencies.

Fifth, if you are trading full-time, set up an office and your schedule. You want to find time to ensure you are self-disciplined enough that you won't struggle with distractions. Take the time to set a start date.

Sixth, once your day arrives, start trading. Make sure that you go through your morning routine, such as reading the paper and seeing how the currencies are doing. Notice any changes that occurred overnight. You also want to ensure you go through your daily schedule and close out your day with your evening routine. For example, check your stocks for the day, and discuss anything about your day in your journal.

How to Profit

Once you start trading, you will want to do what you can to limit your risks. While you will always have some risk, you can find a comfortable level of risk. Another way to profit is by diversifying your portfolio. This means that you will have different currencies and not focus on the same ones.

You also want to be patient. FOREX trading isn't a get-rich-quick scheme. It will take time to start seeing a profit. Don't give up, and don't fall into the wrong mindset. If you need any help, talk to your broker, a mentor, or someone in the forum.

There are many experienced FOREX traders who are happy to help beginners.

Continue to communicate with your broker, and others. Even if you spend months researching, people will always be important when it comes to your success. Don't allow yourself to get into the mindset that you know everything. Continue to learn as much as possible. Take time to practice analyzing reports. You have to do whatever you need to feel so comfortable as a trader.

Chapter 3:

The advantages of FOREX trading

Liquidity

The first and most important benefit of FOREX trading is its liquidity. As you know, the FOREX market is extremely liquid, meaning you can sell your currency at any time. There will be a lot of takers for it, as they will be looking to buy a particular currency. The highly liquid market can help you avoid any loss as you don't have to wait on your currency to be sold. And all of it is automatic. You only have to give the sell order, and within no time, your entire order will be sold.

Timing

The FOREX market is open 24 hours a day, which makes it a great place to invest at. You can keep trading during the day and the night if you are dealing with a country's currency whose day timings coincide with your night timings. You can come up with a schedule that will allow you to conveniently trade with all of the different countries that lie in different time zones. You can also quickly sell off a bad currency without having to wait the whole night or day.

Returns

The rate of returns in a foreign currency trade is quite high. You will see that it is possible for you to invest just $10 and control as much as $1000 with it. All you have to do is look for the best currency pairs and start buying and selling them. The leverage that these investments provide is always on the higher side, which makes them an ideal investment avenue for both beginners and old hands.

Costs

The transaction costs of this type of trade are very low. You don't have to worry about big fees when you buy and sell foreign currencies. That is the one big concern that most stock traders have, as they will worry about having to shell out a lot of money towards transaction costs. But that worry is eliminated in currency exchanges, and you can save on quite a lot of money just by choosing to invest in currency.

Non-directional trade

The FOREX market follows a non-directional trade. This means that it does not matter if the difference in the currencies is going upwards or downwards; you will always have the chance to make profit.

This is mostly because there is scope for you to short a deal or go long on it depending on the situation and rate of difference. You will understand how this works when you partake in it. The main aim of investing in FOREX is to remain with a steady profit, which is only possible if you know when to hold on to an investment and when to sell it off. This very aspect is seen as being a buffer by traders and is the main reason for them choosing to invest in FOREX.

Middlemen eliminated

With FOREX trade, it is possible for you to eliminate any middlemen. They will unnecessarily charge you a fee and your costs will keep piling up. So, you can easily avoid these unnecessary costs and increase your profit margin. These middlemen need not always be brokers and can also be other people who will simply get in the way of your trade just to make a quick buck out of it. You must be careful and stave such people off. Education is key here and the more you know, the better your chances of avoiding any such frauds.

No unfair trade

There is no possibility of anyone rich investor controlling the market. This is quite common in the stock market where a single big investor will end up investing a lot of money in a stock and then withdraw from it quickly and affect the market negatively. This is not a possibility in the foreign currency market as there is no scope for a single large trader to dominate the market. These traders will all belong to different countries, and it will not be possible for them to control the entire market as a whole. There will be free trade, and you can make the most use of it.

No entry barrier

There is no entry barrier, and you can enter and exit the market at any time you like. There is also no limit on the investment amount that you can enter with. You have to try and diversify your currency investments in a way that you minimize your risk potential and increase your profit potential. You can start out with a small sum and then gradually increase it as you go.

Certainty

There is a certain certainty attached with foreign currencies. You will have the chance to avail guaranteed profits if you invest in currency pairs that are doing well. These can be surmised by going through all the different currency pairs that are doing well in the market. With experience, you will be able to cut down on your losses with ease and increase your profits. You have to learn from your experience and ensure that you know exactly what you are doing.

Easy information

Information on the topic of foreign currencies is easily available on the internet and from other sources. This information can be utilized to invest in the best currency pairs. You should do a quick search of which two pairs are doing well and invest in them without wasting too much time. If you need any other information on the topic, then this book will guide you through it. You can directly go to the topic that you seek and look at the details to provide there.

Apart from these, there are certain other benefits like minimal commission charged by the OTC agent and instant execution of your market orders. No agency will be able to control the foreign exchange market.

These form the different benefits of trading in the FOREX market but are not limited to just these. You will be acquainted with the others as and when you start investing in it.

No Fee Prices

The government costs no price for alternate in FOREX, there is no clearing charge, no brokerage rate. Retail foreign exchange agents get their compensation through something referred to as "the unfold".

Low Fee of Transactions

The retail price of a transaction is usually less than 0.1% beneath normal marketplace situations. The unfold should even be as low as zero.07% for large transactions.

There's No Constant Lot Length

Investors can take part in FOREX change with money owed which might be as small as $25. You decide the amount you want to invest i.e. there may be no fixed amount.

The Market Is Open 24-Hours

You do no longer need to wait for the beginning of the running hour. With the distinction in time zones, the foreign exchange marketplace is constantly open. The fact that the foreign exchange market never sleeps is a chunk of amazing information for those who need to alternate on an element-time basis because you may alternate at a while and area of convenience.

No One Can Controlling the Market

The foreign exchange market is so large, and it has so many participants that no unmarried entity can control the marketplace rate for a prolonged time.

Low Access Obstacles

Getting commenced as a currency dealer does no longer necessarily price a ton of money. On-line foreign exchange brokers provide mini and micro trading bills, some with a minimal account as little as $25. This ensures easy access to FOREX trading by using the common person who does now not have quite a few begin-up capitals.

High-profit potential

FOREX trading has a high-profit potential. In fact, there are professional FX traders who have quit their day job and trade currencies for a living. Some people have also attained financial freedom by FOREX trading. Trading currencies has long been established as something that can be very lucrative. Of course, you also need to spend time and efforts in order to make it worthwhile and profitable. When you engage in FX trading, even a small investment of $100 can grow by more than 300% in just a short period of time. Compare this with investing in stocks where a profit of 20% in a year is already considered high. Indeed, if you have money that you can use to invest, learning FOREX trading is most probably the best thing that you can do that can lead you to financial freedom.

Leverage

It is not a secret that many people like FOREX trading because it will allow you to leverage. As we have discussed in the previous chapter, leveraging will allow you to invest a small amount of money but trade using a substantial capital. Needless to say, this will allow you to take in more profits. Many traders do not have enough money to start with a decent capital. Leveraging will allow you to spend and risk less and at the same time have a high-profit return.

Low cost

The main cost in FOREX trading is normally included already in the spread. Therefore, you no longer need to worry about any exchange or clearing fee, and not even a brokerage fee. Under normal market conditions, the retail transaction cost is even lower than 0.1%. If you are working with a large dealer, then it is normally lower than 0.7%. Of course, this may increase depending on your leverage. Since you no longer have to worry about so many costs that you need to cover, you can put all your focus on what really matters, and that is making a profit.

24-hour market

The FOREX market is open round-the-clock. Hence, you can trade in the morning, in the afternoon, in the evening, or evening at 2am or 3am. It is up to you to decide when you want to participate in the market. Although the FOREX market follows a schedule, once it opens for the week, you can rest assured that it will remain open round the clock until it closes by the end of the week.

Fair market

There is no authority that controls or unduly influences the FOREX market. Of course, certain things and event may affect the price of currencies, but they cannot continuously do so for an extended period. The FOREX market is very big with lots of different participants.

Easy to enter

It is easy to enter the FOREX market. You can start participating in the market simply by going online. You can make trades in the comfort of your home. You also do not need a high capital. There

249

are many online brokers that will allow you to trade even with a small investment.

Convenient

FOREX trading is convenient. All you need is to connect to the Internet, and you can start trading using the trading platform that is provided by your broker. You can easily open and close positions with just a few clicks of a mouse.

There is high flexibility for the persons involved in the trade when it comes to trading goods as well as services. You are not restricted to the amount of money to use while trading. There are no excess rules as well as regulations that have been put in place to be followed by the ones involved in trading. It is as well a market that operates for twenty-four hours and throughout the week. Hence, it is wise considering as a part-time engagement by anyone who does a regular job since it has no time restriction. You don't have to wait for the market to open since it never closes. You have the freedom to choose when and at what time you want to get into trading. You are no restrictions for you to waiting for a specific session to trade as it is the case with trading stock. You get into the trade when you have the time to do that. It is always in operation since it is not affected by any situation. You can get updates anytime you need and as well get to view the trend when you have time to see. The different trading styles will enable you to trade at your convenience. If you intend to take the position for a short duration, FOREX trading is an excellent opportunity for you. It is the easily accessible market to any trader.

Central Exchange is not involved

The central exchange interferes with the market in rare cases or either in extreme conditions. It is a guarantee that there will be no cases of prices dropping or either price manipulation. That serves as an advantage to anyone who wants or has invested in FOREX trading. The market does not experience changes as it is the case into the markets that trade in equity shares and many others. There are no regulators since trade is conducted over the counter in the entire globe. The central banks interfere in exceptional cases, and this rarely happens. Localizing, as well as deregulating the market aids in avoiding those interferences.

Low barriers in case you want to enter the market

To invest in currency trade, you are not required to have a vast amount of money. You can quickly get into FOREX trading even with little initial capital. To have a trading account, you are required to have a deposit of $25 as a minimum. Compared to future, options as well as trading stock, which requires you to have the right amount of money. It is relatively cheap since a large amount of capital associated with opening an account does not apply in this case. Hence, it is more accessible to an average person who is interested and does not have much money for a start. The trading to attracts traders with different experience levels, and hence, experience does not serve as a barrier to enter currency trading. For a person entering the market for the first time, there are not many risks involved. They can test, improve as well as organize their new skills, which later turns to be a benefit.

Different methods can be used to trade

The trading method that you will prefer, you will be provided with an opportunity by the FOREX market. The advantage associated is you can buy as well as sell currencies according to specific responses. The world events taking place within a location or either change in the economy can be a determinant. You can as well base on the history of price patterns, and hence, you can identify the trends. Currency linked to an economy known to sustain it. You can as well put several views together to come up with a trade-picking approach that is unique. FOREX trading is used in several trading plan categories. Whether you have a short-term or a long-term goal, FOREX trading will not disappoint you in any way. They have a lot to offer to you as a small beginner.

Leverage will make your finances go further

A contract for differences subjected under a force will make your money go for a long duration. You are then in a position to pay a small portion of the entire value. Profits, as well as losses, made the aggregate value on the time of closure. Doing trade on the margin will give you an opportunity to reaping a good profit even from your small investment. You will be equipped with tools to manage risks, including price alerts, as well as running balances. You can try several strategic positions as a way to curb unwanted risks. Hedging serves as a right approach of mitigating as well as limiting losses to a considerable and known amount. You can choose FOREX pairs, and when failures occur on one pair, the other set in a different position can mitigate. Making a small deposit will help you control an immense contract value. You will reap enticing profits as well as minimize risking capital. You can trade with substantial cash flow compared to your deposit. Choose a reasonable leverage size which will translate to getting a potential profit as well as reducing the losses that you may incur.

You can access tools to aid you in trading

There are numerous trading platforms on tablets, mobile, web, and many more. You can also access a specialist platform in case you want to take your trading on a higher level. There are a lot of trademarks designed to assist you in upgrading your trading and interactive charts as well as consolidated news feeds. Some of the features include stops as well as limits that are vital in managing risks. You will too access products that are designed to assist you in growing the FOREX trading. You will be offered to help you practice trading as well as improve your skills. The demo accounts serve as a variable resource in case you are financially down, and you need to sharpen your trading techniques. You will establish if it's safe for you to open a live marketing account.

Wide range of options

With around 28 major currency pairs to choose from, you'll never run out of currency pairs to trade. This ensures that you will not find a moment to sit idly. Also, considering the nature of FOREX, you're sure that there is always a currency pair among the chances that will make profits.

When you buy one currency, you're likely to sell the other meaning that the transactions should be in pairs. There are numerous options you can put into consideration in FOREX trading. You can trade in multiple pairs by choosing the set based on specific criteria. You can either base on volatility patterns or the level of economic development. It is as well advisable to time when it is convenient. Embrace volatility, and this will help you to shift from on to another currency pair. When you speculate that the value of a currency will decline, you have to sell that and then buy one which to pair with it. FOREX trading provides a wide range of opportunities to trade and not forgetting the budget as well as the risk factor. You sell one currency and buy the other. A FOREX pair cost is like a unit of the money purchased and worth in the selling currency. You will make a profit or loss depending on the accuracy of the prediction you have made. In either case, you are subject to make a profit regardless of the deviation of the market.

The is no fixed amount for you to operate with

In many markets, the contract, as well as lot sizes, are regulated and supposed to be a certain amount. There are no such restrictions in the currency market, and you have the freedom to operate with the amount you are willing to. A reasonable cost is involved in providing you with a great option. It is consistent when it comes to trading as well as investing. It is so because both the buyer and the seller are directly involved in eliminating any broker that can be required.

The cost is low

There are typically considerate transaction costs involved under usual market conditions. The FOREX trading is associated with a little expense since there are rare cases of brokerage as well as commissions given. It is more reliable compared to any other type of trade where you consider brokerage fees. The cost you are supposed to pay to the FOREX broker is relatively small compared to what is paid to get into trading other securities. There is no clearing or government fees as deductions.

There is transparency in any information issued

You can easily access information concerning rates as well as the current forecast since it is accessible to all the public. The period that is involved for any information to be distributed makes the trading fairly judged. It happens in such a short time despite the large market size.

Confidence increase

When you get to the jackpot, your confidence will increase. It will automatically create goodwill, and you become active in trading money, which in turn creates traffic.

Do not emotionally invest in the organization you are trading on behalf. It makes it hard for you to do away with the position even in cases where the market does not go to plan. FOREX trading is an excellent idea to help you detach from such emotion and as well is essential for making the trading success. There are no emotions associated with any spillage that occurs along the way.

Demo account

Most FOREX traders will allow you to preview their services by providing you with a demo account. A demo account will allow you not only to test your broker's trading platform, but it will also allow you to trade in a real-market environment. A demo account can also be used to test your strategy. As a FOREX broker, testing your strategy before using it with real money is a habit that you must have.

Fun

Trading currencies is fun to do. In fact, it is very easy to get addicted to it. It is like a game that adults can truly enjoy, especially if you are making positive profits. It is fun to look at charts and choose the currency pair that you want to invest in. Developing a strategy and making your own market predictions can be fun. Overall, the whole activity of being a FOREX trader can be a truly fun experience.

Ease of Access

FOREX trading requires less compliance from the broker's perspective, and this trickles down to you as a trader. First of all, the commissions you pay your broker when trading FOREX are far less than when trading stocks. FOREX commissions are usually somewhere between $5-$7 per round trip lot.

This means that a single lot of $100,000 will cost you around $7 in commissions to both buy and sell. Thus, the total commission you pay on your trade is around that much. Add to this the higher leverage levels you have access to, and the FX market is far easier to decipher and enter than the stock market.

Chapter 4:

What Is Volatility?

Y ou can easily change to a different currency if there are higher profits or either good investment associated with it. There are higher risks associated with investing in the money-driven market. But volatility provides significant benefits by changing from one currency to another, which yields a good return. It makes it an advantage to lower the risk factors involved as well as increase the profit. You can get some benefit once you speculate on the price changes, either rising or falling. The FOREX trading gives maximum grasp compared to any other financial investing trade out there. It serves as an added advantage to level your investment. The exchange rates are very lively, and profit can be gained anytime when the prices shift anytime you are willing. You require a short duration for you to open as well as closed positions. High volatility attracts opportunities to make huge profits.

The quantity of uncertainty or threat concerned with the scale of the adjustments in a foreign exchange charge in foreign exchange buying and selling is known as volatility.

A better volatility approach that an alternate fee can be probably spread out over a larger range of values. While there's high volatility, the charge of the foreign money can exchange spontaneously over a brief term in either direction. Decrease volatility, on the other hand, will bring about the stagnation of the charge price I-e it does not alternate significantly, its modifies in cost at a gradual tempo over time. The higher the volatility, the riskier the buying and selling of the FOREX pair. Volatility technically method the standard deviation of the exchange within the cost of a monetary instrument over a period. Volatility is generally used to describe the threat of the currency pair over that term. The alternation over the years of a sure currency pair trade price is called volatility. It allows describing the price of threat faced by someone with exposure to that currency pair. The general view of FOREX investors is that volatility is negative as it represents threat and uncertainty. However, higher volatility generally makes foreign exchange buying and selling extra appealing to marketplace gamers. Volatility changes over the years. There are intervals whilst costs go up and down speedy i.e. excessive volatility, and there are periods during which they may not seem to move in any respect i.e. low volatility.

Significance of Volatility for Swing and Day Buying and Selling Strategies

Foreign exchange traders are properly conscious that the volatility of stock adjustments over time, going through intervals of excessive and coffee volatility wherein there are growth and contraction of the price range. This could show to be very beneficial to swing and day buying and selling traders particularly round information events when volatility can rise in a dramatic style, and this will be used to

259

assist within the management of expectations. For instance, if you're holding a role in stock right earlier than an earnings file, and the implied volatility of the front-month or weekly choice rose to a hundred and twenty%. Knowing this, the trader can take better choices in the difficulty of stopping, goals or whether to maintain within the exchange altogether.

Inventory swing traders and day traders are recognized to regularly take a look at technical evaluation tools and indicators handiest for the position and control of trades, however, it may often be beneficial to have a look at implied volatility, although we never change options, with a purpose to see what range of charge swings was priced-in employing the options marketplace.

Chapter 5:

What Is Liquidity?

There are high numbers of the people involved in the foreign exchange market compared to any financial market. Despite its significant size, it is as well extremely liquid. Because of the high liquidity, big players get attracted to FOREX trading. It, in turn, leads to filling the gap of the big orders of money trade with either small or no price deviation. Efficient pricing is promoted since there is no price manipulation, as well as no deviation, is experienced, from the actual price. Under the apparent market conditions, you can buy as well as sell any time since there are always people who are ready to trade. There are constant price patterns throughout the trade despite the level of volatility. The high liquidity makes the FOREX market efficient, and the heat of competition not felt. It is so despite the high number of traders involved on either side. The significant number of persons engaged in the trade ensures there are always transactions going on in the market. You'll be lucky to get an opportunity because the prices do not shift dramatically. Transactions are completed quickly as well as efficiently, and hence the spread, as well as the transaction costs accrued, are relatively low. You can make suppositions of the price movement in the market.

The convenience with the aid of which you may convert an asset into cash without difficulty is known as liquidity. Foreign exchange liquidity is the capability of a currency pair to be bought and offered with outgrowing the first-rate impact on its trade rate. A currency pair is stated to have a high level of liquidity when it can be bought or bought without problems, and there is a sizable quantity of buying and selling interest for that precise pair. FOREX liquidity allows for ease of alternative which makes the marketplace popular among buyers. It ought to be mentioned that foreign money pairs are no longer liquid. In reality, the liquidity stage of currencies tends to differ depending on whether they're primary, minor and exceptional pairs together with rising market currencies. FOREX liquidity tends to dry up as investors pass from essential pairs to minor pairs and ultimately to the exotic pair. The significance of liquidity in FOREX is apparent and its miles a chief element that enables the yield of earnings in a trade. The presence of extra liquidity in a financial marketplace guarantees ease of transaction glide and makes pricing extra competitive. The availability of liquidity is of extraordinary importance for a nicely functioning market and within the case of FOREX trading, there's a notable need for FOREX liquidity.

A marketplace broking or institution which acts as an expert market maker in FOREX operating at both ends of the currency transactions is the liquidity provider. A liquidity company acts as a middleman inside the securities market. They finance or underwrite fairness or debt transactions and then assist inside the buying and selling of the securities. The provider's number one task is to make certain consumers and dealers have on-call to get entry to the securities they represent. Liquidity is provided to the FOREX marketplace by numerous sorts of market participants consequently there's a boom inside the FOREX liquidity volume. Sources of liquidity encompass relevant banks, principally industrial and funding banks, overseas funding managers, hedge funds, retail buyers, foreign exchange agents, retail traders, and high internet worth people. Pinnacle vendors inside the foreign exchange marketplace are known as tier 1 liquidity carriers. These are the biggest investment banks with massive foreign exchange departments who make buy and promote costs available for the foreign exchange pairs that they make markets in, they regularly offer their clients with a range of different services.

Importance of Liquidity

The significance of liquidity in the FOREX market cannot be overemphasized. As already cited, one of the best aspects which allow attractive returns in trading is the presence of a liquid marketplace. The want for FOREX liquidity offerings rises right here. A liquidity provider will take a function in foreign exchange pairs that may be offset with another marketplace maker or joined to the marketplace maker's e-book to be liquidated from time to time later, that is carried out to reap charge balance. A few FOREX market makers can deliver market orders on behalf of their customers. They watch orders and phone tiers for them. It's far impossible for a character dealer to get direct get entry to a tier 1 liquidity provider. To benefit such, get right of entry to, they should go through a web broker. Suitable online agents tend to use as a minimum a few tiers, 1 liquidity providers, which will fill most in their orders and will usually access an ECN/STP network so one can execute trades. Agents who perform a dealing table absorb the position of a liquidity company by using letting their customers buy and sell on their machine with the dealer taking the opposite facet of the transaction, thereby offloading any sort of danger with expert opposite numbers as important. These firms act efficiently as marketplace makers and their business blessings from the fact that most investors lose their money once they trade. Online FOREX agents commonly establish a connection with many liquidity providers to achieve higher-dealing charges and spreads. By doing so, they can provide their customers with the most beneficial price obtainable from a couple of liquidity companies.

That allows you to link up with the pleasant liquidity provider, agents want to examine their express wishes and clear up several elements. Essentially, a broking has to check the overall package on provide when it comes to the kind of property and form of liquidity being supplied. It's far of great significance that multi-asset liquidity is being supplied with the aid of the liquidity issuer along with side access to the repair protocol and historical information. In annexation, a nominated account in distinctive currencies must preferably be an option.

The intensity of the market is any other aspect to be put into consideration. This provides records approximately the liquidity and intensity of specific foreign money. The better the number of trades at every fee, the higher the intensity of the marketplace. A liquidity company needs to be able to offer spontaneous change executions with slippage and re-costs especially all through the times of excessive impact market news. The fee providing of a liquidity issuer should consist of aggressive spreads as well as low fees and swaps and not using a compromise on either aspect. Liquidity carriers and agents must be regulated in an equal manner to ensure they are running below the industry's great practices and that there may be a high broking backing up the liquidity issuer. A liquidity provider with amazing popularity ought to be capable of preventing an automated and robust reporting system to allow compliance with all regulatory necessities.

Chapter 6:

Technical analysis of FOREX

Technical analysis is the study of past marketing trends. This becomes important to day traders because past trends can often help you predict what could happen with the stock in the future. Of course, you will always want to remember that just because it happened in the past, does not mean that the pattern will continue in the future. However, the chances are still high that the trend will continue. You just want to ensure that you don't have the attitude that it will be the exact same because, because even if the pattern continues, there will always be some changes.

Of course, there is more that goes into technical analysis than what the past marketing trends show. Like anything else in your day trading career, you will want to make sure you are educated in technical analysis, so you know how to look at the various graphs that you will encounter along the way. On top of this, you will also want to use other techniques to help you get close to any future prediction. These other techniques you will learn throughout your research on the topic but can include how to make general predictions and gathering your basic understanding of the stock market.

Technical analysis is popular among a lot of different investors and traders. However, not all traders will find technical analysis to be a useful part of their system. It all depends on your personal preference when it comes to how you want to go about choosing your stocks.

In order to ensure that your successful trade percentage only continues to increase as time goes on, you will likely eventually find it useful to branch out from using fundamental analysis exclusively to using technical analysis as well. While some traders consider the two types of analysis to be at odds with one another, the fact of the matter is that a balanced approach that uses each, when required, is always going to be the most effective in both the short and the long-term.

Technical analysis studies past market trends with the goal of accurately predicting those that are likely to occur again in the future. Technical analysis is ideal for those that like the idea of determining future performance by looking at previous prices, without having to dig through mountains of paperwork to find the details you're looking for. While the past will never be able to truly predict the future 100 percent of the time, technical analysis is useful when combined with a basic understanding of market mentality for generating predictions that are accurate within reason.

When you start to read the past marketing trends of stocks, you'll find a variety of graphs and charts that you'll use to conduct technical analysis. We touched on some of these earlier, such as candlestick charts, bar charts, and line charts, but there are several other charts that could be of use to you while you conduct your technical analysis.

Price charts

The price chart is described as the center chart in technical analysis. In this chart, there are two separate lines. One is a vertical line that describes the price, and the horizontal line describes the time.

A price chart is the primary tool of technical analysis. As the name implies, it charts the price of a given currency, on the x axis, as time passes, on the y axis. There are several different types of charts to choose from, but if you're just getting started with technical analysis then you'll want to start with the line chart, the point and click chart, the candlestick chart and the bar chart.

- **Line charts:** The most basic chart of them all is the line chart. It shows the closing price for the currency in question over a set period. The titular line is then formed one the day's grouping of closing prices has been determined and they are then connected with the purpose of determining a trend. While it doesn't include relevant details such as opening price or the results for the day overall, it will tell you if the day is positive or negative while also cutting out all of the noise that is so common in most other charts. As such, it can be an extremely enlightening place to start if you're looking at a new currency for the first time.

- **Bar chart:** When compared to a line chart, a bar chart adds in the additional details related to a currency's movement throughout each day. The top and the bottom of the bar are going to represent the high and low for the day respectively and the closing price is denoted by a dash found on the right side of the bar. Meanwhile, the dash on the left side of the bar is going to show the starting price. Finally, if the overall value of the currency increased for the day then the bar will be black and if it decreased it will be either red or clear depending on your trading software.

- **Candlestick chart:** A candlestick is like a bar chart in many ways, though it also provides additional relevant information that is more detailed overall. It includes the range for the day, expressed as a line, as with a bar graph, but when you view a candlestick chart you'll also notice a wide bar near the vertical line which indicates the degree of difference the price experienced over a given period of time. If the price increases for the day, then the candlestick will not be shaded in and if the price decreased throughout the day then it will typically be shaded in red as well.

- **Point and figure chart:** While the point and figure chart are used less frequently than some of the charts that have been previously discussed, the point and figure chart has been in constant use for more than 100 years and can still provide insight when used correctly. Specifically, this chart is used to determine how much a price is likely to move without taking timing or volume into account. This makes it a pure indicator of price, without any of the market noise that might otherwise be attached.

A point and figure chart can be easily picked out from the crowd as it is made up of Xs and Os rather than lines and points. The Xs will indicate points where positive trends occurred while the Os will indicate periods of downward movement. You will also notice numbers and letters listed along the bottom of the chart which corresponds to months as well as dates. This type of chart will also make it clear how much the price is going to have to move in order for an X to become an O or an O to become an X.

Range and trend

In order to ensure that you can properly profit from the use of technical analysis, it is crucial that you determine if it makes more sense for your trading style to focus on trading via trend or trading via range. While the two are both based on the price of the currency in question, they use that information quite differently in practice which means you're going to want to focus on either one or the other for the best results.

Once you come across a chart you are going to analyze, you'll want to think about where your interest is, whether it is with the range or the trend of the stock. Even though the range and the trend are different, they both have to do with the price which is why they are important for you to look at when it comes to technical analysis.

If you decide that trend is more appealing to follow, then you are more interested in going with the flow. Furthermore, you are probably more comfortable with risk than someone who would pick to follow the range. You will often find out what other people are doing while you look at the trend. While this isn't something that you should get into the habit of as a trader because following others can make you lose sight of your individual trading habits, it is important to follow if this is what is more appealing to you during your analysis. However, the trend is also considered to be the riskier choice of the two.

The reason following the trend is riskier is not because you are going with what other people are doing but because you are using the trend and trying figure out the best future prediction you can on where the stock is going. Because of the risk, you'll want to make sure that you keep your trades small. Remember, the larger your trades are, the riskier they become. Even if you're comfortable with a large level of risk, you don't want to take on too much risk on the same stock.

If you decide that range is more important, then you probably have a lower level of risk that you are comfortable taking on as a trader. There is nothing wrong with having a lower level of risk, in fact, as a beginner it can help you in the long run. On top of this, you can always build up to techniques and stocks that carry more risk as you continue to learn more about the world of day trading.

The reason why range is generally safer is because it allows you to predict where the price of the stock is going to move in the future with more confidence. You can take your education, your analysis, and all the other factors and combine them to give you a more reliable future prediction with the stock.

When you focus on the range, you're looking to see when the stock is going to move positively, which is when you'll make your move and take on the stock. This positive movement will often come before the price declines again, which means that you usually have a very short window to trade this stock, if you decide to take it on. This doesn't mean that you have to find the best point of entry, it simply means that you want to be aware when you believe the time will be and then make yourself available for a possible entry. If you find that you missed your opportunity when you go back to the stock, don't dwell on that. Remember, it is impossible to predict the future of a stock 100%, no matter how well you conducted your analysis.

If you feel as though your personal trading style would benefit from making trades that mostly go with the flow, then you're going to be more interested in trading via trend as this will tell you what other traders are up to. Your goal in situations like this will be to determine which trends are most likely going to be the most robust in the near future, so you have the maximum amount of time to jump on them, reaping a lion's share of the profits in the process. If you are considering this type of trading, then you will want to stick with smaller trades as you can lose out if a trend fails to materialize in the expected way at the wrong time. Trading via trend is ideal for those who prefer high risk and the greater potential for reward it brings along with it.

Range trading, on the other hand, is better suited for those who are willing to forgo some amount of profit for more reliable returns. The range in question is going to be the price that a given currency is going to return to twice or more throughout the time you're holding it, allowing you to profit each time. The market is going to present you with different challenges every single day in the form of different trends and potential opportunities.

Regardless of this fact, the movement typically tends to operate in ways that seem completely random, though its true intentions can be found once you determine where to look. The opening range has been profitable for trading professionals for decades as a profitable way to start off with an idea of the market's mood to make any profits that are coming up even easier to obtain.

When you take advantage of the opening range for a starting point, you'll then be able to locate the truth of the current market to determine if the bulls or bears are going to be in charge at the moment. In order to get the most out of this practice, it's crucial that you understand the opening range for low and high levels as they are of critical importance when it comes to levels of resistance and support throughout the day.

Understanding these details will make it far easier for you to anticipate levels in the market that are more likely to reverse or increase the changes you are seeing. Looking at the trading day from this perspective is going to make it easier for you to make the right moves at the right time to allow you to determine when future movement is forthcoming, so you can be in the right place at the right time.

This doesn't mean you won't be able to act if you can't find the perfect entry point each and every time. All it means is that you will simply need to get in at a point where you'll be in an ideal position for the next time the cycle repeats itself. You should also keep in mind that of the two strategies, range trading can take more resources to utilize properly which means you will want to have a substantial bankroll before you put it into effect.

Point and Figure Chart

While this is the chart that has been around the longest--well over a century—it's also one you won't find very often anymore. However, this doesn't mean that it's less important than any of the other charts you can find when looking at a stock's history. While this chart won't indicate volume or time, it can be an excellent chart that will help you predict where the price of the stock is going to go in the future.

One thing that sets the point and figure chart apart from the rest is that instead of being made up of points and lines, it is made up of x's and o's, which can make it easier to read for some people. When you see an "o" on the chart, this means that the price decreased. When you see an "x" on the chart, it means that the price increased.

People who find the point and figure chart useful will often take a quick glance at the chart and as they can easily spot the x's and o's without having to do a close analysis. For some traders, this quick analysis will give them enough information on whether it is a stock they want to look into further or not. However, the best idea is always to continue your analysis, no matter how the chart looks to you at first glance. It is important to remember that whatever you're doing in the world of trading, you want to be as thorough as you possibly can. If you don't take your time, you can easily miss something of importance that could have given you a sizable profit--or protected you from sizable loss--if you'd only taken it into consideration.

No matter what chart you decide to use when you're conducting technical analysis, you will find the different prices within that chart.

277

These prices will be some of the most important features of your analysis. Through these charts, you'll be able to find out what the price of the stock was when it opened, when it closed, what its peak price was, and what its lowest price was.

Start off on the right foot

In order to use technical analysis effectively, you will need to understand that it functions around the idea that the price of a given currency is going to fluctuate in the future based on a number of identifiable patterns that can be seen in its past. As such, unlike with fundamental analysis where you might have trouble finding enough data to make a rational choice, with technical analysis you'll have more data than you can ever hope to sort through. You'll have plenty of tools to help you sort through all of this information, including things like trends, charts and indicators that will point you in the right direction.

While many of the technical analysis techniques might seem overly complicated at first, at their most basic they are all looking for different ways to determine trends that are going to form in the future along with the strength. Choosing the right trends at the right time is the first step to becoming a successful FOREX trader in the long-term.

- **Understand the market:** Technical analysis is all about measuring the relative value of a trade or underlying asset by using available tools to find otherwise invisible patterns that, ideally, few other people have currently noticed. When it comes to using technical analysis properly you're going to always need to assume three things are true. First and foremost, the market ultimately discounts everything; second, trends will always be an adequate predictor of price and third, history is bound to repeat itself when given enough time to do so.

- Technical analysis also believes that the price of a given underlying asset is ultimately the only metric that truly matters when it comes to understanding the current state of the market. This is the case because any and all other facets of the market have already been factored through to the price before it reached the point it is currently at which means that analyzing anything besides the price is, simply put, a waste of time.

- **All about the trend:** Being aware of the trend and how it can affect the ways you'll analyze a trade is key to your long-term success through technical analysis. When on the lookout for trend, it can be any clear direction that the price of a given currency is taking that is clear enough to cut through all of the noise that naturally infects the market as a whole. Trends can be either strong enough to see from a mile away or weak enough to easily miss even if you are looking for them. Essentially it just means that just because a given trend isn't immediately visible then this doesn't mean it isn't there. Likewise, you're going to always want to ensure that the trend you think you're following is really there as it can be easy to misinterpret false data if you aren't careful.

- **Trend mapping:** After you have picked out the trend you're interested in finding more about, the next thing you'll need to do is create a trendline that will let you map out all of the details as you come across them. This can be accomplished by simply drawing a straight line through the data points to make the trend more visible. If the trend is positive, then you'll want to connect the dots of the various lows that are being measured while if it is a negative trend you'll want to connect the relevant highs.

Technical Analysis and Psychology

If you have any background in psychology, you're going to find technical analysis pretty easy to understand. In fact, you will probably grow to love technical analysis and use it as often as possible. There is a lot of psychology that goes into this because you are essentially analyzing the behavioral patterns of the stocks and traders who took part in creating those patterns.

In fact, psychology can help you in blocking off one of the biggest risk factors when it comes to using technical analysis: getting your emotions tied up in your decisions. As I have discussed before, you want to make sure that you keep your emotions out of your decisions when it comes to trading. Psychology can help you curb your emotions when you are analyzing the stock's behavior because you are more likely to become aware of your emotions when it comes to technical analysis.

One of the biggest emotions you want to make sure you are aware of is greed. This emotion can quickly pop up without people realizing it, especially when their trades are going great and they find themselves making a good amount of money. It is a natural human reaction to feel that once you start profiting from your job, you want to find ways to make more money. In return, you can start to get a sense of greed when you are looking for your next profit, which can cause all kinds of problems and mistakes along the way that could last well into your future.

Another way psychology and technical analysis go together is because of the self-fulfilling prophecy. Because so many other traders have used the same system, you come to realize that the strategies they use do work. This can help you in many ways, including boosting your confidence when making decisions.

Chapter 7:

Guide to the choice of a broker.

A broker refers to a firm or somewhat an individual who charges a certain fee or rather a commission for executing the buying and the selling process. In other words, they play the role of connecting the customer and the seller of the product. Thus, they are generally paid for acting as a link between the two parties. For instance, a client might be willing to buy shares from an organization. However, he might be lacking enough information about the places that he can purchase these shares. Thus, he will be forced to seek a person who understands well the stock exchange markets. The broker will, therefore, educate the client as well as link them with the right sellers. The broker will thus earn by offering such a connection. Other brokers sell insurance policies to individuals. In most cases, the individuals earn a commission once the clients they brought in the organization buy or renews the system. Any insurance companies have utilized the aspect as a way of increasing their sales.

List of Common Brokers

IG

It is rated as one of the best FOREX brokers in the world. It was one of the pioneers in offering contracts for difference as well as spread beating. The organization was founded in the year 1974 and had been growing as a leader in online trading as well as the marketing industry. One of the aspects that have boosted its growth is the fact that it has linked a lot of customers, hence gaining more trust. In other words, a duet to its large customer base, a lot of clients prefers selling and buying their services. The other aspect worth noting is that this organization is London based, and it is among one of the companies that are listed on the London Stock Exchange market for more than 250 times. The aspect is due to the fact that it offers more than 15,000 products across several asset classes. Such classes include CFDs on shares, FOREX, commodities, bonds, crypto currencies as well as indices. Another aspect worth noting is that the 2019 May report, the firm is serving more than 120,000 active clients around the globe. Also, there are more than 350,000 clients that are served daily. The aspect has been critical in boosting its expansion as this group of individuals does more advertisements.

Some of the benefits that one gains by working in this industry are the fact that it allows comprehensive trading and the utilization of tools that enhance the real exchange of data. The other aspect worth noting is that it has a public traded license that allows a regular jurisdiction across the entire globe. In other words, one can acquire the services of this organization across the whole world with ease without the fear of acting against the laws of the nation. Also, the premises offer some of the competitive based commission that enhances pricing as spreading of FOREX. There is also a broad range of markets that are associated with the premises too, there several currencies and multi assets CFDs that are offered by the organization. The aspect has been critical in the sense that it allows the perfect utilization of all the services as well as the resources available across the globe. Some of the services that are offered by the organization are permitted globally, such that even after traveling from one nation to the other, one can still access their services. Since the year 1974, the organization has joined more than 195,000 traders across the entire globe. The aspect has allowed the selling its shares as well as services hence its fame.

Saxo Bank

The FOREX broker was established in 1992 and has then been among the leading organization in offering FOREX services as well as the multi-asset brokerages across more than 15 nations. Some of these nations include the UK, Denmark, and Singapore, among others. One of the aspects of the organization is that it offers services to both retailers as well as institutional clients in the globe. The character has allowed the premises to provide more than one million transactions each day. Thus, it holds over $ 16 billion in asset management. The Saxo bank also offers more services to all her clients. Such services include Spot FX, Non-deliverable Forwards (NDFs), contract difference as well as all the stock exchange options. The aspect has been critical in increasing its customer base across the globe. Some of the services such as crypto and bond services that are offered in the premises has allowed its expansion in the sense that they're sensitive and essentials.

Some of the benefits that one can gain by assessing the services of the premises are that it enhances diverse selection of quality, it increases competitive commissions and FOREX spread as well as an improved multiple financial jurisdiction function that is allowed across the entire globe. In other words, the premises offer services that are allowed in the whole world, and that considers the rules and policies provided in each nation. The aspect has enhanced its continued growth despite the increased competition. One is required to pay a minimum deposit of about $2000 and an automated trading solution for all the traders. There are times when the premises offer bonuses of 182 trade FOREX pairs to all its clients. The aspect has also been the key reason behind its increased expansion. In other words, there are various services offered at a relatively low price hence the widening of its customer base.

CMC Markets

The premises were founded in 1989 and since then, it has grown to be one of the leading retail FOREXes as well as a CFD brokerage. The premises thus serve more than 10,000 CFD instruments that cut

285

across all the classes such as FOREX, commodities as well as security markets. The aspect has allowed the premises to spread its services to more than 60,000 clients across the entire globe. The premises have more than 15 offices that are well distributed in the nation; it offers the services. Most of its actions are thus related in UK, Australia as well as Canada. The aspect is since the premises have its customer bases in some of these nations. In other words, its serves are well are accepted in Canada and the UK.

There are various benefits that one gains by joining the premises. One, the premises offer some of the best competitive spread to all her customers. In other words, there are a variety of services that one can choose from. Also, the premises offer one of the largest selections of currency pairs in the entire industry. There are more than one hundred and eighty currencies that one can access by joining the premises. The other aspect worth noting is that the premises provide some of the best regulated financial agents in the entire globe. In other words, there are policies as well as rules that govern the provision of services in the world. Also, it is easy to identify the premises as there are potent charts as well as patterns that are used as recognition tools.

City Index

The FOREX broker was founded in 1983 in the UK. Since then, the premises have gained popularity and has turned out to be one of the leading brokers in London. It is worth noting that in 2015, the

286

premises acquired GAIN Capital Holding Company that enhanced its increased customer base. Since 2015, the premises have been providing traders with services such as CFDs and spreading-betting derivatives. The premises have been further expanding the FOREX services with the acquisition of markets as well as FX solutions before gaining the capital market. Nowadays, the City Index has been operating as an independent brand under GAIN Capital in Asia as well as the UK. The aspect has allowed a multi-asset solution hence offering traders access to over 12,000 products across the global markets.

Some of the benefits that one gains part of the capital holding, a large selection of CFDs as well as regulated in several jurisdictions. The organization has tight spreads as well as low margins and fast execution. So, the premises have been time from time, offering average ranges to all the clients; hence why it has increased customer base.

XTB Review

The organization was founded in Poland in the year 2002. Since then the organization has been well known for its FOREX and CFDs brokerage. Now, the organization has maintained its offices in several nations; it offers its services. The premise has been working as a multi-asset broker that is regulated in several centers, hence increasing their competitive advantage. The premises have been trading as multiple financial centers offering a lot of services to all her traders. With a wide range of more than 2000 functions, the premises have been trading in almost all nations hence an increase in its customer base. The premises also provide excellent services that have been the reason behind its expansion. One of the aspects that have made the FOREX broker be thriving in such a competitive environment.

Signs of Illegitimate Brokers

Although numerous brokers have been working in the FOREX industry, the aspect of legitimacy has been an issue affecting the progress of some these premises. One of the elements that are considered is the vulnerability of the clients. In most cases premises illegitimate brokers tend to rob their customers. Most of them are self-reliant and optimistic and operate above their financial knowledge, hence making numerous mistakes. Most of these organizations record big losses as they are relatively weak in term of management. The organization offers a lot of transactions that tend to be cumbersome in terms of management. It's worth noting that most of their operations aren't legitimate and never approved by the necessary authorities. Thus, when deciding on the kind of FOREX premises to seek services from, it's essential to consider some factors. Avoid assumptions that are exaggerative in terms of offering services that are above their knowledge. The aspect is harmful in the sense that they provide services that aren't well planned hence recording a number of loses that befalls many clients in the long run. In other words, the drops recorded in the organization

Signs of Legitimate Brokers

Although there are numerous illegitimate brokers in the market, there are legitimate brokers who offer excellent services. Most of them provide a few unique functions. In other words, they don't give a lot of transactions. Thus, they can manage their operations and command profits on their premises. The other aspect worth noting is that most of the services are approved by both the clients as well as the governing bodies in the organization. The other issue worth noting is that most of these premises have employed excellent knowledge in a range the progress of the customers. In short, their services are focused on advancing the clients.

In a nutshell, when selecting a FOREX broker, it is good to consider several factors. It is critical to find whether the premises are approved by both the governments as well as the clients. It is good to view the number of services as well as the transactions that are offered by the premise. The aspect is true because most of the wrong assumptions tend to provide numerous services that are poorly managed. The reviews offered by the clients of each of these premises need to be considered as they reflect whether the brokers are legitimate or not. Clients of consistent clients tend to offer reviews that are good as the services they receive manage to be excellent. The financial reports of these organization tend to be considered. The aspect is linked to the fact that they tend to reflect whether the brokers are making loses or profits. It is critical to find premises that record gains since the benefits tend to be high.

The fact that the FOREX market is open 24 hours a day 5 days a week, and more than 4 trillion worth of transactions move through it each day means that there are always going to be new brokers or dealers coming onto the scene in hopes of making a profit somewhere along the line. As such, if you ever hope to have any real success in the FOREX market, the first thing you're going to need to do is separate the wheat from the chaff and find the broker or dealer that actually suits your needs.

While one might hope the process of finding a dealer or broker that is honest and easy to work with would be as simple as finding any other type of review online, unfortunately that is not the case. This is because two different companies might phrase the same costs and benefits in very different ways, and many FOREX dealers will actually call themselves brokers, simply because this is a word that more people are already familiar with. Luckily, there are a few things you can always do to ensure you're getting off on the right foot.

- **Understand what separates brokers from dealers:** The first thing you're going to want to do when looking for a company to work with when it comes to actually making trades is determine if you're dealing with an actual broker, a dealer in broker's clothing or just an honest dealer. For starters, you're going to be able to easily determine if you're working with a dealer instead of a broker if they are willing to take trades themselves, instead of simply setting them up for the clients that they see.

- **Know the level of regulation:** When looking for the dealer or broker that most accurately meets your needs, you're always going to want to take in to consideration the amount of regulation that they are operating under, not just what their rates and promises are. Simply put, the greater degree of regulation they are subject too, the less likely you have to worry about them walking away with your money. This is a not insubstantial concern when working with online brokers or dealers which is why you need to always speak with a real person and ask to see proof that they are regulated in the way they appear to be.

- **Be aware of capitalization concerns:** Outside of ensuring that your dealer or broker is regulated, you will also want to know what amount of capital that they are working with. While brick and mortar institutions are likely not going to have to close up shop after a bad week, you never know what an online dealer is working with unless you ask. If you're looking for brokers or dealers outside of the United States, checking with a local regulatory body for this type of information is typically the best place to start.

- **Know what platforms they support:** If you are completely new to all types of trading them you won't have any trading platform preferences that you'll need to take into account when it comes to choosing a dealer or broker to work with. If you're already committed to a specific platform, however, then you're going to want to ensure that the dealer or broker that you're working with is compatible as well.

- **Factor in the costs:** If you end up working with a dealer then you're going to be working with a fee structure that is set by someone known as the market maker. The market maker is the person who you can count on to buy when you want to sell and sell when you want to buy. To factor in how much a given dealer is going to charge you, you're going to want to consider the number of pips in the spread between what buyers are paying and what sellers are receiving. The bigger the spread, the more that dealer is going to end up costing you in the long run.

- **Compare available services:** When looking for the right type of broker or dealer for you, it is important to make sure that you take the time to shop around for long enough that you get a sense of the various amenities and services being offered currently. You will also want to determine what types of accounts they have that are currently available (options typically include demo accounts, micro accounts, mini accounts and standard accounts) the biggest difference between them is the size of the largest trade that the account is cleared ahead of time to make. The amount that is connected to each will likely vary between individual brokers and dealers, another reason why it will pay for you to ask around and determine what a fair going rate currently is.

- **Ask the right questions:** After you have narrowed down your search to the best possible dealers and brokers, the last thing you're going to want to do is speak with a representative from each of the companies in question and ask them numerous questions just to make sure that everyone is on the same page. Some of the questions you're already going to want to be familiar with, but it is important to understand how they are answered as much as it is to know the answer at face value.

It is important to know what countries they are currently regulated in as well as the currency pairs that they offer for trade. You will want to know if the customer deposits are separated from any operating capital, what trading platforms they support and if they utilize the Electronic Communications Network and if there are any limits placed on account types. Finally, you will want to ask about customer service and the process for depositing or withdrawing money.

Chapter 8:

Information on FOREX Specifications.

The Main Mechanisms that govern the FOREX

T he FOREX market is governed by mechanisms that are simple enough to understand, as it is focused on currency trading. This does not mean, however, that trading is easy.

Simplicity lies in the fact that, unlike the stock market and the commodity market, FOREX excludes the presence of companies. The value of currencies, that is of the elements of exchange in FOREX, is mainly influenced by central banks, which through the implementation of certain monetary policies, influences interest rates and, consequently, the nominal value of money. So, in order to be efficient within FOREX, traders will always need to be informed about all the economic and financial events that may affect the FOREX market and the items traded in it. As a currency market, it is subject to real fluctuations rather than to trends, which concern stocks and indices.

This difference derives from the fact that, while the indices depend on the willingness of the individual companies to earn, the currencies are tools that represent the economy, and in particular the import and export data of a single nation, and for this reason, they tend more floating in the market. This is to be considered a very favorable characteristic for traders, as it makes FOREX much more predictable than all other financial markets.

If the mechanisms of FOREX are too complicated to understand, then it is possible to rely on some tricks that allow you to copy the strategies implemented by professional traders. These techniques, known as Copy-trading, can be adapted on the basis of the capital held, allocating only a low percentage of the same for each individual transaction and increasing the investments only if the ratio between yield and risk is sufficiently high.

The Pareto principle

The Pareto principle is one of the laws that govern the entire universe. It is a non-physical law, as it has no certain thesis that identifies it, but at the same time, it appears very valid. It is possible to speak of a sort of golden relationship between contrasting elements, in a complete antithesis between them. One of the two elements, in fact, will be numerically or volumetrically larger or wider than the other, in a ratio that is around 80% against 20%.

This principle, as mentioned, regulates the entire universe and, consequently, also the financial markets and specifically the FOREX market. Many traders can avoid or disregard this principle, but really, it has been statistically stated that about 80% of traders investing in FOREX lose the allocated capital. Of course, this data also includes traders who have never studied the basics of trading,

295

nor even analyzed the market. Therefore, going deeper into the mechanisms that govern the FOREX would allow traders to move away from 80% Pareto. Nevertheless, it is still statistically confirmed that only 20% of investors manage to pursue a strategy that allows them to constantly make profits.

The Paretian principle applies especially to human psychology and this also applies to the world of trading. The approach to the market and the psychological aspect of the traders are indeed fundamental to understand if the road taken will lead to success or failure. The strategies often fail because the investors don't follow them assiduously, letting themselves be carried away by temptations and not acting on the market with rationality.

The openings of the positions are also regulated by the absolute principle of Pareto. In fact, it's statistically proven that in a well-defined time interval, 80% of it does not allow safe entry into the market, while in the remaining 20%, it is possible to make profitable transactions. Also, in this case, the psychological errors detectable in the haste to open a position or an attempt to redeem immediately from a negative operation, are considered the main elements that lead to failure.

As long as a human remains the architect of his or her own investment, psychological errors will always be protagonists of the financial markets, and the Pareto concept will always be valid.

Cryptocurrencies

Cryptocurrencies can be considered as digital currencies without any control by supervisory bodies, and for this reason, it is decentralized. Just the lack of real control has allowed this type of currency to spread easily around the world and to be traded within the financial markets. The main feature of cryptocurrencies is the presence of a very high volatility rate.

The trader will naturally have to foresee the possible evolution of the cryptocurrency observed in the market, trying to buy at relatively low values and then selling at high values. Moreover, even in this market, it is possible to invest by anticipating any future declines in cryptocurrencies, thus selling out in the open.

The best-known cryptocurrency in the world is certainly Bitcoin, which was born in Japan in 2009. Bitcoin was the first cryptocurrency to be accepted as a form of payment on the web. Of course, being totally based on cryptography and on a centralized payment system, known as Proof of Work, Bitcoin has managed to break free from traditional banking circuits, while still guaranteeing the same level of security in digital money exchanges.

To date, cryptocurrencies are therefore used both to buy certain goods or services and to transfer or receive monetary values.

Spread and the pip to get profits

Trading in FOREX and in all other markets is carried out by considering two essential elements. The first is certainly the price at which a given transaction is sold, and this value is referred to as Bid. The second element is the purchase price of the same operation and it is referred to in a technical jargon as Ask.

The difference between the two elements, namely between Bid and Ask, gives the trader the value of the spread. This difference is nothing more than the commission that each broker receives as gain for every single transaction opened on the market. The calculation of the spread is fundamental for a trader as it helps identify which transactions are advantageous, based on the forecasts made and the strategy that the investor has decided to adopt.

Another fundamental element is the percentage of point, also known with the acronym pip. The pip represents the basic unit of the entire FOREX, as it indicates the smallest possible fluctuation for a currency pair. Calculating the percentage of point is very simple. It's, in fact, represented by the difference between the fourth decimal digit of the values of a currency pair observed at two different time points.

Since the pip is the unit of measurement of fluctuations within FOREX, it's natural that the spread is also expressed in terms of pips. The value of the spread is in any case decided by the broker to whom the trader has decided to rely on. Each investor is therefore required to evaluate the convenience of opening the same transaction with different brokers.

FOREX trading today

The trading activity has undergone profound changes over the years. The most important of these transformations has certainly occurred with the advent of the web that has practically liberalized the FOREX, making it accessible to all.

Today, FOREX is considered the safest financial market in the world, as risks are minimized, and returns are optimized.

The main advantage of modern online trading is the elimination of commission costs. The brokers, in fact, now make gains only from the spreads calculated on the currency pairs traded in the FOREX.

Furthermore, today's FOREX allows you to trade at any time of day or night, taking advantage of market openings and closures, depending on their business hours.

Modern trading allows profits to be made despite very low investments. This is possible thanks to the effect of financial leverage, which makes it possible to amplify the investment made even by 300 or 400 times. The higher the possibility of increasing any profit, the greater the risk associated with the transaction. Therefore, it is up to the trader to define and implement his or her own strategy, contemplating all these elements, choosing the most profitable hours and deciding the amount of optimal capital to be allocated for each market segment.

But what most distinguishes modern trading is the fundamental need to understand the market in all its aspects in order to correctly anticipate currency fluctuations. Imagining FOREX as a random market is completely wrong. The fluctuations, according to the most important technical analysis theories, are indeed predictable, and there are several tools that facilitate the identification of trends and possible future values.

In particular, modern FOREX requires the alienation of the emotional component from the investment activity. In fact, humans are excessively exposed to stress and tension, and sometimes open positions on the market driven more by the desire for revenge against a loss just suffered than by rationality. In this sense, we risk sending an entire strategy, even well-designed, into the air with investments that are completely entrusted to chance. This attitude does not characterize successful traders, who follow what they had previously implemented to the letter, accepting losses and waiting patiently for the right time to make the investment.

Chapter 9:

Market analysis

Making an Analysis of the Worldwide Economy

To make gains and profits and gains in trades that you're going to make, analyzing the economic trends of the worldwide economy is of great import to be fully aware of the factors that may trigger the currencies to increase or decrease in value. This is important in making a correct prediction on the pair of currencies you're exchanging, whether they will make a profit or a loss. Factors that are important to look into when evaluating the global economy are like the political climate of countries whose currencies have a strong value, natural factors that may influence the economy of countries, the Gross Domestic Product of the country whose currency you want to exchange with your base currency, and other minor factors such as the investment rate of the said country. Evaluating which countries are looking up to growth and development opportunities is also important in determining the quote currency to use impairing up currencies to make a trade. Also, on the analysis of the worldwide economy, when the currency of the country you seek to purchase in exchange of your base currency is doing well and is set to increase in its value, convert your base currency into the quote currency. On the other hand, convert the quote currency into the base currency in case its value increases. There are various online sites that provide analysis tools on the economic performance of different countries with your potential quote currency. Others rank counties in terms of their GDP that makes it easier for you to choose the countries projected for growth and development. Being in touch with the trending news globally is a plus in getting information relevant to trading FOREX. A new FOREX trader may subscribe to a few FOREX trading channels and outlets to be constantly on toes of events and happenings that may trigger the value of currencies to either increase or decrease, which may result in the reversal of the outlook of the trade. Having relevant information always is key in making gains and preventing the loss of your money and probably your account is cleared.

Without having to get into a deep philosophical discussion, most readers will be aware that as soon as we developed beyond the tribal hunter-gatherer stage, and on to this day, people have bartered. They trade one item for another, thus doing away with the need for every individual to produce or grow everything they need in order to get through life.

This was a key innovation, usually relying on an accepted authority (the King) minting some form of coin, made of precious metal, such as gold or silver, that everyone agreed had an intrinsic value. People could trade their products or services for a mutually agreed-upon number of coins, that they could then stockpile for future need or exchange at will for other products and services.

Several other innovations came about thanks to this, which are beyond the scope of this book, but suffice it to say that along with money came taxation, class differences, banking, and many other things we take for granted today. It also created some complexities as people and kingdoms themselves started trading with people belonging to other kingdoms.

Money Changers

Moneychangers were the first foreign-exchange traders. They had a deep knowledge of the different kinds of coins from the different kingdom states, and how much each was worth relative to the others. We find them mentioned in ancient texts, such as the Bible. In one passage, Jesus famously expelled several them from the Temple in Jerusalem. These money changers would be conveniently located where travelers could find them and would exchange foreign coins for local ones and take a percentage for their services. For example, if a coin from Kingdom A were worth exactly the same as a coin from Kingdom B (just to keep it simple), the money changer would take 100 coins from the one, and in return give 99 coins from the second, keeping one coin as their fee.

Note that this still required that travelers move around what was potentially a very dangerous terrain, with bandits and other hazards, carrying their wealth in the form of metal coins. If the wealth were significant, this would involve caravans moving the gold in chests on wagons pulled by beasts of burden or men serving the same purpose, and a large number of guards to provide security, all of whom had to be paid and kept fed. It was quite an endeavor in those days to go shopping to the neighboring Kingdoms.

As commerce increased, it quickly became impractical to cart heavy gold and silver coins around all the time. With time, this wealth was stored in the equivalent of banks, and representative money was invented. A piece of paper or other inexpensive and easy to carry marker was used to represent the actual gold coin. These markers would be guaranteed by a trusted authority, be it a bank or a nation, that would promise to redeem them on demand for a set amount of gold. The money changers didn't care, and they simply continued converting this new money as if it were the actual gold or silver coins each represented and taking their usual fee.

Fiat Currencies

The earliest experiments in history with fiat currencies failed miserably; newer ones have yet to fail. Fiat currency is a form of money that is not backed by the storage of an equivalent amount of gold, silver, or other precious commodities, and thus not redeemable for it. It simply exists because someone created it and has forced or convinced the populace to accept it. Since this money isn't backed by anything tangible, it is highly vulnerable to inflation, where the currency has less, and less buying power as people with real goods demand more and more of it in exchange for the same items. There is a saying that bad money drives out good money. Those who can accumulate the real money, and the "fake" money loses more and more value until there is a collapse and the fiat currency is so worthless that no one accepts it. Some of the first experiments with fiat currency happened in China, with results similar to what was just explained.

In modern times, of course, fiat money is the norm, and no one expects to be able to walk into a bank and demand they produce the gold or silver that once backed each bill. But when did this become the norm? Well, by the late 19th century, all major powers had pegged an amount of their currency to an ounce of gold, with this determining the official exchange rate between one currency and another.

At said times, the books were balanced, with one country exchanging the amount of currency they held from another country, and vice versa, and whoever had the greater quantity would receive the equivalent amount in physical gold from the other. This worked, for the most, though there were still inefficiencies, such as a new gold mine being discovered, thus increasing the amount of available gold, making gold cheaper. And it still required shipping gold from one place to another to settle the accounts.

Modern Currencies

After Bretton Woods broke down, we come to the age of floating exchange rates, which may seem cryptic to most people. What makes a US dollar worth 110 Japanese yen? And why was it worth

120 Japanese yen 3 weeks ago? First, we need to understand the most common ways modern governments handle their monetary systems. The three typical ways are:

- **Dollarization**: When a country opts to use another country's currency, typically the dollar, instead of printing their own. Examples today include Ecuador, Panama, and El Salvador. The governments of these countries have opted not to print any local money, and the US dollar is legal tender there.

- **Pegged Rate:** This is when a government pegs its currency to another country's currency. For example, until 2005, the Chinese had their yuan pegged at 8.28 yuan to 1 US dollar. As the dollar gained in value, so did the yuan, and if the dollar dropped, so did the yuan. The Chinese peg ended in July of 2005.

- **Managed Floating Rate:** This is the most common method in use today, where governments allow the exchange rate to fluctuate based on supply and demand freedom. However, they can and do routinely intervene to strategically weaken or strengthen their currency against others by manipulating other variables such as short-term interest rates.

So, in simple terms, most of the world's governments use a floating rate and allow the market to decide what their currency is worth against other currencies. And they manage their economy and its variables at times if they need to nudge their currencies value in one direction or another. While it might seem logical at first to think that a stronger currency is better for a country it often works the other way around, especially for countries that are large exporters.

The more their currency is worth compared to others, the more expensive their products appear to be to the outside world, and this can make their exported goods less attractive. For large importers, the same applies in reverse; a stronger currency makes imported goods less expensive. Many countries in today's global economy are both importers and exporters, and they try to balance the value of their currency carefully.

These boards show unit prices for each foreign currency accepted, with the prices indicating how many units of the foreign currency are needed to acquire one unit of the local currency. You will also note that there are two slightly different prices for each foreign currency. This is because the exchange shop will both buy and sell these currencies, so one is a selling price, and the other a buy price. The difference between one and the other is called the spread and represents the profit the money changer will make. They sell the local currency at a higher price and buy it back at the lower one. So in the example above they would sell dollars to Japanese visitors at a rate of 109 Japanese yen per dollar, and when the Japanese visitor leaves the country, they will buy back any remaining dollars the visitor has, but only give 102 Japanese yen for each dollar returned, essentially making a 7 yen profit on each dollar.

The prices quoted may change multiple times a day, based on the fluctuating market values. As you can see, the board in the image is electronic and easily updated.

Now, these are retail rates for changing relatively small amounts of currency. International trade, banking, and similar activities will often require that millions of US dollars or their equivalents be exchanged at the same time. We'll take a look at that next.

International Trade

Countries have always traded with each other, sometimes directly, but more commonly through companies that handle the production and/or buying of the goods being traded, as well as the logistics of importing and exporting the goods themselves. Sometimes this may involve multiple individuals and companies cooperating in order to get the products from one country to another, and bill for them. For example, coffee is grown in Colombia by small, often artisanal farmers. It would not be cost-effective for a small farmer to reach out directly to, say, Walmart in the United States to offer their coffee. So, the small farms will sell to cooperatives that bundle the coffee producer of a larger geographical area that has multiple farms.

They, in turn, may sell to larger companies, and this may continue until we finally get to a large Colombian operator with enough quality coffee to sell a big shipment to Walmart. Note that all the companies upstream have paid and been paid for the coffee they've bought and sold using local currency, so everyone involved so far

309

has been compensated. Now, the large operator sells the entire shipment to Walmart and delivers the coffee to a logistics company that will transport it from Colombia to the USA.

At this point, we have a dilemma. The Colombian company uses Colombian pesos, and Walmart uses US dollars. To resolve this situation for all parties involved, commercial banks have foreign currency desks that provide exchange services for businesses. Today everything is handled electronically so that Walmart will transfer the funds in dollars, and the Colombian supplier will receive payment in pesos or even receive US dollars directly but must still exchange them for pesos at some point. Either way, some banks or entities must provide this service. An added bit of complexity comes from the fact that most commercial trade is not paid on the spot, but instead with the advantage of payment terms or even letters of credit. Which means that a company can buy something today and have, perhaps, 90 days to deliver payment?

When we are talking about payment in the same currency, that's not a problem, but suppose payment needs to be made or received in a foreign currency. Suppose Walmart bought it at the equivalent of a dollar per pound of coffee, but when it comes time to submit payment, the rates have changed, and they now owe two dollars per pound. It could also work in Walmart's favor, of course, and come time to make a payment; they only owe 75 cents per pound. However, businesses cannot operate with that kind of financial risk and uncertainty. Many of today's large corporations engaging in international business will acquire foreign currency in advance of the time. It needs to be paid in order to lock in the price. These same companies discovered that these transactions sometimes resulted in significant windfall profits as rates changed between the time, they acquired the foreign currency and the time when the invoice comes due. FOREX trading as speculation and investment is born!

Institutional Trading

A company like General Electric will have its own internal department dedicated to nothing but foreign currency transactions, and these departments often become significant sources of profit for the company. Sometimes they'll engage in currency trades for no other purpose than generating profit. Banks, governments, and other large entities also routinely engage in currency trading, for different purposes, but ultimately for their own benefit, not for any third-party clients. Collectively these are the institutional traders and represent the majority of the volume of trades happening in the FOREX market at any given time. Originally, they represented the entire FOREX market virtually. Until the 1980s, the institutional FOREX market required a minimum of US $1 million per trade. That effectively locked out everyone except the large traders.

Retail Trading

With the PC Revolution in the 90s, we finally come to retail trading, which is the ability for small traders, like you and me, to participate in the FOREX Market. The personal computer and the modem, later the Internet, allowed individuals to open a brokerage account and trade directly from their homes or offices. Trading software became available that would allow traders to follow an instrument, chart its price history, and enter and exit trades.

The FOREX Market today is the single largest market based on the amount of money traded daily. $5.3 trillion dollars are traded every single day, 24 hours a day, except weekends and some holidays.

Trades are immediately executed as there is always a guaranteed buyer or seller for any traded currency pair, so liquidity is not an issue. Trading stocks, for example, you may end up owning a stock that no one is buying at any price, so your sell order will remain unfilled until such a time as there is a buyer, not so with FOREX. This is one of the many advantages this market offers.

With retail trading also came the ability to trade sums lower than a million dollars at a time. Currency pairs today are traded by full lot (US$100,000), mini lot (US$10,000), and micro-lot (US$1,000). And, thanks to margin, you only need to have a fraction of those amounts in your account. You can trade with as little as US$20 for a micro-lot, with a margin of 1:50, which is quite common. Some brokers can go as high as 1:500 leverage, though I would not recommend taking them up on that, as will be explained later.

You should at this point have a basic understanding of the history of money, what modern fiat currencies represent, why they're not all worth exactly the same, and more importantly, that we have the ability to trade them from our computers in order to make money, 24 hours a day, 5 days a week.

Opening the First Trade

Pairing currencies and making the first trade; opening and closing a trade happens when the quote currency to be paired by the base currency have been paired and there is an opportune trading window. Opening a trade is making an order to purchase a certain currency and in exchange for your base current through your broker firm. You'll have the analysis tools, that are commonly offered by the brokers in software programs. The execution of making an order in some platforms might be instant while in some other platforms, it might be a tad bit slower. Nonetheless, most brokerage firms offer live prices and values of the currencies that are to be traded and their exchange rates and the instant changes to their values are displayed. The first trade for a new trader might just be one or others might open up new trades over a short period of time. It is advisable that just several enough trades be opened, which the new trader is comfortable and at ease in trading.

Chapter 10:

Exceptional FOREX day trading structures

Scalping

Scalping is a totally different way to trade when compared to swing trading. If you have an idea what day trading is, it is entering and exiting a position on the same trading day. In FOREX, scalping is an extreme form of day trading.

The idea behind scalping is to enter and exit positions multiple times a day over short time periods, taking small profits with each trade.

This works on FOREX because it is a highly volatile market. At any given time, you can look for a new low price or high price, and then trade accordingly exiting the position when it does a "mini swing" in the opposite direction, if you're willing to only get a small profit off each trade.

This is an approach to trading that is kind of like saving nickels and then adding them up to a million dollars over time.

If scalping is your style, you are hoping to do a lot of trades. Scalping is pretty popular on the FOREX markets.

If you would rather have small but consistent profit, then you should learn scalping. Since the potential profit is small, your risk will also be small. Of course, the key to profit with this strategy is having multiple small profits. Therefore, you need to be patient and diligent at the same time. If you are the type of trader who only wants to profit a big amount quickly, then this isn't for you. Basically, scalping is where you enter a position and then leave it the moment that you realize a profit. Hence, this strategy is perfect for day traders. An important element of scalping is identifying the currency pair to invest in. Some traders merely rely on the volatility that is inherent in the FOREX market. However, it's worth noting that merely relying on volatility isn't good enough. Instead, you need to rely on the hard facts and actual details. Therefore, as a trader, you are expected to do as much research as possible to help you develop your own understanding of the market.

315

When you use scalping, you should keep a close eye on the market while your position is open. All you need is a small profit, and then you should close your position. It is an excellent short-term strategy. Another important element of scalping is to know when to close your position. It can be very tempting to continuously hold a position, especially when you're profiting from it. However, keep in mind that holding on to a position for a longer time also increases your risk. After all, the fact remains that no matter how profitable a position may be, the market can still suddenly fall at any time. When you use scalping, you should minimize your risk as much as possible. Do not worry; if your position is truly profitable, you can still get back to it. The important thing about scalping is to be able to profit a little by risking also a little. Do not be greedy. Scalping is effective, but it takes time and you'll have to do it many times to earn a significant amount of profit.

A notable disadvantage of using scalping is that it requires a large deposit; otherwise, the profit that you'll get per successful trade would be almost negligible. If you don't invest a big amount, then you'll earn very little even after ten successful trades using scalping.

Scalpers will use tick charts or trade on one-minute candlesticks. This is a very active form of trading, and you might have to trade 10 or more times per day to make significant profits. The goal for a scalper is to make small profits of 3-10 pips per trade. Your hope is that they will add up to big profits over long time periods.

316

Let's remember the size of a pip related to lot size. If you're talking about a micro lot, a pip is 10 cents. So, 3 pips are a mere 30 cents, and even 10 pips are just a dollar. So, scalping doesn't make too much sense for someone who is trading micro-lots. At the max end, you're only making a dollar per trade, and so you'd have to make 100 trades to make $100 a day, and that would be if all the trades produced the maximum amount of profit, something that is unlikely to happen.

With a mini lot, a pip is a dollar, so now you're looking at around $3, $5, and up to $10 profit per trade. It's easier to get to a significant amount of money at this level, but still very difficult.

It seems that to make significant profits scalping without having to do huge numbers of trades, you'd have to trade standard lots. Remember, in this case, a pip is $10, so if you make 5 pip profits that is $50, so you only have to do a few trades per day to make decent money. Even then, it's still going to be a rather active type of trading, and you're definitely looking at this being a full-time living. The less you make per trade, the more time you're going to have to devote to it, which almost ensures that you're going to have to trade standard lots to make a living doing it.

Scalping is also going to involve having the get in and out of positions quickly. A 10-pip move can evaporate in a flash, and so if you get a 10-pip profit, you want to exit the trade immediately. That means you are going to have to select currency pairs that are going to be liquid. That way, you will be able to quickly close your position and take the profits that you are seeking.

Scalping is a high-risk strategy, and it's not for everyone.

Intraday Trading

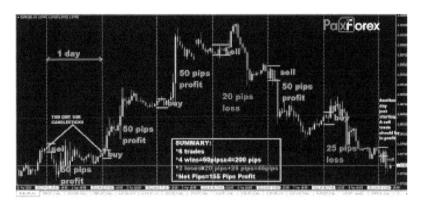

Intraday trading is another day trading style, but it's more relaxed than scalping. So, you are looking to enter and exit a position on the same trading day. However, rather than getting out of the position quickly, you're going to be doing fewer trades and looking for a larger amount of profit per trade. This will give you some flexibility to trade with smaller lot sizes, but you'll probably have to trade multiple lots at a time. While a scalper is probably going to do 10 or 20 trades per day, you're going to be looking for larger profits in the 3-10 trade per day range.

Position Trading

If you are a position trader, you are willing to hold a position for a very long time (in FOREX terms). That means you'll hold the

318

position at least for weeks, and you're willing to hold it for months, or even more than a year.

Think of position trading as longer-term swing trading. The techniques are going to be about the same, but you are willing to wait long term in order to take the kind of profits that you are looking for. Position traders are not people who frequently trade, and they may spend a long time on the sidelines waiting for the right time to enter a position.

News Traders

Items in the news, including political, economic, and trade news, can have a big impact on currency prices. The impact is probably not going to be very long-lived in most cases, but while it's working, it can cause big price moves. These days with the 24-hour news cycle, there are always new controversies coming up that increase volatility and send the markets going one way or another. A news trader seeks to follow the news and enter trades when this happens

319

to ride the wave of the trend that gets created from the result. For example, the president may remark (or issue a tweet) that would cause the U.S. dollar to either rise in value or fall by a large amount. As soon as the tweet was issued, the news trader would enter positions that they think are going to move a large amount as a result of the remark. So, if the remark were one that would probably lead to a rise in the dollar against the Euro, the news trader would sell Euro/USD currency pairs. Then they would use the techniques of chart analysis to look for a reversal after the trend takes on momentum and exit the trade when the trend shows signs of beginning to reverse.

Trend trading

Many traders simply trade with the trend when a long-term trend one way or the other can be identified. This technique can also be used in conjunction with swing trading or position trading. The trick is accurately identifying trends that appear to be set up for a long ride upward or downward. This is called trading with the trend, or some traders say the trend is your friend. If you are trend trading, you have the luxury of being able to trade less liquid currency pairs, provided that the trend is stable. Of course, no trend is going to be stable forever, but it should be stable enough, so that you can ride the trend for a long period to earn profits and then remain in the trend for a time, when you try and exit the position. If you're looking at currency pairs that are not as liquid, getting out of the position is not going to be as easy, but you should be able to do it while still making good profits. Trend trading works with any lot size, and you can do fewer numbers of trades and seek larger profits per trade.

NZDUSD Daily Uptrend

End of Day Trading

If you are an end of day trader, you are taking a more relaxed approach to trading, looking at the markets at the end of your day, and doing your technical analysis to enter or exit trades. This type of trading can be used within the context of other trading styles like swing trading and position trading, but of course, it's not going to be used with scalping or intraday trading. People who will retain a full-time commitment and don't have time to follow the markets all day long may use end of day trading. End of day is a figurative phrase, since FOREX markets are open 24 hours, so it's a time of day that you pick in order to do your trades. You can do your analysis at this time and determine which trades to enter or exit. The low-key aspect of this trading style makes it suitable for all lot sizes, and it does require some patience. You'll have more flexibility and be able to wait for the size of profits you are hoping to take, and so you don't necessarily have to enter a large number of trades.

Fundamental Analysis

This analysis is sometimes referred to as the 'lifeblood of investment' for good reasons. As its name suggests, fundamental analysis deals with the fundamentals or the basics. Take note that basics does not mean that it is composed of elements that are easy to understand. Rather, it refers to the very foundation of things. In FOREX trading, this involves knowing and analyzing fundamental indicators to see if a currency is undervalued or overvalued relative to another currency.

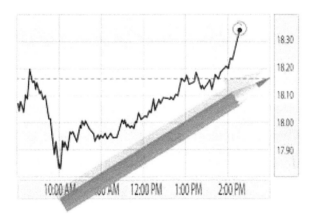

Fundamental analysis also analyzes the different factors or elements that affect the prices of the different currencies. An important part of fundamental analysis is to be updated in the news. In fact, some people refer to fundamental analysis as news analysis since this approach is primarily concerned about being updated on the news and analyzing it. When you apply fundamental analysis, the step is to be aware of the news that may have an effect upon the prices of different currencies, especially those that may affect the currencies that you want to trade. Keep in mind that there are many factors that can influence the price of a currency, such as the economy, technological developments, market acceptance and use, the level of competition, government relations and regulations, and businesses, among other things. So, if you read in a newspaper that there is underemployment in the United States, and all other things being equal, then there is a good chance that the price of the U.S. dollar can decrease. So, you can take appropriate actions to take advantage of it. You should also check the record of the currency inflows and outflows. This is published by the central bank. Of course, when you use fundamental analysis, you are expected to spend lots of time doing research and analysis.

As a professional trader, fundamental analysis should be a part of your life. When it come to the FOREX market, the amount and quality of information that you have play a crucial role since trading decisions are based on what you know about the market. Hence, the more that you understand the market, the more that you'll be able to come up with a sound investment decision. Fundamental analysis is also a strategy that you can combine with other strategies, such as technical analysis. Keep in mind that knowing the basics is important. In fact, many of the changes that occur in the prices of different currencies can easily be explained just by understanding the basics or the fundamentals.

Technical Analysis

If you're more of a visual person, then you might want to learn technical analysis. Most traders use this strategy due to its effectiveness and simplicity. If you think that fundamental analysis is too tiring, then technical analysis combines everything altogether that all that you need to do is to analyze graphs and charts. The concept behind this strategy is that all the factors or elements that affect the different currencies have their final effect upon the price. Therefore, by simply analyzing the price movements of the different currencies as shown by the graphs, you get to deal with all the said elements. After all, regardless of what is happening in the world, the only thing that truly matters is how the prices of the currencies move in the market. If you can predict their movements, then you can easily take appropriate actions and earn a decent profit.

The key to technical analysis is to be able to read patterns. Yes, patterns do exist. In fact, if you allow a random generator to play for some time, it will also create some patterns. It is worth remembering that patterns come and go. Therefore, do not expect to see a pattern every time that you look at a graph. A common problem with traders who use technical analysis is that they force to see a pattern even when it does not really exist. Do not delude yourself. Keep in mind that you are not obliged to enter a trade. Therefore, only make a trade when you see a good opportunity to profit. Just because you have spent about an hour or two analyzing a pattern does not mean that you should decide to trade right away. When you use technical analysis, patience is an important virtue that you should learn. Now, if you identify a pattern, then you should act quickly and take advantage of it.Technical analysis is definitely one of the strategies that you should learn as a trader. It is also not uncommon to see traders who use this strategy with another strategy. Once you learn how to read graphs and charts, you will easily be able to draw information simply by looking at them. Hence, no matter what strategy you use, you can always use your skill in reading charts to help you come up with a better trading decision. Once again, the more information and understanding that you have about a currency or currencies, the more likely that you will be able to predict their movement. Needless to say, this kind of knowledge is something that you can turn into a profit.

Momentum trading

The key to this strategy is to identify strong price movements. The idea behind this strategy is that a strong price movement that is headed towards a direction is most likely going to continue for some more time. After all, the fluctuation caused by a strong price movement cannot be expected to counterbalance itself quickly. Momentum trading usually uses the same graphs and charts used in technical analysis since it deals directly with the price movements of a currency pair. Since momentum trading only aims to take advantage of the momentum of a strong price movement by following its direction, it is only suitable for short-term trading. This strategy is easy to use. You simply need to spot a strong price movement and take advantage of it before the trend changes. Another important part of momentum trading is knowing when to close your position. It can sometimes be very tempting to hold your position.The problem is that by the time you realize that the momentum has already stopped, your profits might have already turned into losses. Therefore, in order to avoid this from happening, you should avoid getting greedy. The key is to exit the momentum trade even before it stops. Now, there is no hard and fast rule as to how you can determine up to how long a momentum trade is going to last. To be safe, just aim for a small profit and exit the position once you hit it. Do not forget that this strategy is about taking advantage of the momentum, which means that a strong price movement has already taken place, so do not hold on to the position for too long.

Swing trading

Swing trading is where a trader holds an asset between one and several days to try to capture gains in the financial market. These traders don't monitor the screens all day instead only a few hours a day. Swing traders usually rely on technical analysis to look for trading opportunities. Swing trading position is held longer than day trading position but shorter than buy and hold investments. They have larger profit targets than day traders. Swing trading is a long-term trading strategy. As a swing trader, you should expect to experience multiple price fluctuations. This is norm on the FOREX market, especially if you hold a position for a long period. A good thing about being a swing trader is that you can earn a high amount of profit by the time that you close your position. Another advantage of using this strategy is that you don't have to study the market every day. Although it's still advised that you at least check on the market daily. This is just to ensure that your position is not being compromised. From time to time, you might see that you are losing the trade, but do not panic.

Again, you should expect for some price fluctuations to take place. The important thing is to be in a profitable position when you exit the trade. Hence, do not allow yourself to be affected by the day-to-day volatility of the FOREX market for such is bound to happen.

Of course, you cannot expect to make a profit simply by holding on to a position for a long term. It is still important for you to choose the right currency to invest in. How you pick a currency depends on you. You may use financial analysis, technical analysis, or any other approach that you prefer. Unlike momentum trading where you normally just aim for a small profit, swing trading usually brings a significant amount of profit since it has a much longer trading period. The drawback is that this is also the style of trading that can lead to a serious loss since it involves holding your position for a long time. Although swing traders usually ignore the daily fluctuations in price even in the case of a loss, these can easily pile up over time and turn into a significant amount. This is also an excellent strategy to use for part-time traders as you don't have to follow the market regularly. Most swing traders only make a few trades in a month. The key is to focus on the quality of the trade than on quantity.

Hedging

Simply put, hedging is a way to protect yourself against a big loss. Consider it as an insurance in case something unexpected happens that can adversely affect you as a trader. There are brokers that will allow you to hedge directly where you can purchase a currency pair and at the same time place a trade to sell the said pair. Although you won't have a net profit while both trades are open, you can earn more without taking on addition risk if you observe proper timing.

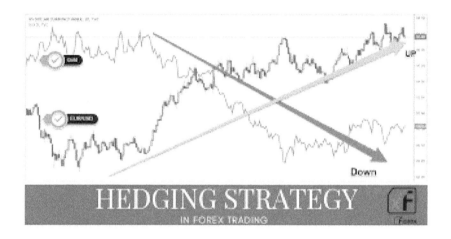

The way a hedge protects you is by allowing you to open an opposite trade while you're also trading the same currency pair. Of course, as a trader, you're free to just close your initial trade and then move to a new trade. A good thing about hedging is that you can save your trade and even make money if the market suddenly moves against your initial position. Now, in case the market reverses and takes a direction that is favorable to your first trade/position, then you can place a stop on the hedging trade or simply close it. This is the simplest way of hedging.

It is worth noting that hedging isn't suggested to be used by beginners. Its proper application requires adequate knowledge of the market, price swings, and proper timing.

Fading

Fading may be a trading method throughout which a trader assumes that a fast upward motion is overdone and takes a quick role on a probable reversal.

This method is regularly very volatile in trending markets due to the fact going against a strong fashion reduces the possibility of profitability.

This approach is regularly probably worthwhile in variety bound markets due to the fact a robust resistance degree has been installed, increasing the opportunity of destiny resistance and reversals at that stage.

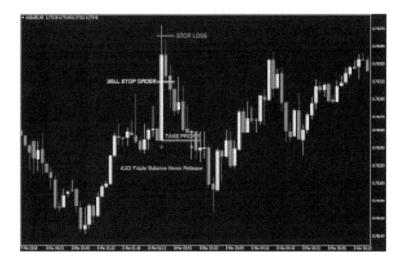

'Fading the marketplace' is normally a high chance strategy and is generally deployed with the aid of seasoned investors who are cognizant of the inherent hazard involved in an approach that goes towards conventional market knowledge. A less common use of the time fade refers to the failure of a dealer (market maker) to honor a printed quote whilst a customer or another dealer desires to change.

A dealer who fades could sell while a rate is rising and purchase whilst it is falling. The idea at the back of a fade strategy is that the marketplace has already factored altogether facts and consequently the latter degrees of a circulate is powered with the aid of investors who are slower to react, for this reason increasing the possibility of a reversal of the preliminary thrust. 'dogs of the Dow' may be a famous fade strategy.

An instance of a fade strategy could include buying on a dip in rate and promoting when costs rally. Fading is mostly a risky method, but it offers the ability for giant brief-term profits. It requires little inside the manner of complex analysis, but the chance that the trend continues is usually gifted. A company's fundamentals or charge movement, or a mixture of the two could also be diminished. For example, an investor may also purchase an inventory after an income warning because he or she believes the market has overreacted. Buyers who use fade strategies, often get noted as "contrarian buyers."

A market maker would possibly, at times, 'ignore' an order to transact at a printed quote. As an example, if a miles higher bid is posted on any other alternate for security then the marketplace maker might not be inclined to suit it for a consumer order. Instead,

331

the marketplace maker may also provide to alternate with the other marketplace maker (with a higher rate). The marketplace maker providing the better charge has to be given the offer and change at the well worth supplied or adjust the rate.

Fading economic facts can be a famous foreign exchange strategy. Each week, an international economic calendar lists crucial economic events, like the rate of hobby bulletins, employment statistics, monetary hobby reviews, and monetary organization speeches. Buyers who fade the monetary news trade the opposite course of the quantity released.

For example, if the monthly non-farm payroll document beats economists' expectancies, a trader may promote U.S. Greenback pairs, like the USD/JPY and USD/CHF, and purchase pairs just like the EUR/USD and GBP/USD.

Experienced buyers considered it a prudent exercise to wait for a hint after a news launch earlier than coming into a trade. This allows time for the bigger players, and nowadays algorithmic buying and selling fashions, to behave on the information but presents sufficient possibility for everyday traders to digest and seize much of the trend if the information is diminished.

Volatility is typically high for numerous hours after monetary reviews are launched, so employing a wider forestall may additionally assist to avoid getting whipsawed out of a part.

Scaling in

Scaling in is where you enter a trade little by little instead of putting everything in one position all at once. A trader who is looking to scale in may want to divide his position into quarters or in any way he deems best. Scaling in is an effective way to control your risk as you get to have a better understanding of how the market moves.For example, if the total amount that you're willing to invest in a trade is $200, you divide it in half (or in quarters or in any way that you want) to start scaling in. Let us say that you open a position and invest $100, if the position turns out to be favorable, then you realize a profit.

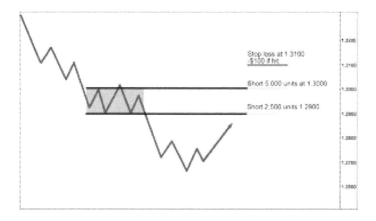

It is now up to you whether you still want to add the other $100. Now, let's assume that after adding the other $100, the price movement reverses and you start to lose the trade, since you have an initial investment at a much lower cost and has already profited, then you'll be able to lower your total losses. Of course, the drawback here is that in the vent that the trade continues to be profitable, you will not earn as much as if you just invested the whole $200 at once on the first trade. Still, this strategy is worth learning since it effectively lowers your risk. As you may already know, being too aggressive is not a suggested approach as it can exhaust your funds quickly. To stay longer in the market and remain profitable, you need to control your risk and minimize your losses.

Scaling out

If scaling in is about adding and having more open positions, scaling out is about lowering your exposure to risk by closing out some of your positions. Hence, the opposite of scaling in. Let's say that you are very confident about a certain trade and you make a big investment into it. However, with time, you realize that it isn't as profitable as you had thought. This usually happens when a news piece with a negative impact on a trade gets featured. Suddenly, you start feeling less confident of your trade; however, you still think that it can be profitable.

Now, since you find it hard to predict how the market will respond and are quite unsure of the profitability of your position, you can start scaling out by closing some of your positions or lowering your invested amount in a trade. This way you can still profit if the market turns out to be favorable; however, in case that the market becomes unfavorable, then scaling out would be able to cut back your losses effectively.

So, how do you know when to scale in and when to scale out? This depends on how you think the market will move. If you predict that the market will move favorably, then scaling in would be the better option. However, if you become unsure of the profitability of your position, then scaling out would be the better option. In a volatile market where your position earns a profit but you're aware that it will soon take a downhill, scaling out will allow you to continuously take advantage of the current price movement with a much lower risk.

Averaging down

Averaging down is an effective way to invest in a currency pair at a bargain price. It is also a good way to earn a high amount of profit. However, it is considered an aggressive approach, so be cautious of using this strategy. The key to this strategy is to identify as currency pair that you think would be profitable soon. You then invest in that currency pair. Let's say that the price drops and you experience some losses, instead of closing your position, you should make another investment in the same currency pair. Since the price has also dropped, then the cost of the pair will now also be lower. Continue to do this as the price of the currency pair decreases.

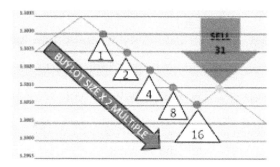

Okay, although this may seem like a losing strategy at first, it can turn out to be highly profitable after some time. Just imagine what could happen if its price finally reverses and increases back either to its original value when you first applied this strategy, or higher. As you see, all your open positions will experience a nice profit. This is an effective and highly profitable strategy. The important thing is to be able to identify a currency pair that would be profitable in the future and then hold on to it. To do this, you may want to research as much as you can about the currencies involved in a pair, so that you can have a better understanding of how likely their prices are going to change in the next few days or weeks. Although this strategy seems very practical and highly profitable, it is noteworthy that you should be very careful doing this. If you fail to pick a profitable currency pair, then you will most likely lose a lot of money. Use this strategy with caution. Be sure to follow on the market and stay updated on the latest news that may be relevant to your investment/trade.

Pin bar strategy

This is a strategy that you can apply when you are using technical analysis. You can easily identify the right time to use this strategy by looking at a graph. The signal is when you see a horizontal line which means that the price fluctuations have been stagnant over some time. This horizontal line is what is referred to as the 'bullish pin bar'. The concept behind this theory is that the resistance will serve as a new support for a price increase. Hence, if you make an investment at any point in the bullish pin bar, you will most likely experience a profit in the near future. Hence, when you see a bullish pin bar, you should consider entering the market and opening a position depending on the currency pair where it applies.

Take note that this does not work 100% of the time. However, there's a good chance that it will turn out to be a good investment. A better approach is to spot for a bullish pin bar and make some more research before investing your money in a trade. This way you will be more confident and increase your chances of making the right trading decision.

FOREX wedge breakout

There are many breakout strategies. With this one, what you are looking for is a wedge pattern where the price goes up and down. However, unlike a usual wedge, you'll see that the differences between the price increase and decrease gets smaller over time. You'll know that if the pattern continues then it will soon to an end and become a mere horizontal line. The key is to take advantage of this pattern before it disappears. So, you should open a position just immediately after a price decrease. Keep in mind that you should not hold on to the position for so long; otherwise, you will more likely experience a bad loss.

To be safe, stay conservative. Once you make a profit by a few pips, close down your position. How much you will profit will depend on the behavior of the pattern, but it will most likely be lower than the previous increase in value. Be sure to take advantage of this opportunity and close your position while still at a profit.

Retracement

The concept behind this strategy is that prices do not move in a straight line especially during highs and lows. Instead, they usually make a pause or only change in the middle of a larger path. Hence, when you apply retracement, you will wait for the price to "retrace" itself or pull back.

This is to confirm that a pattern is being made. Once you identify this, you can make use of the pattern that is being formed by taking appropriate actions. When trading currencies, knowing the most probable movement of the price in a graph is a big advantage that can lead to profit.

Reversal trading

As its name already suggests, this is where you expected a reversal in the price trend, and your objective here is to make an entrance into a trade that is ahead of the market. This is not really a strategy for beginners as it requires you to have more understanding of how the market moves. Reversals don't always occur but they can be highly profitable if you are able to take advantage of them. There are tools that traders use in order to identify a reversal, such as visual cues, as well as volume and momentum indicators.

Go with the flow

Sometimes the best way to trade is simply to go with the flow. The key to this is simply to be updated on the news. If the US economy is doing really well, then you may want to start going long on it,

340

especially if the economy of the other currency is not showing any development.

You have to simply watch which one is going strong in the market. You can also apply this using technical analysis.

If you see a strong price movement, then you can take advantage of it. Still, when you use this approach, no matter what strategy you use, you should apply fundamental analysis in order to significantly increase your chances of making a profit.

If you do not want to make any research, you might want to read the posts on FOREX trading forums and see how the traders respond. Sometimes you may be able to spot interesting ideas and profitable opportunities.

However, just make sure not to rely completely on whatever you read from other people. It's still important for you to develop your own understanding of the FOREX market.

Conservative

This strategy simply encourages that you should be conservative in your approach. Avoid trades that are aggressive, especially those that lack sufficient research. The key to this approach is to make small but multiple trades. Instead of focusing on how much you can earn from every trade, you should focus on increasing your rate of success. The idea behind this approach is that once you're able to establish an effective strategy, you can always increase the amount that you trade with.

As a beginner, what's important is for you to work on a powerful strategy that can give you a high rate of success. Be as conservative as possible and never commence a trade that uses more than 5% of your total funds. The key is to stay low and let your small, yet continuous gains turn into a significant profit. Also, by remaining conservative, you will not be provoked to turn into an emotional trader.

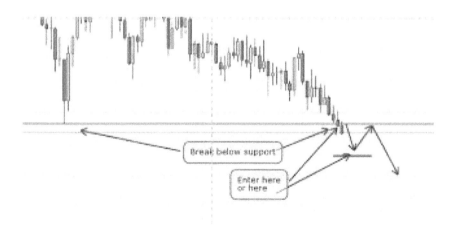

This is also an excellent strategy to stay longer in the market. It's also strongly suggested if it's your first time to trade in a real FOREX market using real money.

Be as conservative as possible and cut back on your risks and losses. Last but not least, keep your focus on making continuous small profits. Being consistent is the key. Once you're able to streamline a good flow of profits and if you are already confident enough in your strategy, then that is the time for you to increase the amount that you invest per trade. Still, be sure not to use more than 5% of your total funds per trade.

Copy trade

Some brokers have a copy trade feature. What this does is to copy the trades of other traders.

Of course, it is you who will choose the trader whose trades you want to copy. Needless to say, when you use this strategy, you need to identify an experienced and successful trader among the majority of traders who either earn a little or even lose their investment.

Be sure to check the profile page of a trader and look at his success rate. Also find out about his current open positions and analyze it. Again, having your own understanding of the market is important.

If you can spot a really skillful and successful trader, then all it takes is a few clicks of a mouse to follow and copy all his trades.

Another way of using copy trade is by plotting the trades and success rate of a certain trader. You will not find a trader with 100% success rate, except if he is a new trader who has not yet encountered any losses. The trick here is to track his trades and only join him if you think that his trade is going to be successful. By doing this, you can "skip" the trades that will most probably not turn out favorably. You should be careful about this as it is not easy to predict when a certain trader will lose in a trade. A good way to apply this is by making your own analysis of the situation. It should be noted that although there are some people who are already happy just by copying other people's trading decisions, it is still advised that you, as a professional trader, should not copy a trade just for the sake of copying. You won't grow as a trader if all you do is copy another person's trades.

Make your own

Although there are many strategies that you can find about FOREX trading, the best approach for you is to devise your own strategy. After all, different circumstances may require a different approach. You must adapt a strategy that is both effective and flexible. You are also free to modify already existing strategies, but you can also come up with something that is completely of your own invention. It doesn't really matter what strategy you use, what is important is if it's effective enough to yield into profits. A strategy also doesn't have to be complicated to be effective. After all, as you already know by now, trading currencies is not a complicated activity. Mostly, it's just about identifying the right currency to invest in and predicting whether the value of the currency will increase or decrease against the other currency in its pair.

Do not expect to develop your own strategy quickly. It takes time to come up with an effective strategy. To test just how effective your strategy is, you should test it many times in a live market and see how it performs. Strategies also change over time just as the market also changes. Hence, professional traders are known for always working on their strategy.

Day Trading

Day trading is a short-term trading style designed to buy and sell financial securities within the same trading day. That is closing all positions by the end of the trading day. In Day Trading, you can hold your trades for minutes or even hours. Day traders deal with financial instruments like options, stock, currencies, and contracts for difference. Many day traders are investment firms and banks. Day traders use technical analysis to make trading decisions.

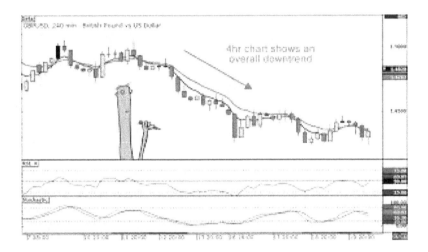

Trend Trading Strategy

Another popular and common FOREX Trading strategy is the trend trading strategy. This strategy attempts to make profits by analyzing trends.

The process involves identifying an upward or downward trend in a currency price movement and choosing trade entry and exit points based on the currency price within the trend.

Trend traders use these four common indicators to evaluate trends; moving averages, relative strength index (RSI), On-Balance-Volume (OBV), and Moving Average Convergence Divergence (MACD). These indicators provide trend trade signals, warn of

346

reversals, and simplify price information. A trader can combine several indicators to trade.

Pairs Trade

This is a neutral trading strategy, which allows pair traders to gain profits in any market conditions. This strategy uses two key strategies:

Convergence trading - this strategy focuses on two historically correlated securities, where the trader buys one asset forward and sells a similar asset forward for a higher price anticipating that prices will become equal. Profits are made when the underperforming position gains value, and the outperforming position's price deflates.

Short Facebook Stock

Statistical trading - this is a short-term strategy that uses the mean reversion models involving broadly diversified Security Portfolios. This strategy uses data mining and statistical methods.

Price Action Trading

This FOREX Trading strategy involves analyzing the historical prices of securities to come up with a trading strategy. Price action trading can be used in short, medium, and long periods.

348

The most used price action indicator is the price bar, which shows detailed information like high and low-price levels   during a specific period. However, most traders use more than one strategy to recognize trading patterns, stop-losses, and entry, and exit levels. Technical analysis tools also help price action traders make decisions.

Carry Trade Strategy

Carry trade strategy involves borrowing a low-interest currency to buy a currency that has a high rate; the goal is to make a profit with the interest rate difference. For example, one can buy currency pairs like the Japanese yen (low interest) and the Australian dollar (high interest) because the interest rate spreads are very high. Initially, carry trade was used as a one-way trade that moved upwards without reversals, but carry traders soon discovered that everything went downhill once the trade collapsed.

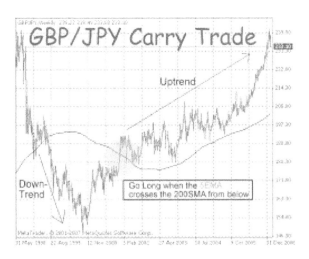

Momentum Trading

This strategy involves buying and selling assets according to the strength of recent price trends. The basis for this strategy is that an asset price that is moving strongly in a direction will continue to move in the same direction until the trend loses strength. When assets reach a higher price, they tend to attract many investors and traders who push the market price even higher.

This continues until large pools of sellers enter the market and force the asset price down. Momentum traders identify how strong trends are in a given direction. They open positions to take advantage of the expected price change and close positions when the prices go down.

Pivot Points

This strategy determines resistance and support levels using the average of the previous trading sessions, which predict the next prices. They take the average of the high, low, and closing prices. A pivot point is a price level used to indicate market movements.

350

Bullish sentiment occurs when one trades above the pivot point while bearish sentiment occurs when one trades below the pivot point.

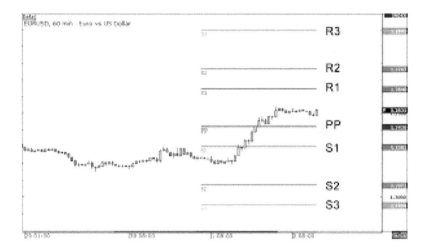

Inside Bar Trading Strategy

This highly effective strategy is a two-bar price action strategy with an inside bar and a prior/mother bar. The inside bar is usually smaller and within the high and low range of the prior bar. There are many variations of the inside bar, but what remains constant is that the prior bar always fully engulfs the inside bar. Although very profitable, the inside bar setup does not occur often.

There are two main ways you can trade using inside bars:

- As a continuation move - This is the easiest way to trade inside bars. The inside bars are traded in trending markets following the direction of the trend.

351

- As a reversal pattern - the inside bars are traded countertrend

- When using this strategy, it's important to look for these characteristics when evaluating the pattern:

- Time frame matters - avoid any time frame less than the daily.

- Focus on the breakout - best inside bar trades happen after a break of consolidation where the preceding trend is set to resume.

- The trend is your friend - trading with the trend is the only way to trade an inside bar

- A favorable risk to reward ratio is needed when trading an inside bar

- The size of the inside bar in comparison to the prior bar is extremely important

Pin Bar Trading Strategy

This strategy is highly recommended for beginners because it is easy to learn due to a better visual representation of price action on a chart. It's one of the easiest strategies to trade.

Pin bars show a reversal in the market and, therefore, can be useful in predicting the direction of the price.

Pin bars consist of one price bar, known as a candlestick price bar, which represents a sharp reversal and rejection of price.

Candlestick charts are the clearest at showing price action.

There are various ways traders trading with pin bars can enter the market:

- At the current market price

- Using an on-stop entry

- At limit entry, which is at the 50% retrace of the pin bar

- To improve your odds when using the pin bar strategy:

- Trade with the trend

- Wait for a break of structure

- Trade from an area of value

- Some of the mistakes pin bar traders should avoid include the following:

- Assuming the market will reverse because of a pin bar

- Focus too much on the pin bars and miss out on other trading opportunities

- All pin bars are not the same and should not be treated as such

FOREX Breakout Strategy

A breakout strategy is where investors find stocks that have built strong support or resistance level, wait for a breakout, and enter the market when momentum is in their favor.

This strategy is important because it can offer expansions in volatility, major price moves, and limited risk.

A breakout occurs when the price moves beyond the support or resistance level. The breakout strategy is good for beginners because they can catch every trend in the market. Breakouts occur in all types of market environments.

Traders establish a bullish position when prices are set to close above a resistance level and a bearish position when prices close below a support level. Sometimes traders can be caught on a false breakout, and the only way to determine if it's a false breakout is to wait for confirmation. False breakout prices usually go beyond the support and resistance level; however, they return to a prior trading range by the end of the day.

Good investors plan how they will exit the markets before establishing a position. With breakouts, there are two exit plans:

Where to exit with profit - traders can assess the stock recent behaviors to determine reasonable objectives. When traders meet their goals, they can exit the position. They can either raise a stop-loss to lock in profits or exit a portion of the position to let the rest run.

Where to exit with a loss - breakout trading show traders clearly when a trade has failed, and therefore they can determine where to set stop-loss order. Traders can use the old support or resistance level to close a losing trade.

Chapter 11:

Platforms

In a bid to understand what the various platforms for FOREX are, an individual need to be equipped with the knowledge of what FOREX is. From the face value of FOREX, it is a combination of the world's foreign currency exchange. Foreign currency exchange from its terminologies refers to the process of converting from one currency to another usually for purposes of trade. Other purposes may include tourism and even commerce. FOREX happens in the market for foreign exchange because this is the place where the value of currencies is determined. In order to acquire an item of your choice, one needs to have currency. Currency is of key importance since this is the only medium of exchange. Take for instance you are a citizen of the United Kingdom and you wish to acquire cloth wear from The United States, you will have to pay for the clothing wear in dollars rather than sterling pounds.

For this to happen, the importer based in the United Kingdom will have to convert an equivalent amount of sterling pounds into US dollars. This is because the medium of exchange in the US is limited to US dollars. The transport industry experiences the same. This mostly happens when it comes to air transport. A United States' tourist coming to Africa to witness the famous Wild beast migration cannot pay dollars to see the animals migrate. He or she will have to convert the currency into one that is favorable. The act of converting one currency to another is governed by a rate known as the currency exchange rate.

The exchange for these currencies from one currency to another has no defined place. This means that these exchanges can take place anywhere. The exchange is controlled by a computer network thus enabling the exchange to occur in an over-the-counter manner. Thus OTC. The market operates on a 24hr basis and runs till Saturday noon. Here, currency exchange takes place on a worldwide perspective. This means that the exchange happens across every time zone. For instance, when commerce day ends in Hong Kong, it commences in the US.

In the past before the onset of Bretton Woods institutions, the currency would be left to float freely, and the value of a currency would be determined by the desire of those particular people to engage in trade. Most people do not engage in FOREX directly but rather indirectly. They leave their banks to engage in such kind of transactions.

There are three internationally accepted means of trading in FOREX. These methods are usually employed by individuals, corporations, and institutions. They include:

- The spot markets

- Forwards market

- The future market

The spot market refers to a platform where goods are bought and sold for immediate delivery. The spot market often sets the basis upon which the forwards and futures market ensues. With the introduction of the electronic OTC mode of exchange and the onset of various middlemen in this field, the spot market has been in a booming business since people are always buying and traveling to various parts of the world. In a nutshell, the spot market is where the exchange of currencies occurs according to the reigning exchange rates. It has been a common behavior of people mistaking the FOREX for the spot market.

The prices and exchange rates in the market are often affected by the curves of supply and demand. There are many aspects that lie beneath the curves of demand and supply. These factors are not limited to economic performance, current interest rates, and political stability. Take for instance the scenario of Somalia. A tourist from the US would not be inclined to visit Somalia because of the various reasons associated with political instability. When the conditions at home don't favor trade, the FOREX in that country drops drastically.

The mentality of how a currency will perform in the future is also a key factor that needs to be taken into consideration. A spot deal is the finality of an agreement of performance. Here, an individual ought to deliver a specified amount of currency to counter the other specified amount of currency. This exchange is usually akin to the reigning exchange rates.

The Forwards and futures markets assume a different kind of path. Whereas the spot market is keen to deal with the current actual currencies, the forwards and futures markets focus on contracts. These particular contracts are often to the effect that a claim towards a particular currency is due. The focus is often on the specific type of currencies and the future date for settlement. For instance, when it comes to the forwards market, two parties come together and determine the terms of the agreement in the contract. They then proceed to purchase a contract in the OTC.

The futures market involves an exchange where one can trade on commodities or financial instruments at an explicit price for delivery at an explicit time in the coming days. Here, future contracts availed based on size and the date upon which the amount will be settled. The US has an association that regulates the futures market. This association is known as the National Futures Association. The future contract contains explicit details which cut across all the factors discussed underneath the contract.

The contracts have a binding effect on the parties in that the parties are obliged to perform their duties to the latter. It is important to note that the contracts can be repurchased or resold before the period of expiry is due. The effect of the forwards and futures market is to shield the corporation or individual against risk.

FOREX markets act as a shield for firms especially those engaging in businesses in foreign countries. The phobia is often directed towards the rising and falling tides of currency values when they trade in goods outside domestic jurisdictions. FOREX markets act as a shield to these kinds of firms through having an already set up timeline that governs the whole transaction. For instance, a trader can purchase or dismiss currencies in anticipation. This then creates an exchange rate that is binding to the particular transaction. This type of arrangement is popular in future markets whereby it is governed by a central authority.

However, there are factors that affect the supply and demand curve for currencies whic include; political instability, economic strength, and tourism. An increase or decrease in currency value will always mean that there is an opportunity to make a profit. Speculating that one currency's value will diminish is like saying that the other currency's value will dominate. This will lead to pairing. For instance, Japan and the US are paired with speculation that the interest rates will fall in the US (YEN/USD). This means that you will require fewer yen to match up the dollar.

Various Platforms for Investing in FOREX

An individual, corporation or company who has the desire to invest in FOREX may settle on any of the following channels of investment. On the FOREX market, the price of the national currency, for instance, is the way the market views the initial position of the economy. With an initial comprehension of what FOREX means, an individual can understand that most of these transactions occur online. With that in mind, the various platforms for investing in FOREX include:

Commercial and prop platforms are the two major types of trading platforms. Commercial platforms are fashioned to meet the expectations of daily traders, retailers, and investors. Their characteristics involve an easy to use a feature that enables ease of use by any individual. They also encompass other features that may be of aid to the trader such as news reports that may improve the investor's knowledge in the market. The investor knowledge is improved by continuous interaction with such feeds.

Prop platforms occur on a larger basis in that they are fashioned to allow a particular mode and requirement of trading to ensue. In order to settle on a proper trading platform, an individual needs to take note of the following factors: the kind of fees and features that are provided should be a driving factor towards settling on a trading platform. Traders who engage in FOREX daily are often inclined to be in need of features that may be of aid to them in making decisions. Before deciding, one needs a complete in-depth on the issue at hand.

Investors require a candid view of the available options and gaps to exploit. The amount of fees payable is also of great importance since traders will always be inclined to be pulled towards the direction of fewer fees. A scenario where trade-offs will occur should be anticipated. This refers to the compromising of quality or quantity in order to increase on another variable.

When you pay fewer fees and thus get lessor information, this will, in turn, take a toll on your whole investment. Several platforms may be tied to explicit middlemen whereas others are only tied to a particular broker.

Thus, the reputation of middleman is key when contemplating on which investment road to take. There are other trading platforms that have an already formed threshold.

If an individual or corporation seeking to invest does not meet the threshold set, then they do not qualify to invest. There are numerous trading platforms which surpass even numbers.

The most renowned ones include:

Network of middlemen

They are a channel that allows the sharing of numerous amounts of information across the FOREX. They act as pointers to where the business is most favorable. Middlemen will always be favored by the minimum trade barriers.

Trade Station

This is a type of platform that uses automated scripts to perform trading strategies. It is most popular among algorithmic traders

Robinhood

This type of platform operates on a free-commission manner. This is because this type of platforms makes money from various sources. The sources include interest on cash in its savings.

Meta Trader

This is the most popular trading platform. Its key features are that it combines many platforms of middlemen and has a scripting language that is handy when automating FOREX.

Interactive Brokers

A party trading in FOREX will face a lot of challenges. Among these challenges, there will be a bag of goodies. For instance, the markets amerce up to 5 trillion a day. This is a direct fact that they are the giants in terms of volumes of trade daily. The conversion of one currency to another and the entry and exit from the FOREX markets becomes less subtle because all these happen in a fraction of a second. Besides that, a trader needs to understand the importance of leverage. When a bank or a financial lending institution lends trader money, it allows him or her to control a large position when the reality is that there is very little to it that they actually own.

The FOREX market operates on a 24-hour basis. This means that you can conduct your business at any time of the day having no setback. In order to trade soundly, a trader needs in-depth on the various factors that affect various shifts. He or she should visualize every key aspect before trading. There are various factors that are inherent in a currency and these are usually the factors that control the currency values.

Traders with relatively fewer funds or those trading in fewer amounts of capital have a chance of venturing in the FOREX market and becoming successful rather than in other markets. These types of traders should focus on understanding the trends in the market since they partake in exchange daily. Traders with larger funds, such as long-term investors should focus on the tides of the market. An inner comprehension of the requisites of the macroeconomic environment and the factors behind the shift in the currency values will be of great aid to traders seeking to assume FOREX trading.

The feature of this platform is one of the best and comprehensive in the market. Meta Trader 4 has strong analysis functions. The chart is clear and easy to understand. Traders can put in currency pairs directly to the chart to comparing the up and down of the market.

Meta Trader 4 has a lot of advantages. Many traders use it, so if you run into the problems, you can easily to find the right answer quickly. Meta Trader 4 can operate and link with other software. Users can run automated trading with this platform smoothly.

Meta Trader 4 is not only used for FOREX trade but also used for different types of trading such as stocks, bonds, gold and much more. Traders can download Meta Trader 4 on its online website. They can try, test their data. This platform is really for the serious traders.

Chapter 12:

FOREX tools

This is a term used to help a person decide the kind of property they should use to earn and make a living. According to bankruptcy law, the exemption for tools of the trade is usually determined by the state in the state exemption statutes. The exemption can also be determined by federal law in the federal bankruptcy exemptions. The period in which a person lived in a state before filing could also be a determinant of the exemption. Lawyers assist their clients to understand which properties are exempt and the exemptions apply.

Anything a person can prove they use as a tool for trade is marked as a separate exemption from assets they own. This means that a person can be allowed an exemption for households separately from assets they use to make a living. One person may provide their vehicle as a property they own while another may produce their vehicle as a taxi which earns him his daily bread.

Having the right tools for trading will guarantee success for anyone starting. An experienced trader may not really be concerned about the tools they use but for beginners, the tools count.

Trade ideas stock scanning software

After establishing a good broker, the next step is finding the stock to trade with. The ability to determine stocks before they make a big move is what determines a more profitable trader. Trade ideas software helps in stock scanning for volume spikes, HOD movers to establish the gainers and the losers and things like that. This is the best software there is that scans the market and finds the winning stocks.

Signal charting

The third step is getting high-quality charts. The broker you chose makes come his standard charts. Those will work for you for some time until you decide to use ones that allow you to draw and write formulas. Signal allows one to run charts on 8 monitors without time delay. This is advantageous to people who like observing several stocks at once. it also allows installation of custom scripts. Custom scripts can be used as custom indicators for reversals and drawing support and resistance lines.

Breaking news provider

Every morning, a trader should start by reviewing the market. After the review, you look at the catalyst to determine why stocks are moving higher. Reasons for the stocks could be moving up in consideration to the market, or a strong sector while other times it may be a unique catalyst like earnings. Breaking news provide the headlines for when the stocks are spiking.

TAS market profile

This software is best in helping make trade decisions. It has several tools in it. Among them is a TAS scanner which allows one to observe stocks moving at different timings with different levels of buying and selling.

Having the right tool may not guarantee success in the trading world but it will give the right directions that will help make trading easier. The right tool will also provide an advantage to you over other traders who do not have the tools.

The right hardware

While you don't necessarily need the latest and greatest in computer hardware to run most types of trading software, that doesn't mean you can get by with the bare minimum either. The better your computer, the faster and smoother the software will run and the less lag and fewer crashes you will experience. First and foremost, it is important that you have adequate RAM which will make it easier to multitask without issue as you will frequently have several different programs as well as your web browser open at the same time. Additionally, as your software needs increase, the base level of hardware required will do the same.

370

While these costs can easily add up dramatically if you have to purchase an entirely new rig all at once, there will rarely be a need to do so. Rather, you can purchase parts overtime as needed, or when they are on sale, in a more piecemeal fashion most of the time. With this strategy, you can grow your hardware capabilities slowly as your need for the increased power manifests itself.

As you get more serious about day trading, you're also likely going to want to run at least 2 monitors at a time, if not more, then you can dedicate one to trading and the other to research and tracking results. This mean you will likely need a better video card with enough HDMI ports to account for the additional monitor. Once this is done, depending on the quality of your system and its available cooling power, you may need to look into liquid cooling solutions as well to ensure that things don't overheat in the midst of an important trade.

Regardless, you are going to want to invest in the best internet speed available that your current system can reasonably take advantage of. The current high-end standard is 1-gigabyte MBPS which can be found in most major markets, though something around 100 MBPS is typically fast enough for most systems. In addition to having access to the speed, you are going to need to be sure that your router and modem can keep up as well or they will bottleneck your efficiency to a noticeable degree. When you contact your internet service provider, you will also want to consider reinstalling a landline as a type of emergency backup in case you find yourself unable to make a specific trade in any other fashion. While this might seem like overkill, the $10 per month will seem reasonable the first time you find yourself using it to place a major trade, and you can think of it as a hardline to your broker in case the worst occurs.

Brokerage

Many traders stick with the first brokerage they come across without ever thinking twice about it. This can be a serious mistake; however, as an experienced trader has needs that are frequently quite different than those of a beginner. As such, once you get used to the day trading experience, it will generally behoove you to reevaluate your choice of broker and determine if you ultimately made the right decision.

First you should determine the best options for what you're looking for, the best place to start is on your favorite day trading website and see what the people who frequent their forums have to say. After you have determined a suitable list, the next thing you will want to do is determine the fees that they charge in exchange for the services that they offer. If you've already found what trading platform or online tools you prefer, then make sure that the brokerages you are looking for support them as not all brokerages support all trading platforms. Otherwise, you risk having to learn an entirely new platform from scratch.

Finally, it is important to make a concentrated effort when it comes to determining the type of customer service the brokerages you are interested in providing. To determine this, you'll want to do more than listen to reviews which can easily be skewed in one way or another; it is instead best to see for yourself. This means you are going to want to call the brokerage personally and see how long it takes for you to speak with a real person. While you won't have to actually call your brokerage very often, when you do it is likely to be an emergency which means you are going to want the time it takes to find someone to talk to, to be as short as it possibly can be.

As a new customer, it is likely that you'll receive a call back from someone associated with the brokerage who will try and sell you their service. If this call takes more than one business day to occur, then you will know that you are better off going somewhere else. After all, if the company treats new customers with that level of disdain, consider how much worse things will be once they already have your money and aren't actively trying to make a good impression. Finally, assuming that their customer service is up to mark, you will also want to email them with questions a few different times, just to see what their level of response is like. While this process may be a bit time consuming, once you find a brokerage that is on point, it will be more than worth the effort in the long run.

Online trading tools

There are plenty of different tools online that claim to help you maximize your trade efficiency, so the ones you choose to use are ultimately up to you. First things first, you are going to want to find a financial calendar that works for you to ensure that you don't miss any important dates when it comes to financial earnings reports. The program you choose should automatically populate with various important events as well as offer many different customizable dates and provide details on multiple different markets.

If you ever trade in the FOREX market, then you will want to find a good currency converter that shows any changes to specified currencies in real time. You will also want a currency converter that shows the range a specific currency pair has operated in over a predetermined period.

Additionally, you'll want to ensure that you have a calculator that makes it easy to determine pivot points along with Fibonacci numbers. These tools will make it easy for you to keep up to date on relevant trends and help you stay informed on relevant indicators that are otherwise easy to miss if you aren't careful. Along similar lines, you are going to want to track down a heat map that is reliable, and that shows you the trades that are currently trending along with a volatility monitor to make it easy for you to keep tabs on the mood of the market.

Indicators of Trade

This is a measure or gauge of trade that allows analyzing of prices and provides trade signals. Indicators provide trade signals that alert a trader when it is time to trade. Day trading indicators are not to be used as the only plan. They should be used along with a well laid out though to make it a useful trading tool. No matter the kind of trade one is involved in, having many trading indicators may bring inconsistency with trading decisions due to the complexities involved. Keeping it simple could simply be the trick to making clear and less stressful trading decisions.

Trading indicators should not be taken as the only method relied on trading. Although, using indicators alongside other trading variables may come in handy. Getting rid of the many indicators helps traders have a simplistic approach to the market.

Role of Technical Indicators are:

- Find the direction of the trend

- Determine the momentum or lack of momentum in the market

- Determine whether the market is growing

- Get the volume to determine how popular a market is with traders

Getting the same type of indicators that on the chart that give the same information is where the issue is. This is because you may give conflicting information or get more information than you need to stress you out. The main shortcoming of most indicators is that since they are gotten from price, they delay the price. There are rules that one can use to determine useful indicators for day trading, swing trading, and position trading. This include among others:

- Choosing one trend indicator such as moving average and one momentum trading indicator is the simplest rule.

- Knowing well the perimeters you want to investigate before you decide on the trading indicators which you will use on your charts. Then learn the indicator you chose in terms of how it works, calculations it does and the effects it will bring for your trading decisions.

Indicators work only depending on how they are incorporated into the trading plan. Some indicators like MACD and CCI are best at calculating information. Others like alligator indicator are fast at showing a market that is trending and ranging. Other indicators will show directions and act as entry and exit signals of trade. The usage of a basic indicator along with a well laid out trading plan by back, forward and demo can you put you ahead of trade with many complicated indicators. NetPicks offers systems that test trade plans, prove trading systems and trading indicators.

Economic calendar

The economic calendar is helping the traders get the fresh and updated news such as what the future of the market looks like, pieces related to trading economic data, new policies from the central bank, the elections and monetary policies updated around the

376

world and much more. These are really important for trading especially FOREX market.

You can get the economic calendar from brokers or financial websites. It will provide the big picture about the economy such as the events that impact the economy in what level, unemployment rate, expecting the market conditions. Traders have to keep close eyes on these things because trading currencies will be effective.

Pip calculator

Pip is the measure unit, and it is the most popular and smallest measure unit in FOREX trading especially between the currency pair. The pip calculate is convenient to use. Many traders use this FOREX trading tool to easy in exchange the pair currency. The users just have to enter the detail of their position, the amount of the currency, size of trade, currency pair and also the leverage.

Time zone converter

FOREX market has 3 biggest markets around the world. One market closes, then another market opens. That is why some traders can trade 24 hours. Besides that, the market also overlaps with each other so the traders can also trade 2 markets at the same time.

With the right strategies, traders can get double profit. Time zone converter helps traders know exactly which market is opening in exactly what time. The experienced traders often trade around 3 or 4 morning Eastern time because they can trade in London market which is the biggest market for FOREX. It also overlaps with the Asia FOREX market.

Volatility calculator

Traders should focus and always keep eyes on the market volatility. It can help you have the good view about which is a good currency pairs to choose for trading. You don't want the currency pairs with limited scope of volatility because it won't make the best trade.

Volatility calculator will give the general the history exchange of these currency pairs and give you the overall of how much volatility the pairs will be. You'll decide if you want to trade on those pairs or not.

The history exchange can help the user pick what is the time frame that they want to focus on week, month, quarter or even years. The more market volatility is the better chance for traders to make the profit.

The traders can see the time frame with the currency pairs yield the most return, and they can start to trade on that time frame when it comes. It's working both ways that high return will also be high risk included. The traders can manage to diversify the trading to protect the money by risk management strategies.

Currency correlation

FOREX trading is all about currency pairs. Traders is sure to not ignore the correlation between the currency pairs. The easy way to signal the currency pairs correlation is mark them positive or negative correlation.

The correlations range from -1.0 to 0.0 to +1.0. These are easy to understand: -1.0 is the perfect negative or inverse that often marked with color red color, 0.0 is no correlation, +1.0 is the perfect positive that often marked with blue.

The correlations between of currency pairs are calculating based on the history data between them. One of the popular currency correlation tools that many traders know of is Mataf. Besides, you can also search and will see a lot of online websites offering this tool for free.

Chapter 13:

The Right Mindset to Make Money

W e'll talk about what you should do, to make sure that you aren't failing in your endeavors to start your FOREX trading journey without making it too hard on yourself. Many successful people have followed these habits, to get optimal results in all their aspects of life, whether it be job-related or anything else. Make sure you start implementing all these habits after you are done reading this book as it will help make FOREX trading much easier for you. So, you need to change your current lifestyle by being more productive and disciplined. You must remember, being successful in FOREX trading is more of a lifestyle.

Plan your day ahead

Planning your day ahead of time is crucial, not only does planning out your day help you be more prepared for your day moving forward, but it'll also help you to become more aware of the things you shouldn't be doing, hence wasting your time.

Moreover, planning your day will truly help you with making the most out of your time, that being said we'll talk about two things:

Benefits of planning out your day

How to go about planning out your day. So, without further ado, let us dive into the benefits of planning out your day.

It will help you prioritize

Yes, planning out your day will help you prioritize a lot of things in your day to day life. You can allow time limits to the things you want to work on the most to least, for example, if you're going to write your book and you're serious about it. Then you need a specific time limit every day in which you work on a task wholeheartedly without any worries of other things until the time is up. Then you move on to the next job in line, so when you schedule out your whole day, and you give yourself time limits, then you can prioritize your entire day. The same thing goes for your trading, make sure you allocate time for trading, which will allow you to focus on your research, hence making you more successful.

Summarize your normal day

Now, before we start getting into planning out your whole day ahead, you need to realize that to plan your entire day, you need to know precisely what you are doing that day. Which means you need to write down every single thing you do on a typical day and write down the time you start and end, it needs to be detailed in terms of how long does it take for your transportation to get to work, etc.

Now after you've figured out your whole day, you can decide how to prioritize your day moving on could be cutting out a task that you don't require or shortening your time for a job that doesn't need that much time. Now, you can add pleasurable tasks into your day like hanging out with your friends, etc.

Arrange your day

It is crucial that you arrange your day correctly, so the best way to organize your day is to make sure you get all your essential stuff done earlier in the day when your mind is fresh. After that's done, you can have some time for yourself to relax and do whatever you want. But make sure you get all the things that need to be done before you can move on to free time for yourself. Another thing that will help you is to set time limits on each task, that way you'll be more likely to get the job done.

Remove all the fluff

So, what I mean by that is remove all the things that are holding you back from achieving your goals. If you have time for the fluff, do it if not, then work on your priorities first. In conclusion, planning out your day will help you tremendously! Make sure you plan out your day daily to ensure successful and accomplished days.

Cut out negative people

This task might be the hardest to do, but it is quite essential, see the people who you are around are the people who will create your personality. So if you're around negative people, you'll develop adverse circumstances for yourself. If you're surrounded by people who aren't upbeat about life and find everything wrong and never see the good in anyone, you need to cut them out and be around people who are happy and ready for what life has to offer. Now I get it, some cynical people can be your family members, and you can't cut them out, the ideal thing to do is. 1) Make them understand what they are doing wrong. 2) Show them how they can change their life. And if they still want to remain the same, then keep your distance. In conclusion, it's essential that you are in a grateful "vibe" as it'ill not only help you with your mental and physical health, but it'll also help you attract better people and better circumstances.

Stop multitasking

I think we're all guilty of this at a time, and if you're multitasking right now, I need you to stop. Now multitasking could be a lot of things, and it could be as small as cooking and texting at the same time, or it could be as big as working on two projects at the same time. Studies are showing how multitasking can reduce your quality of work, which something you don't want to do if your goal is to get the best result out of the thing that you are doing. That being said, there are a lot more reasons as to why you shouldn't be multitasking, so without further ado, let's get into the primary reasons why multitasking can be harmful.

You're not as productive.

Believe it or not, you tend to be a lot less productive when you are multitasking. When you go from one project to another or anything else for that matter, you don't put all your effort into your work. You're always worried about the project that you will be moving into next. So moving back and forth from one project to another will affect your productivity if you want to get the most out of your work you need to be focused on one thing at a time and make sure you get it done to the best of your abilities. Plus, you're more likely to make mistakes, which will not help you work at the best of your ability.

You become slower at your work.

When you are multitasking, chances are you will end up being slower at completing your projects. You would be in a better position if you were to focus on one project at a time instead of going back and forth, which of course helps you complete them faster. So, the thing that enables you to be faster at your projects when you're not multitasking is the mindset, we often don't realize how much mindset comes into play. When you're going back and forth from one project to another, you're in a different mental state going into another project which takes time to build and break. So by the time you manage to get into the mindset of project A you are already moving into project B, it is always best that you devote your time and energy one project at a time if you want it to be done at a faster pace.

Set yourself a goal (time, quality, etc.)

All in all, multitasking will do you no good. It will only make you slower at your work and make you less productive. Making sure you

384

stop multitasking is essential, as it'll only help you live a better life. If you want to be more successful and live a better life, you need to make sure your projects are quality as I can't stress this point enough.

You are probably reading this book because you want to get better at living your life or achieve goals which you haven't yet. The reason why you're not living the life that you want or haven't reached your goal could be a lot of things but, one of the items could be the quality of your work which could be taking a hit because of your multitasking.

So, review yourself, and find out why you haven't achieved your goals and why you're not living the life that you want.

Then if you happen to stumble upon multitasking being the limiting factor or the quality of your work, I want you to work on one project at a time while giving it your full attention.

What you'll notice is that your work will have a higher quality and will be completed in a quicker amount of time following the steps listed above, which will change your life and help you achieve your life goals in a better more efficient way.

Now that we have talked about some action items regarding making FOREX trading more of a lifestyle by changing the way you set up your day. Let's talk about some of the lifestyle changes you need to make, so that trading is easier for you.

Get more sleep

It is essential that you get your 8 hours of sleep. Many people don't know this but, even if your eating is perfect but you're not getting the sleep, chances are you are not going to see any changes. Getting your 8 hours of sleep helps you a lot. When you get the right amount of deep sleep, you'll see results such as better recovery and better mental health. You don't want your FOREX trading endeavors to go in vain. Not only that, if you don't get enough sleep, the chances of you staying awake the next morning will drop down tremendously. You will feel drowsy the days you don't get your full sleep. Keep that in mind moving on, and as always make sure to get your total 8 hours of sleep.

Physical activity

It is very crucial for you to take part in physical activities, for a straightforward reason it will help you to assist your motivation to trade. The same thing as getting proper sleep, the role of you being physically active will give you a great balance of you being energized and motivated throughout the day. Many people don't know this but being physically active can help you to stay more motivated. There have been many studies backing these claims up, that being said, let's talk about some of the benefits which might come along with you following a working out plan.

Regular exercising changes your brain

No, regular exercises don't change the way your brain is shaped by any means if that's what you're thinking. But what it will help with, is better memory and better-thinking skills. If you were to do your research, you'll find that out for yourself, how big of a role regular exercising plays when it comes to brain functions. Make sure you start implementing this physical activity, it'll only help you get better at your trading skills and to see better results out of it.

By now you can see the benefits of exercising, not only does regular exercising help you stay healthy physically, but also enables you to optimize your mind and helps you with better brain function which will allow you to work for an extended period at any given task.

Improves your mood

This is one of the most significant differences you will notice once you start working on your health is that your mood will stay elevated through the day! Which is a great thing to have as you will be able to get more things done and be more successful. See when you work out you release a chemical called dopamine, which is a feel-good hormone and of course working out will help you become less stressed.

Improves physical health

Yes, this isn't one of the most salient points to bring up but let's discuss it anyway. Once you start to implement healthy habits to your day, you'll become more physically fit, which will not only give you more energy through the day, it'll also help you keep up with things like your daily chores and not get tired so quickly. You will see a difference in the quality of your life and your work ethic once you start to implement daily health habits and become more physically healthy.

Helps boost your immune system

This ties into improved physical health, but working out will boost your immune system and lower your risk of diseases like diabetes, hypertension, etc. Once you have a boost in your immune system, you will be less likely to get even the common flu. I know of someone who hasn't gotten flu in fifteen years simply because he started to live a healthy life, now I am not saying that you will see the same results but staying healthy will definitely help you with boosting your immune system which will help you not get sick so often and enjoy some quality time with your family and get more stuff done.

Now that we have discussed how staying in shape can help you live a better life; we will now move on to the ways you can help yourself live a healthier life.

Start easy

Now, if you have never worked out in your life, you need to realize that you won't be going hard at the gym as Arnold Schwarzenegger did in his hay days. So, don't push yourself too much in the gym because you are not ready for it, and you might lose motivation. So, if you are starting off getting in shape perhaps light jogs, some resistance training couple times a week to get the blood moving. But make sure you get up to the point where you are working out at least three hours a week to see some health benefits. Start once a week then twice, and so on.

After reading this chapter, many might be thinking that this is more of a self-help book than it is FOREX trading. The Truth is that we want you to understand how to live a better life by changing the habits that you are currently following. Doing FOREX trading and making it a lifestyle is a lot more work than you think it is. For you to make it easy, you need to understand that you need to change your habits to be successful at FOREX trading, which means you need to change the way you move the way you think and the way you perform. The reason why it will be straightforward for you is that you will change the way you move and the change the way you live your life in general. Changing the way you live your life will not only help you get better results, but it will also help you to make FOREX trading a lifestyle, many people confuse income source as not being a part of a lifestyle, and it is something that they're supporting to better their health. But the Truth is that when they're working on trading, they don't realize that it needs to be a lifestyle for it to be a health benefit, if you want to be healthier then you need to make sure that you're taking care of your health 24/7 365 days a year.

Which means you need to make this a lifestyle, and for you to make this a lifestyle, we need to understand some self-help techniques to keep it sustained for a more extended period. The way we're going to be delivering it is by showing you how to change your lifestyle for the better instead of the worst.

Research

When you deal with the FOREX market, doing research will go a long way. In fact, it is your research that will give the direction of the overall trade since you will use the information in your research to come up with a trading decision. Therefore, your research plays a critical role in every trade.

Make sure that you do sufficient research. Take note that just because you have spent five hours in researching in one day does not mean that it is already enough. When you're an FX trader, research should be a normal part of your day-to-day activity as a trader.

The more that you know about the currencies being traded, the higher the chance of being able to identify the best currency to invest in and trade. Also, don't forget to research the different factors that can affect the prices of currencies in the market. Although it is virtually impossible to analyze every detail when you trade foreign currencies, it's still worth studying since having more knowledge and understanding will allow you to make the right trading decisions.

Of course, the information that you get from your research will not dictate or directly show you the right decisions to make. Therefore, you also need to dedicate some time to analyze the information that you have. This is another crucial part since your analysis will be the one that will lead to your trading decision. This is also a tricky part since you will most probably have several conclusions on what profitable currencies to trade may be, and some of them may even conflict with one another. Of course, you're free to make multiple trades at once; however, for a beginner, it is recommended that you only do one trade at a time to monitor your progress more easily. Also, doing multiple trades when you are just starting out is also too aggressive for a beginner. Do not worry; the more that you get used to trading in a real and live FX market situation, the more trades you can make. But, for now, as a beginner, focus on making one trade at a time and strive to increase your rate of success.

Money Management

Even if you use a winning strategy, there is still a chance that you may lose all your money if you don't manage your money properly. This is true not only when you deal with FOREX but also in any investment or business. You have to manage your money properly.

Pay attention to how much you spend and the money that comes in. Of course, to make a profit, the money that comes in must be higher than your overall expenses. It is also worth noting that a good way to manage your money is to manage the trades that you make. After all, the money that you will come or will be spent for trading. Hence, your trading activities are closely connected to the money that you need to manage. It is best to have a plan; a short-term and a long-term plan even before you initiate any trade. Be sure that your objectives for entering a transaction are clear.

Of course, part of money management is to only invest the money that you can afford to lose. Therefore, do not use the money that you need to pay for your household bills and other obligations. Keep in mind that FOREX trading still has its risks even if you do all the necessary research. Just like any other business or investment, there is a chance that you can lose your money. Also, by not using the "important" money, it will be easy for you to stay calm and just enjoy the process of trading.

Another issue to discuss is if you should use OPM or other people's money. Some people say that you do not need to spend money to be a trader since you can always use OPM once you can develop a winning strategy. However, this book does not recommend this practice. Yes, you can use OPM and probably be successful, but you should also consider what can happen in case your trades do not work out the way you would want them to be. And, take note that this is a common scenario when you deal with the FOREX market.

In case the worst happens, then you risk being drowned in debt. So, instead of taking such risk, you should only use any extra money that you have and work on your strategy to grow it without having to worry that you will be in debt if your trades do not work out.

Part of money management is time management. You should also pay attention to how much time you spend on things that are related to the FX market. If you spend too many hours a day but only earn a little, then perhaps you are not productive. It isn't just a matter of earning a profit but also how much profit you can earn.

Right Mindset

Having the right trading mindset is important to success. Your mindset can influence your analysis, as well as the decisions that you make. Without the right mindset, there is even a chance that you may miss out on opportunities. There are many things that can characterize the right trading mindset, such as:

- Always calm and thinks clearly

- Not greedy

- Objective

- From an emotional standpoint, it is not affected by the outcome of a trade

- Patient

- Knows how to take advantage of opportunities when they arise

- Thinks positively yet remains practical and reasonable

- Remains full of enthusiasm

- Willing to research and analyze various information on a regular basis

- Has a strong will

- Learns from mistakes

- Applies tested strategies and does not rely on luck

- Seeks more knowledge and understanding

- Strives for continuous development

Many things can be said about the right trading mindset. If, while reading the short list above, you feel like you're being described, then you're probably on the right track to achieving the right trading mindset.

Take note that no matter how much you want to have this mindset; you cannot expect to achieve it overnight. After all, it takes time to break old habits and be able to learn new and more effective habits as a trader. The good news is that it is possible. If you persist and practice enough, then soon enough you will achieve the right mindset that is the optimum mindset for trading currencies.

It takes lots of practice and study to acquire the optimum practice for trading. It is not really composed of complicated steps or features, but rather a strong habit of the best practices and rich experience.

FOREX Trading Journal

Do you really need to keep a journal to trade currencies? The answer is no. However, it is worth noting that having a journal can be very helpful, especially in the long run. A journal will allow you to:

- View yourself from a different and unbiased perspective

- Find things that can be improved which you would otherwise overlook

- Have a better view of your trading journey

- Learn new things

- Remind yourself of your goals and objectives for trading

Do not worry; you don't have to be a professional writer to keep a trading journal. However, you do need to do two things: You have to update your journal on a regular basis, and you have to be completely honest with everything that you write in your trading journal.

You can write your experiences and goals in any notebook. Other traders do not use a notebook but make use of technology. They keep a file in any writing software like Microsoft Word or WPS (Kingsoft) Office. You can also use your mobile phone instead of a traditional notebook. The important thing is to be able to keep a record easily. Of course, you should also make sure that you do not lose such record easily. Writing a trading may not seem that helpful the first few times that you are doing it; however, in the long run, you will get to appreciate its value and importance to you as a currency trader.

Follow on the News

The news usually reveals useful information that can help you predict the movement of the different currencies in the market. This is true, especially when you deal with the four major currency pairs. Therefore, it is important that you be updated with the latest news, especially concerning the factors that can affect the value of different foreign currencies. For example, all things being equal, if there is a news that there is a problem of underemployment in the U.S., and it appears hard to solve immediately, then you can expect for the value of the U.S. currency to drop. This, of course, will allow you to make right trading decisions.

Be careful because the news can be tricky. Although it is advised that you follow the news, do not let it decide the course of your trade. Normally, when the news highlights or promotes a certain currency, the expected outcome is that the price of the said currency should increase. However, this isn't always the case. Don't forget that many factors affect the price of currencies. You should also consider how the market (people) responds to the news. After all, consumer behavior is one of the things that can influence the prices of the different currencies.

Stay Conservative

Be conservative and stay conservative. Whether regarding the investment that you make per trade or how you compute the likelihood or outcome of a trade, it is important to be conservative. The FX market is full of speculations. Although it is a given that you intend to make money, it is important that you keep your expectations and projections as conservative as possible. This will help minimize your risks and losses. Being conservative is important especially when you deal with an environment that is highly speculative such as the FOREX market.

Many professional and successful traders only spend around 1% of their total funds per trade. Hence, they can make at least 100 trades (minimum). After all, no matter what strategy you use, even if it is highly effective, negative outcomes are inevitable. The best way to see just how effective a strategy is by applying it in the long run, which means that you will have to make multiple trades using the same strategy. This is another reason why it is helpful to be conservative. It'll allow you to see the full potential of your strategy.

Develop Your Strategy

When you engage in the FOREX market, you need to work on a reliable strategy. Pat of being a trader is to work on and develop your trading strategy continuously. Do not forget that the market continues to move and evolve. As such, your strategy must also be flexible enough to adapt to changes. Also, there are many things and variations that take place in the FOREX market. The best strategy today may not be as effective by next week. Hence, you need to develop your strategy on an ongoing basis.

It is worth noting that before you apply any strategy, you need to be sure to test it first multiple times. Some traders get too lazy and only run a single test. This is wrong. Be sure to test your strategy more than five times before you use it with real money involved. A good way to test your strategy is by using the demo account provided by your broker.

It's also common to make continuous adjustments or changes in your strategy. Remember that even a minor adjustment can have a big impact on the effectiveness of a strategy. Therefore, even if you only change a small part of your strategy, make it a point to test it for several times before you use it with real money.

398

Professional traders continuously work on their strategies. It's also not uncommon to completely abandon a strategy that you have been working on for weeks and months. It is a never-ending test of trial and error. Strategies that perform well can be further developed, while those that fail should be abandoned. Of course, you won't be paid for testing and developing countless of strategies, but this part is crucial to your success as a trader since the strategy that you use is the key to making continuous profits in the FX market.

Take Advantage of the Demo Account

As we already discussed it is common for brokers to provide you with a demo account. It's a good way to have an experience of actual trading in a live market environment without risking any money and you can test the trading platform of your broker before you deposit real money in your account. Also, demo account will be useful whenever you want to test your strategy, which is a regular thing for professional brokers. Well-established brokers always offer a demo account, so that won't be a problem. Don't be too lazy to use your demo account. Don't rush to participate in a market using real money. When you use a demo account, you still have to research and do all the things that you would do as a trader who wants to earn a profit. Hence, you might as well do it for real so that you can get paid for your efforts. Well, the problem is that this is not always the case. It is not uncommon to find traders who lose a trade despite doing lots of research and analysis. What you need is to develop a reliable strategy. To do this, you can expect to encounter many failures or losing trades. These failures are the ones that will lead you to a more effective strategy. By using a demo account, you can come up with a better strategy without risking a dime, and once you develop a winning strategy, you can always back up your strategy with real money.

Take A Break

Allow yourself to take a break from time to time. Doing research and analysis can be tiring in the long run. Also, by giving yourself some break, you will be able to relax your body and clear your mind. This is important to allow you to come up with better ideas and make better decisions. It's also worth noting that it takes time to learn how to trade foreign currencies effectively. Take, for example, juggling. Even if you have the complete instructions on how you can juggle four balls, you will most like not be able to do it right away. You need to practice more. The same applies in trading currencies. Just because you have read good books on the subject does not mean that you can already make continuous profits with your knowledge. You also need to practice. Of course, exerting too many efforts and time in practice is also not good for you. You also need to rest. Take note that with all the research and analysis that you do on a regular basis, you deserve to take a break from time to time.

A good way to take a break isn't to think about anything that is related to the FX market. Some people commit the mistake of taking a break by spending the time with the demo account or looking for new strategies. That is not taking a break. That is still considered as working. It is true that the FX market can be very addicting, but you need to control it. Therefore, when you take a break, do something that will get your mind out of the things that are related to FOREX. Go to the beach or go on a vacation with your family somewhere. You can also watch a good movie or go for a run — anything fun and will not make you think and worry about FOREX and your pending trades if any. Just enjoy. Do not worry; you will go back to your life as a trader immediately right after the break. When that happens, be sure that you are more ready to face the evolving FX market.

Economics of It

Trading is all about economics. You need to know what is in high supply (and will not cost you a lot) and what is in high demand (and will cost you a lot). If you can buy stocks that are in high supply at the beginning of the day and sell them off at the end because they are in high demand, you'll be better able to make sure that you are truly benefitting from the economic factors that come along with trading. It's a good idea always to try and make sure that you are getting the stock for the lowest amount possible and that you're selling it for the highest amount possible. This is the only way that you will be able to make a lot of money.

Knowing that the higher the demand, the higher the price is will help you to have an easier time when it comes to trading. You should make sure that you are only doing things that are in high supply when you first buy them. If you do find something that is in high demand and it is at a good price, snatch it up and then turn right around and sell it for higher. This is the best situation when it comes to day trading and one of the easiest ways that you can make a lot of money at once.

The Reward with the Risk

Similarly, to how you need to make sure that you are comparing the demand and the supply of the stocks that you are purchasing, you need to compare the risk of the stock to the reward that you can get from it. This'll help you to decide how you are going to get the stock and how much it is going to work for you.

The risk is what happens when you are buying the stock. This is the amount of money that you can lose on the stock if it does not end up being one that you can win. You should always make sure that the risk is much smaller than the reward that comes along with the stock. This means that the amount of money that you could lose on it is smaller than the amount of money that you could make on it. This doesn't necessarily mean that you're going to lose money or make money on it, but it does mean that you need to be careful about the money that you are spending on different stocks.

On the other end of the spectrum, you should always look at the reward. Do you think that you'll be able to sell it for double what you paid for it? While this isn't likely, it's a good way to look at the rewards that are associated with it. If the rewards seem like they are good and like they are something that you will be able to deal with in the long term, you need to take the stock and go with it. Even if you don't get the highest amount possible for the stock when you sell it toward the end of the day, you will be able to make some money from it.

Don't Put Your Eggs in One Basket

Always be careful when you are buying stocks. Even if you find a stock or any investment that seems is, you shouldn't spend all of your money on that one stock. Buy a few of them or even buy more than what you really think is necessary but then stop and move onto a different good stock that'll allow you to make even more money. It's important that you do this so that you're safe with your stocks even if you don't have the right type of investment going on.

By trying out different stocks and making sure that you are investing your money in the right way, you will give yourself a chance to get even more money from the investments that you have made. This means that you need to be sure that you are getting a lot of different stocks that are in different categories and that will allow you the chance to try to do more with the options that you do have. It doesn't always have to be hard for people who are trying to get more out of the day trading options, but it is something that you need to make sure that you are doing the right way.

It can sometimes be hard for you when you are trying to find different stocks. You may not always be able to find exactly what you want, and the expected returns may not be the greatest, but it will be a way for you to make sure that you are going to have something different than one thousand dollars of the same things. If you try to find different stocks that are going to be profitable, you'll be able to make money from them. You just have to try.

Invest in Different Types of Stocks

There are so many different types of stocks that you can invest in. The different investments will give you a chance to broaden the horizons of your portfolio and will give you a better chance at being able to sell off the ones that you have before the day is over. It can sometimes be complicated to learn all of the aspects of trading so make sure that you are doing it the right way and that you are going to be able to get the most out of it. If you work to make sure that you are getting the right type of stocks, you'll have a much easier time when it comes to making money.

You will also be able to sell the stocks more easily. For example, you may struggle to sell 15 of the same stock because that is a big bulk sale. You probably won't struggle, though, selling 15 different stocks that all have different aspects to them. Just make sure that they are all profitable and that they are all going to bring of money that you want to make.

If you can create a profile that is varied and different, you'll have a better chance at selling the stocks and getting your money back for them when you are done with the process. It can sometimes be complicated to get the options that you have with selling stocks so make sure that you know what you are doing and that you are going to be able to include everything in the sale of the stocks that you do have. You may even be surprised that some people will want to buy all the stocks that you have in your portfolio at the end of the day.

The First Hour

Just like how the first part of your trading is the most important when you start to day trade, the first hour of the day is also going to be the most important part of the trading day. You need to make sure that you get to it early and that you buy your stocks as soon as you can. This is important for two reasons.

The first reason is that you'll be one of the first people there and you'll have access to the best stocks possible. There are many benefits that come with being the first to get to a specific trading option, but one of the biggest is that you will not have to compete with other people to be able to buy your stocks. You can get the best price possible, and you will have a handle on the day long before anyone else even shows up to buy stocks.

The second reason is that you will then have all day to sell off the stocks that you just bought. You need to make sure that you have as long as possible so that you don't have to worry about getting stuck with them at the end of the day (which is any day trader's worst nightmare). If you buy the stocks at the beginning of the day, you can then take the rest of the day and make sure that you're selling them so that you don't have to worry about having them left over. You will always have a fresh start.

Trading plan

A FOREX trader should have a trading plan that should be prepared well in advance. The trading plan should list out his entry and exit conditions as well as his money management rules. This is of utmost importance, and he should religiously follow his trading plan to the tee. In order to become a successful FOREX trader, he should never deviate from the trading plan.

Discipline

This is one of the most important qualities needed to be a successful FOREX trader. A trader should be disciplined and methodical in the way he goes about with FOREX trading. He should not only meticulously plan his trading but should also be disciplined enough to follow it.

Ability to do analysis

A FOREX trader should have the ability to analyze the technical charts and other financial data in order to become a successful FOREX trader. He should invest in himself and learn how to use the financial tools that would help in becoming a better trader.

Trading is a very competitive job; one needs to always be a step ahead of others in order to be successful.

Emotional stability

It is very important to keep emotions and trading separate. In order to be successful, the trader should be able to trade like a machine and not let emotions affect his trades. He shouldn't let losses affect him, nor should he get overly excited about the winning trades.

Hard work

Nothing beats hard work for becoming a successful FOREX trader. The trader should be prepared to put in a lot of hours and research the FOREX market thoroughly before each trading day. Most successful FOREX traders have a pre-trading session wherein they analyze the global markets, check charts, read various financial newspapers, note down key economic events of the day, etc. before they start their trades.

Good knowledge of charting and analysis tool

In order to be a successful FOREX trader, it is very important to have good knowledge on the usage of charting and other analytic software. The usage of this trading software raises the odds of success considerably, so it is important to have a good understanding of them.

Constant Learning

The Trading field requires constant learning. The trader should be prepared to learn throughout his trading career.

Something that might work now might not work after five years. So, it's very important to constantly adapt and keep learning in order to be a step ahead of others. A good trader should be on the constant lookout of learning new things that might help him with his trading, be it the usage of trading software or a new way of analysis.

Mastering fear

It is very important to master fear in order to be a successful FOREX trader. The trader should be prepared to take losses now and again and should understand that it's part and parcel of the game. The inability to book losses and holding on to a losing position can result in more losses. The trader should also be ready to take a trade when a good opportunity arises and should not allow fear to hold him back.

Thinking on your own

It is very important to think on your own and make trading decisions and not just blindly follow the crowd. As the saying goes, "buy into the fear and sell into the greed!" Now, this does not always mean doing the opposite of what others do. It just means that the trader should have an open mind and the ability to think on his own and make decisions accordingly.

Awareness of global events

FOREX markets are affected by the major international events that occur. The key economic events happening globally as the FOREX markets are traded globally and affected by these economic events.

A few examples of the key economic events are Federal Bank interest rate decision, ECB rate decision, GDP data of key economies, job data of key economies, inflation data of key economies, etc.

Never blame the market

The market might behave irrationally, but the trader should be responsible for reading the market cues and making trading decisions. Instead of playing the blame game, he should learn from each mistake. The trader should understand the risks associated with trading and have a proper money management rule in place.

Trading journal

It is important to maintain a trading journal and make an entry of all the trades he makes. The reasons for taking that trade should also be noted down. This would help in analyzing the trades later and help in avoiding the mistakes made. This would also help in identifying the good trades made and look for similar patterns later.

Choosing the right broker

It is important to choose the right broker. Some of the factors that should be considered while selecting a broker should be A) low brokerage B) fast and reliable trading terminal C) ease of trading and good research and charting software's that the broker provides.

Money management rules

This is perhaps the most important among all things that are mentioned now. A money management rule is basically the rules that define the maximum loss a trader can afford to take per trade or at a point of time. Most FOREX traders never risk more than 2-5 % per trade. They also never risk more than 10-20 % at a particular point across all trades. It is very important to follow these rules; else, you run the risk of wiping out your entire trading account in a matter of days, if not hours! It's always better to limit your losses and live to fight another day!

Conclusion

Many people are turning to trade in order to generate their income, invest in their future, or simply give themselves extra cash for the month. Whatever your reason is for getting into trading, you learned four different types of trading strategies within the contents of this book.

To become a successful trader, you need to continue your education, studying in more detail the type of strategy you want to focus on.

Investment requires discipline, patience, and commitment in order to achieve the maximum returns from your capital. By implementing the skills and strategies you have learned in this book you can develop a sound trading plan that will chart your way to success in FOREX trading.

Taking advantage of this extensive global market that is foreign exchange will increase your money-making opportunities and open you up to learning new ways of multiplying your money. By using your disposable income to generate more money you'll be in effect ensuring your financial future and creating a path to a wealthy and financially stable future.

You now understand that the trading scenes that you have imagined and seen in several movies do not provide the whole story of trading.

Through the pages of this book, you have learned how important research is. Not only do you want to spend months researching trading markets and strategies before you make your first trade, but you also want to continue to research while you are trading. This means you will watch your daily reports, pay attention to the news, join a forum, and do whatever else you need to do in order to help you reach bigger profits as a trader.

You also understand the importance of confidence and the winning mindset. Even if you are scared to jump into the world of trading, you'll be able to reach your full potential through working hard and making sure you continue to believe in yourself. Instead of looking at mistakes as something you did wrong, you want to look at them as a learning experience. Take your mistakes and grow from them, then move on. Don't continue to dwell on your mistakes as this can lead you to second-guess your decisions in the trading market. While you want to be careful when you make decisions, you don't want to become anxious and push your exit strategy or trading plan aside. You want to follow what your plans state and do your research in order to make the best decision possible.

Determination is another important factor. Without your willpower, you won't have the ambition or mindset in order to become a master of the market. You won't take the time to perform the research or keep everything between your investments and the market aligned. It's important to think of trading as any other type of career you have had over the years. You must do whatever you can to ensure you are successful. You will be able to do this with strong determination.

Taking charge of your life when it comes to finances means that you will be willing to take calculated risks to make your money work for you. Investment is a double-edged sword that creates the opportunity for making either loss or profit on your capital. Provided you follow the guidelines provided in this book on risk management, your FOREX trading investment is bound to be a success in the long term.

By reading this book you have already taken the first step towards improving your knowledge in FOREX trading and equipped yourself with the tools you will need to get started. The next step is to start incorporating the strategies and critical tips recommended in this book and take your first move into FOREX trading.

You will also want to look at the trend charts, which will give you a variety of colored lines to explain how well the currencies are performing and if they're good for you. Taking into consideration all these different factors, you will become a successful trader no matter what strategy you decide to use. One of the biggest parts of becoming successful is believing you can be successful. By following the tips and tricks outlined in this book, you'll be able to reach the goal you have set or are about to set for yourself.

Through all the information you have read in this book, you will be able to apply your favorite FOREX trading strategy.

Through practice, you will be able to master your preferred strategy, which will allow you to gain bigger profits. It doesn't matter which strategy you decide to use. What matters is that you're confident in your abilities and remain consistent with your strategy.

Don't enter the market at any time just because you want to trade. Trade when you know for sure what is about to happen, and you clearly know where stop loss order must be placed and for how long the market might be going. If you find yourself in doubts at any time, do not enter a trade.

Specifically, if you are dedicated to the idea of making the most money possible from the FOREX market while putting in as little day-to-day work as possible, then you are always going to be on the lookout for additional ways to streamline the experience. Whether this is by improving the way in which you determine your trades, removing your bad habits from the equation, researching more efficiently or some combination of the three, the only way to ever improve is through hard work and dedication.

Letting your money work for you will give you an incredible feeling, especially at the beginning, when you make the first gains. We are thrilled for you to start and we cannot wait to see your results coming.

CPSIA information can be obtained
at www.ICGtesting.com
Printed in the USA
LVHW042024291020
670161LV00001B/144

9 781801 097659